"Never has it been more important for Christians to study the book of Revelation and understand God's plan and purpose for Israel and the world in the last days. That's why my friend Skip Heitzig's exploration of Revelation is a must-read! Skip is a first-rate Bible teacher. He has a great passion for helping people understand Bible prophecy, what it means, and why it should motivate believers to live more faithfully for Jesus Christ as we see the Day approaching."

—JOEL C. ROSENBERG, *New York Times* best-selling
author of *The Last Jihad*, *The Last Days*, and *Epicenter*

"When I preached for Pastor Skip Heitzig some time ago I was amazed to find 12,000 people in attendance at his church. I knew this tall, lean, cowboy-looking preacher must be something special...He is a warmhearted communicator of the Word of God who faithfully teaches divine truth with a practical application to everyday life."

—TIM LAHAYE, author of the best-selling Left Behind™ series

"Skip Heitzig has given us a very readable and accurate commentary on the book of Revelation. Throughout its 22 chapters, we are constantly reminded that this is the Revelation of Jesus Christ. If you are looking for a way to study the future, you've just found it!"

—DAVID JEREMIAH, senior pastor, Shadow Mountain Community Church;
founder of Turning Point Ministries

YOU CAN UNDERSTAND *the* BOOK OF REVELATION

SKIP HEITZIG

HARVEST HOUSE PUBLISHERS
EUGENE, OREGON

Cover by Dugan Design Group, Bloomington, Minnesota

Cover photos © Adam Gryko, Amyn Hooda / Fotolia

Author photo copyright © 2010 by Jeff LeFever, www.lefever.com

YOU CAN UNDERSTAND THE BOOK OF REVELATION
Copyright © 2011 by Skip Heitzig
Published by Harvest House Publishers
Eugene, Oregon 97402
www.harvesthousepublishers.com

Library of Congress Cataloging-in-Publication Data
Heitzig, Skip.
You can understand the book of Revelation / Skip Heitzig.
     p. cm.
ISBN 978-0-7369-4331-4 (pbk.)
ISBN 978-0-7369-4332-1 (eBook)
1. Bible. N.T. Revelation—Commentaries. I. Title.
BS2825.53.H45 2011
228'.07—dc22

                                                                2010051982

Printed in the United States of America

16 17 18 19 / LB-SK / 10 9 8 7

To my grandson, Seth Nathaniel Heitzig,
who for me represents the future.
May your life in this uncertain world be filled with fun and joy,
knowing that it will one day be eclipsed
by a far more certain and wonderful existence!

Acknowledgments

This book is not the stand-alone work of its author. Many have contributed to making it come to life. First I am thankful to the wonderful congregation at Calvary of Albuquerque, New Mexico, whose encouragement and voracious spiritual appetite made it possible for me to preach the book of Revelation throughout an entire year. Thank you for wanting *everything* in the 22 chapters of Revelation explained and applied and for giving me the time and space in which to do it.

I also must acknowledge the writings and research of the many authors and commentators who have preceded me and whose tomes grace my library. Those 110 volumes that deal with the book of Revelation have greatly enriched my life. I stand on the shoulders of such giants.

Likewise I am indebted to the wonderful team at Harvest House Publishers who helped make this book possible. Steve Miller and his team have helped enormously with careful editing skills and insights. The whole Harvest House team has worked so diligently to make this book a blessing to those who read it.

Special thanks goes to Steve Halliday—he's a literary superstar! Steve was masterful in editing large portions of material and paring down the information into bite-sized nuggets. Thanks for your writing skills, Steve!

Also, thanks to Brian Nixon and Rebekah Hanson and the entire Connection Publishing Team. Your research and input has been invaluable. You guys make serving Jesus a lot of fun.

Finally, I want to give special acknowledgment to my wife, Lenya, whose love for Scripture and the God of Scripture has prompted me to study, write, and preach. Thank you, sweetheart, for knowing how to keep one foot stepping toward eternity while grounding the other foot in earthly responsibility. We've had a great journey so far. The best is still to come!

Skip Heitzig

Contents

Why Study the Book of Revelation?

Many years ago a church asked me to serve as a guest speaker. The people seemed excited to have me there—until they found out I planned to teach on the book of Revelation. They quickly suggested that I "stay out of that stuff."

Welcome to the book of Revelation, one of the most mysterious, controversial, and neglected books in all the Bible!

This final book of Scripture is so filled with mystery—in fact, at times it can get downright spooky—that many people have said, "I'm not going to read it." Some seminaries refuse to teach the book. Many churches nearly ban it altogether. What accounts for these negative attitudes? Perhaps these people are a little afraid of the book. After all, what if the scenarios described in it come true? What if they're not just symbolic? We don't want things like *that* to come true on planet Earth!

Back in 1870, a clergyman made a grave and ironic mistake. He visited a small denominational college and stayed at the home of a school instructor. One evening the clergyman said to his host, "I believe the Bible states that nothing else can be invented."

"I totally disagree," the educator replied. "In fact, I believe within fifty years men will be able to soar through the sky like birds."

The clergyman shook his head and answered, "I suggest that you not share your opinion, lest you be accused of blasphemy. Flight is reserved for the angels."

The irony? The clergyman's name was Milton Wright, the father of two famous boys who, thirty years later, made history when they flew in their heavier-than-air machine. Every time we fly today, we testify to Milton Wright's error. Although the educator's prediction seemed unlikely at the time, it came true.

Many people read the book of Revelation with a skepticism much like that voiced by Milton Wright. "These things will never come true," they say. "It can never happen!" The great reformer Martin Luther expressed a similar sentiment. He wrote, "My spirit cannot adapt itself to the book and a sufficient reason why I do not esteem it highly is that Christ is neither taught nor recognized in it."

As great a reformer as he was, however, Luther could not have been more wrong. From beginning to end, the book of Revelation focuses on Jesus Christ. In chapters 1 through 3, we see Jesus as the exalted King and Priest over His church, ministering to His body. In chapters 4 and 5, we see Jesus in heaven as the glorified Lamb of God. In chapters 6 through 18, we see Jesus Christ as the Judge over all the earth. In chapter 19, we see Jesus Christ as the returning King of kings and Lord of lords. And the book closes with Jesus Christ as the Bridegroom, taking His bride into the heavenly city.

From first to last, it's a revelation of Jesus the Christ!

Perhaps Luther also discounted the book because he lived during an era when it simply didn't seem possible that many of the amazing things described in Revelation could actually take place. Their fulfillment seemed impossible, even ludicrous.

How times have changed! We live in a day when not only are those things possible, but it looks as though they're lining up left and right. Newspaper headlines daily remind us of events in the book of Revelation. Think of how many Bible prophecies already have come true. I challenge any skeptic to do a study of biblical prophecy. Find out how much God has said that already has come true. Don't discount the book of Revelation because the events it describes don't seem possible; when God talks about the future, He's not guessing. He *knows*.

Does that make you uncomfortable? Does prophecy make you uneasy? I know it has that effect on some people. Yet consider that a full *one-fourth* of the Bible is prophecy. It's all over the place! And it doesn't make predictions that may or may not come true, like the weatherman. God loves to bless weathermen and meteorologists, but oftentimes they say, "It's not going to rain this week. It'll be clear and hot!" And the very next day a rainstorm blows in.

I heard about a tourist driving through west Texas. He pulled into a gas station and noticed a rope dangling from a sign that read "Weather Forecaster." He studied the rope for a while and asked the attendant, "How can a rope tell you the weather?"

"Very simple, sonny," the old Texan replied. "See when that rope wags back and forth? It's windy. When that rope's wet? It's raining. And when it's frozen stiff? There's snow. When that rope is gone? Yep, tornado."

God's predictions are *very* different. When He makes a prediction, He does so because He knows the end from the beginning. And in the book of Revelation, He makes *very* definite predictions.

Why should this matter to us? Because we live in an age of high anxiety when people want to know what's going to happen. What does the future hold? Will there be an Armageddon? Will this world come to an end? Will Jesus really return to the earth visibly and physically? If so, when will He come back? These are real questions to which real people are grasping at straws to get the answers. They'll read a horoscope to find out "what the stars say." Or they'll get their palms read or turn to the tabloid prophets of the *National Enquirer* and *Star* magazines. Or they'll call a late night psychic hotline to find out what some psycho might predict about their personal future. All the while, God has written—not only in Revelation, but also in Daniel, Ezekiel, and other places in the Bible—all about the future of planet Earth, the human race, and what we can expect to come.

As we look into the book of Revelation, we'll define the rapture and the second coming of Christ. We'll be introduced to a coming world ruler who will try to impose an economic system on every human on the planet. We'll see a severe seven-year judgment that God brings upon the earth. We'll meet a group called the 144,000, find out who they are, and learn what they'll be doing. We'll examine when and why the Jews will rebuild their temple in Jerusalem. We'll see the emergence and ultimate destruction of Babylon and discover its meaning. We'll look at the battle of Armageddon. All this and more we'll consider as we go through the book of Revelation.

As we do so, I have a personal prayer for us. I pray that we won't content ourselves with walking away with interesting tidbits of information about Gog and Magog and constructing cool charts about the end times that we can use to impress people. Instead, I pray that after we study God's prophecies about the future, we will walk away with a greater trust in Him than ever. I pray that we'll come to the firm conviction that we serve a God who has a perfectly accurate prophetic track record, who knows the end from the beginning, and who holds all of our lives in the palm of His hand.

Every tomorrow has two handles: the handle of anxiety and the handle of faith. Many people grab the handle of anxiety: "What's going to happen? The worst may come upon me!" But every time God makes a promise and we watch Him fulfill it, we move to the handle of faith and say, "This is a God I can trust—even with my life." That's what I pray happens as we explore this wonderful, mysterious book of Revelation.

So let's begin this exciting journey. Let's move forward with both hope and expectation. Jesus is coming again! And until He returns, let's remember that He has crucial things for all of us to do.

I

What Have We Got Here?

Revelation 1

SUMMARY

While the book of Revelation is certainly a mysterious book full of curious symbols and imagery, the central theme of the book could not be clearer: Jesus Christ. From beginning to end, this book is all about Jesus and what He has done, is doing, and will do to bring about the eternal plan of His Father.

RELATED SCRIPTURES FOR STUDY

Psalm 22:6; Isaiah 53:5; Daniel 7:13-14; 1 Peter 2:5-9; Revelation 21:6; 22:13

Through the centuries, the book of Revelation has sparked as much controversy and disagreement as it has fascination and awe. In the fourth century, Gregory of Nazianzus and other bishops argued against including it in the Bible because it presented so many problems with interpretation. Although the Council of Carthage in 397 fully accepted Revelation into the canon of Scripture, the Eastern Orthodox church still doesn't include it among the church's Divine Liturgy. Although the reformer John Calvin accepted Revelation as canonical, it's the only New Testament book for which he did not write a commentary. And Martin Luther included it among the books he classified as "antilegomena"—books he considered of questionable use or origin.

Without question, the book *is* difficult to interpret. It is deeply mysterious. And yet God has given it to us not only to set our minds at ease about the future, but also to spur us on to "love and good deeds" (Hebrews 10:24). So let's briefly investigate why we have this book, why it is so different, who wrote it, and the identity of its main character.

A Quick Look at the Book

Back when we announced at our church that we were going to tackle the book of Revelation, you could hear a ripple skitter across the auditorium: "Wow, Revelation!" The congregation had mixed sentiments. I'm sure some thought, *Hot diggety dog! I can't wait to give Skip some tips.* Others gasped, "Oh *no*! Not the book of *Revelation*! You've gotta stay out of that book—that's one of those closed books. That's a sealed-up book."

Many folks no doubt got a surprise when they discovered that the word "revelation" comes from the Greek word *apokalupsis*, from which we get our word "apocalypse." Most people who hear of an apocalypse think of a catastrophe or a cataclysm—but that's not what the word means. In fact, it signifies an unveiling or a disclosure. It speaks of uncovering or revealing something that had been hidden. Imagine a new statue placed in front of city hall, covered with a sheet. At the dedication ceremony a band plays, the mayor gives a spiel, and finally the artist talks about his commissioning. At the precise appointed moment, the sheet comes off and the statue is *apokalupsis*—unveiled. What once was hidden now stands in the open.

In a similar way, the Holy Spirit draws back the curtains on the book of Revelation and reveals things to us. Remember that this book is a prophecy (v. 3). It's not an allegory; it's not mere symbols to be spiritualized however one may choose. It makes specific predictions about the future. Verse 1 speaks of things that Jesus "signified" by an angel "to His servant John." The word "signify" means "to reveal through signs."

The book of Revelation employs symbol after symbol, many of them deeply mysterious. The opening vision of Jesus, for example, portrays Him with white hair, fiery brass feet, and a sword flashing out of His mouth. Revelation also speaks of many "sevens": seven lampstands, seven spirits before the throne of God, seven trumpets, seven seals, seven thunders. You might wonder, *Why such an emphasis on the number seven?* In the Bible, seven is the number of completeness. Even as seven days make a complete week, so the number seven denotes completeness—a complete revelation of God, a complete judgment, a complete church.

But why the symbols and weird language? Why didn't God just say, "Point number one: This is the rapture of the church. Point number two: After the rapture, this will happen." Why such an extensive use of symbols?

I can think of several reasons. First, the text of Revelation functioned like a spiritual code for the early church. The Roman government fiercely persecuted first-century Christians, carefully examining any documents they confiscated. A Roman official reading the book of Revelation would respond, "What's up with *this*? This is weird." But a New Testament Christian would grasp its meaning. It feels very Old Testament, and early Christians practically bathed in the Hebrew Scriptures. In fact, out of 404 passages in Revelation, at least 360 quote or allude to the Old Testament. First-century believers understood apocalyptic literature from the Old Testament books of Daniel and Ezekiel, so when they read this book, they *got* it.

Second, the passing of time does not weaken symbolism. Symbolism tends to transcend cultures, language groups, and people groups. It can bless all people of all times—and God inspired this book in order to bless all ages of the church.

Third, symbolism arouses strong emotions. Symbols create mental images that other forms of literature simply can't duplicate. As my son was growing up, for example, we would read a Bible story, then act out the Bible story. We dressed up as certain characters and put on towels as headdresses and robes—he was always David and I always got the rock. And then afterward we would pray about the lesson. Our games gave my son a visual handle on the stories. He grasped as a child what it took me until my mid-twenties to understand. John uses a similar approach in Revelation by employing vivid images and potent symbolism.

Fourth, verse 1 speaks of the "things which must shortly take place."

My son once said to me, "Dad, this was written 2000 years ago—and John said it will 'shortly take place.' Wasn't he wrong?" You might have the same question. Did John think the events he described in Revelation would happen during his lifetime? In fact, the word translated "shortly take place" comes from the Greek term *en tachi*, which means "swiftly." From this term we get our word "tachometer," a device that measures velocity. It means to unfold in a brief period of time. In other words, once these events start occurring, they will unfold swiftly until they reach their conclusion. A time will come when the machinery of world history will kick into high gear; and then, as suddenly as it began, it will all end.

A Look at the Biographer

The book of Revelation came from God the Father, to His Son Jesus Christ, to an angel, and then finally to the apostle John, who wrote it down. In his early years, John worked as a Galilean fisherman. His dad was Zebedee, his mom was Salome, his older brother was the martyr James (who had his head cut off; see Acts 12:2).

John became part of Jesus' inner circle, along with James and Peter. This trio was privy to things from which the other disciples were excluded. When Jesus healed Jarius's daughter in Capernaum, for example, the Lord took with Him Peter, James, and John. On the Mount of Transfiguration, Jesus again took Peter, James, and John. In the Garden of Gethsemane, these three again accompanied Jesus further into the garden than the other disciples.

Beyond this, John apparently had a certain intimacy with Jesus Christ that the others lacked. In his Gospel, John repeatedly called himself "the disciple whom Jesus loved." Jesus loved all His disciples, of course, but He felt a special bond with John. At the Last Supper, it was John who laid his head on the bosom of Jesus, hearing His heartbeat—as if to grasp every word from His master's mouth. Among the disciples, only John stood at the foot of the cross as Jesus gave His life for the sins of the world. It was John to whom Jesus entrusted the care of His elderly mother. And it was John who ran to the tomb first and believed first.

John wrote this book on the island of Patmos, a Roman penal colony about twenty-five miles off the coast of Asia Minor. To this day, the island has no source of fresh water. In John's day, Patmos was merely a barren rock jutting out of the Aegean Sea, a perfect place to isolate prisoners. John probably was in his nineties when he wrote this book—an old guy isolated and alone on a dreary, forsaken island. Tradition tells us he didn't die there; rather, he returned to Ephesus, where he lived out his remaining days. A beautiful church tradition says that shortly before John died, fellow believers carried him in a chair to all the churches of Asia Minor. Wherever he would go, he'd raise his arms, smile, and say, "Little children, love one another!" His harsh experiences didn't fill him with bitterness, but with the love of Jesus Christ. John wrote Revelation to suffering Christians in order to encourage them in their faith.

Could it be that *you* are one of those suffering Christians? Do you feel exiled on your own desolate Patmos? Do you feel imprisoned by life's circumstances? Or perhaps you feel trapped by another person, or maybe your Patmos is a hospital bed. Regardless of your situation, the book of Revelation will encourage you. Remember that John received his greatest revelation from God in a place of extreme isolation.

If you feel exiled on your own personal Patmos, understand that God has brought you there in order to reveal Himself to you. While a little faith may bring your soul to heaven, a lot of faith—clinging to God despite your circumstances—will bring heaven to your soul.

A Look at the Benefits

Of all the books in the Bible, only Revelation offers a promise like the one in verse 3. Only this book opens by saying, in essence, "Read me and you'll be blessed."

To be blessed means "to get happy." The more you read this book, the more you will understand Jesus Christ and His plan for your future—and the happier you will feel. The text says *read* it, *hear* it, and *keep* it. While you can read it for yourself and listen to others as they read it aloud to you, only you can keep it and apply these truths to your life.

As we move through this book, I encourage you to keep asking yourself, *What did I learn that I can apply both today and tomorrow?* The real joy, John said, comes when you *do* what the Bible says. Happiness comes when you apply God's Word to your life.

A Look at the Blessed One

John began by introducing us to the central character and capstone of the book of Revelation: Jesus Christ (vv. 4-8). The book explains who He is, what He has done, and what He will do. Jesus is the main thing, and John keeps Him the main thing throughout this book.

Notice that the book is called *the* Revelation of Jesus Christ—singular, not plural. It's not the book of revelation*s*, but the book of Revelation. It's not a bunch of analogies or a collection of predictions regarding the future. Rather, it offers a revelation of a Person, Jesus Christ. The Savior takes center stage.

For that reason alone it could be that you desperately need this book. You require a fresh revelation of Jesus Christ. Maybe you have heard about Jesus, but you don't yet know Him personally. To you, perhaps, He's still a little baby in a Christmas manger. Revelation pictures Jesus as the ruling Lord of the earth. In fact, when John saw Jesus, he "fell at His feet as dead." John said Jesus responded by laying "His right hand on me, saying to me, 'Do not be afraid; I am the First and the Last'" (v. 17). John remembered Jesus in the flesh—the man with tattered robes and beat-up sandals, the carpenter from Nazareth—but now recognized Him as God in human flesh. He saw Jesus as a glorious, reigning King, ruling with an iron scepter over the whole world.

Jesus is the central character of the book of Revelation not merely because of His exalted status, but also because of what He has done for us: "Jesus Christ, the faithful witness, the firstborn from the dead, and the ruler over the kings of the earth. To Him who loved us and washed us from our sins in His own blood…" (v. 5). Jesus has every right to rule your life because He's done everything to redeem your life.

And of course, Jesus is coming to earth again (v. 7). This is the major theme of the book. Jesus Christ, the One who died and rose again, will return to this planet—and not as a common servant, but as an exalted King. He will rule! The theme of Revelation and of all history is simply this: *Jesus wins.*

A Startling Beginning

John tells us that he *heard* something, *saw* something, and *did* something. He heard a voice, he saw a vision, and he fell and worshiped. Then he wrote down what God directed him to record. In other words, this is *not* original material. John didn't sit down and say, "Here I am on Patmos. I've got time to kill, so maybe I can write a best-seller." No, he wrote down the heavenly message that Jesus Christ gave to him.

Because John's account is utterly faithful to the vision he received from God, in verse 2 he calls what he sees "the word of God." It's the testimony of the Holy Spirit, supervised by Jesus Himself. As John finds himself catapulted into the future, he is given a preview of amazing events and records everything he sees and hears.

A Loud Voice Like a Trumpet

John heard a voice so loud that it sounded like a trumpet blast. This wasn't some quiet whisper! Jesus spoke in a piercing, brassy voice that John compared to "the sound of many waters" (v. 15). John remembered the sound of Jesus' mortal voice—but now it's different, thunderous, and utterly unmistakable.

Did you realize that the voice of God changes depending on the circumstances? The prophet Elijah wanted it loud, and yet it came to him in a still, small voice. On Mount Sinai, by contrast, the great Lawgiver roared forth His Law, accompanied by thunder and lightning. Since John wasn't used to such a roar coming from his Savior, the blaring voice of the mystery-revealing Jesus startled him. Today on the Isle of Patmos, guides direct you to the grotto of Saint John—a little cave with a church built up around it. Locals will point to a crack in the rock and tell you that's where the trumpet voice came from; they claim the sound split the rock. While it may be a fanciful story, the voice certainly startled John.

Jesus loudly emphasized that He is God (vv. 8,11,17). *Jesus Christ is deity in a body. Alpha* is the first letter in the Greek alphabet; *omega* is the last. Any Jew would have replied, "Wait a minute! That's a title reserved for God alone" (see Isaiah 41). So when Jesus reintroduces Himself as the Alpha and the Omega, the Almighty, He plainly describes Himself as God.

And then Jesus speaks of His eternal nature: "I am…[the One] who is and who was and who is to come" (v. 8). When Moses first spoke with God at the burning bush, the Lord used this name to describe Himself: "I AM THAT I AM." This special name in Hebrew means, "I was, I am, and I will be." And here is Jesus, taking that eternal name upon Himself! The fact is, if you try to remove the deity of Christ from the person of Christ, Christianity collapses. It's not optional. *Jesus Christ is God.* That's the underlying fact of the New Testament.

A Captivating Vision

As soon as John heard the unearthly voice, he turned to see the face that went with it. Instantly he saw Jesus in all His glory, standing in the midst of some golden lampstands. A Jewish person reading about seven lampstands would think of the menorah, the seven-branch candlestick that stood in the holy place of the tabernacle. Verse 20 tells us this image refers to the church. What a fitting description! A lampstand is meant to give light, to dispel darkness, to show people the way out. Jesus not only claimed to be the light of the world (John 8:12), He also told His disciples that they were the light of the world (Matthew 5:14). Jesus is like the sun, the source of our light. We are like the moon, reflecting His glory. And so Jesus stands in the midst of His church, the body He designed, to dispel darkness and show people the way out.

Verse 13 describes a garment that reaches to Jesus' feet, speaking of His majesty and greatness. Verse 14 tells us, "His head and hair were white like wool." How do you picture Jesus Christ? Maybe you see Him as a fair-skinned Anglo-Saxon, as in so many paintings. Since Jesus was Semitic, He probably had dark skin and dark hair; but when you see Him in His glory, He's going to blow your mind. He's *not* going to be what you pictured! This isn't Jesus as John remembered Him. This Jesus had "eyes like a flame of fire." Perhaps that refers to Jesus' ability to see into everybody's heart. I think the eyes of fire are related to His feet, "like fine brass, as if refined in a furnace" (v. 15). Whenever you read of brass in the Scriptures, think of judgment. John had never seen *anything* like this! But now he sees the holy Jesus of righteous judgment…a prelude to Revelation chapter 4, when a series of judgments begins.

In verse 16 we see Jesus holding seven stars in His right hand and a sharp, two-edged sword flashing out of His mouth. In the Bible, a person's right hand represents power and authority. So in great power and authority, Jesus holds the stars, the messengers of the churches (v. 20). In response, John fell on his face not only because of Jesus' majesty, but also because he recognized that God was speaking to *him*. When people in the Bible had a real encounter with God, they didn't get puffed up about it. They didn't say, "Hey, I've had a vision! I should write a book." Instead, they became extremely self-conscious and meek. Far from exalting them, such an otherworldly experience humbled them.

I believe that the modern church desperately needs a new awareness of Jesus Christ. We need to see Him as high and lifted up and in total charge of His church. Too many Christians tend to think of Jesus as "my good old Buddy in the sky." I believe we speak too much about standing on our own two feet when we ought to fall down at *His* feet. Have you prostrated yourself before Him in humility, worshiping Him? Charles Spurgeon wrote, "Why is it that some people are often in a place of worship and yet they are not holy? It is because they've neglected their prayer closets. They love wheat but they do not grind it. The water flows at their feet, but they do not stoop to drink of it."[1] Then he asked a penetrating, uncomfortable question:

> Are we tired of God? If not, how is it that we do not walk with Him from day to day? Really, spiritual worship is not much cared for in these days, even by professing Christians. Many will go to a place of worship if they can be entertained with fine music or grand oratory; but if communion with God is the only attraction, they are not drawn thereby.[2]

By contrast, John immediately fell down on his face, recognizing that this Jesus he followed was *God in the flesh*. This awareness overwhelmed and humbled him, as it should us.

Obedient to a Vocation

Jesus instructed John to write what he saw to seven churches of Asia Minor (v. 19). This verse is the key to interpreting the book of Revelation, because in it Jesus gives John an outline of the whole book.

"John," He said, "first write down the things that you *have* seen." And what had John already seen? A vision of Jesus. "After that," Jesus said, "write down the things that *are*." Here Jesus points ahead to His words intended for the seven churches of Asia Minor (chapters 2–3). "Finally," Jesus continued, "write down the things that will take place after this," referring to the events detailed in chapters 4–22. And John faithfully obeyed what Jesus had commanded.

If you remember nothing else from the book of Revelation, remember this: When Jesus speaks, obey Him. John heard, John saw, and John obeyed. John understood that God had a call upon his life, and he pursued it faithfully.

God has a calling upon your life too. Because the Lord wants to minister to others through you, give fresh attention to His voice. Get a fresh perspective of Jesus Christ. Seek a fresh experience of worship. Surrender your life in total humility to God, and expect to hear His voice. When you do, obey what you hear. Follow whatever vocation He gives you, and do so with all of your heart.

Our Real Hope

One day a weary father returned home, exhausted after a long day at work. He couldn't wait to hit his favorite chair, put up his feet, kick off his shoes, and read the newspaper. When he dragged himself through the door, he plopped down, opened the newspaper—and his five-year-old son launched himself into his lap.

"Daddy! Let's play!" the little boy shouted. The father knew his son needed time with Daddy, but he thought, *I have a greater need, for just a few minutes. I need time alone.* He didn't want to tell his excited son to bug off, so he mentally constructed a brilliant scheme. He noticed that one section of the newspaper featured a picture of the earth, taken from a moon probe. "Give me that section," he instructed his son. Using some scissors, the father cut the picture into puzzle-shaped pieces, piled them up, then gave them to his son, along with some cellophane tape. "Put this puzzle together," he said. "When you're all done, bring it to me, and then we'll play."

The boy whizzed off and the father thought he had bought himself a chunk of time. But a few moments later, the boy returned with the picture of the earth, perfectly taped together.

"How did you do it so quickly?" the startled father asked.

"Dad," the boy replied, "it was simple! On the back is a picture of a man, and when you put the man together, the world comes together."

That little boy is on to something. The world *will* come together when Jesus Christ returns. Judgment will fall, Jesus will begin to reign, and God will create His perfect world order. But until that day, the Lord puts the world back together one person at a time. He rebuilds and reshapes and tapes each of us together until we start functioning in the way He designed us to operate.

Let God put you back together, and then start living as the Lord has always meant for you to live.

2

The Churches of Revelation, Part I

Revelation 2

Summary

In the first four of His short letters to seven first-century churches in Asia Minor, Jesus evaluates the condition, performance, and ministry of each church. He looks not only for things to commend, but also things to rebuke or admonish, and then gives each church His prescription for improved spiritual health.

Related Scriptures for Study

Luke 10:38-42; Acts 20; 2 Corinthians 11; Hebrews 11

Before Jesus talks about the ominous judgments described throughout most of Revelation, He has a few crucial words to say to His church. He writes short letters to seven individual congregations located in what is now modern-day Turkey. And while each letter has a specific local application to the churches addressed, each letter also has a personal application to us today.

Ephesus: When Love Grows Cold (2:1-7)

Jesus says in essence to this church, "I know everything about you— and you have some good points, some bad points, and some work to do." First He commends them, then He confronts them, and finally He gives them a commandment.

Jesus commends the church because its members labored for Him and did not become weary. That's a mark of a healthy church! James said, "Be doers of the word, and not hearers only, deceiving yourselves" (James 1:22).

The people in the church at Ephesus also patiently persevered. In the original Greek text, the word translated "patience" means "to bear up under a load." It could be translated "to persevere under difficult circumstances with a steady determination to go on." Under tremendous opposition and persecution, the Ephesians hung in there. Ephesus was not only a key center of culture and trade in Asia Minor, it was also a center of religious activity—not Christian, but pagan. The city sat on a seaport trade route that ran from the east to the west and therefore had imported emperor worship from Rome. Once a year, citizens had to look at a statue of Caesar and say publicly, "Caesar is my lord." Because Christians refused to do that, they got into trouble. Ephesus was also a hub for Eastern mystical and magical worship, as well as the center for Diana (sometimes called the mother goddess of all of Asia) worship. But despite tremendous persecution, the Christians in Ephesus persevered. They bore up under the load and, like a soldier who stays at his task, did not swerve.

Third, they had discernment. Jesus tells them, "You are doctrinally sound. You know how to discern truth from error." Some shady itinerant preachers traveled from congregation to congregation in the early church, claiming to be apostles or prophets. These teachers would say, "I'm an apostle, and thus says the Lord."

"And who sent you?" someone would ask.

"I don't need human credentials," they'd reply. "God sent me."

These questionable teachers became such a problem that the church wrote a manual called *The Teaching of the Twelve Apostles for the Gentile Churches*. Part of it reads:

> If any missioner comes, he should be welcomed as the Lord. But he is not to stay more than a day or two days, if really necessary. If he stays three days, he is not genuine. If anyone comes to you speaking in a trance or with visions from God and says, "Give me money" or anything else, do not

listen to him. Let him not live in idleness simply because
he says he is a Christian.

The Ephesians also hated the "deeds of the Nicolaitans" (v. 6). Scholars debate the identity of these Nicolaitans; they probably followed
Nicolas of Antioch, who appears to have taken grace to an unscru-
pulous extreme: "Live any way you want to, because you're a believer
under grace. Sin it up!" A lot of people thought, *Now this is my style of
religion!* But Jesus commended the Ephesians for hating such teaching and practice.

Jesus commended the Ephesians as a model church that worked
hard, persevered under persecution, and discerned error from truth.
But He also chastised them: "I have this against you, that you have left
your first love" (v. 4). Notice He does *not* say, as is often misquoted,
"You have lost your first love." Love for Christ is not something you lose;
it's something you leave. The words here imply a process that happens
over time. Erosion has taken place. In the original Greek text, the term
"first" is emphasized to mean something like, "You have left behind your
love, the first one." One translator rendered it, "You no longer love Me
like you did at first."

How is it possible to serve God, and even to suffer for Him, without doing so out of love? Experience tells us that we can serve the Lord
out of many motivations: guilt, a desire to be noticed, sheer duty. But
the highest motivation for serving Him is love. And therefore Jesus is
far more interested in what you do *with* Him than what you do *for* Him.

Jesus then tells the Ephesians to remember, to repent, and to repeat
(v. 5). First, He urges them to remember. Think back to the time when
you received Jesus Christ and with tears said, "O Lord, save me. O
Lord, I love You." Go back to that place of intimacy where you felt so
very close to Jesus. Oscar Wilde once said, "Memory is the diary that
we always carry around with us." Open that diary of your memory and
recall those first weeks and months with Jesus.

Second, repent. John wrote, "If we confess our sins, He is faithful
and just to forgive us our sins and to cleanse us from all unrighteousness" (1 John 1:9).

And third, repeat your first works. Get back into Bible study, prayer, and telling others about Jesus. Do these things even if you don't feel like doing them because feelings follow the will in the same way a caboose follows an engine.

All of this is crucial because Jesus tells us that He won't stay around a church that doesn't love Him (v. 5). And if He removes the lampstand, we'll lose the opportunity to make an impact on our world and community. So don't put your spiritual life on cruise control. In some areas of your life you may find it necessary to put the brakes on and turn around. In other areas, you may need to hit the accelerator—remember that a dynamic walk with the Lord is not self-maintaining. God rewards those who diligently seek Him, so seek Him with all of your heart. And whatever you do, don't get so busy about the affairs of the kingdom that you neglect the King Himself, who wants your love.

Smyrna: Postcard to Those in Pain (vv. 8-11)

The church in Smyrna was a church in pain, suffering because of persecution for its Christian faith. Now, whenever we suffer, we have a choice. We will either become better or bitter. Pain can work like a chisel to shape us, or it can become a heavy stone that crushes us. Pain is inevitable; misery is optional. In this short letter—really, not much more than a postcard—Jesus is sensitive, direct, and brief, and encourages the Smyrnans to remain faithful even to the point of death.

The prosperous city of Smyrna lay only forty miles north of Ephesus; today it is called Ismere. Because of its natural harbor, it became an important stop on the east-west trade route. It was named for its chief export, myrrh, an aromatic resin used in perfume that releases a beautiful scent when crushed. The city was filled with Greek pride and Roman arrogance, and Jesus said to the church, "I know your tribulation." The term used in the original Greek text means "to be crushed"; the word picture is of a heavy stone set upon wheat so that through pressure it might grind the grain. Likewise, the suffering and persecuted church at Smyrna was being crushed, and yet the members gave off a beautiful aroma as they remained faithful to God.

The huge city was filled with all sorts of shrines and temples. One major thoroughfare, called The Golden Street, ran all the way from

Ephesus through Smyrna and ended up at the Acropolis on Mount Pagas. It was dotted with the temples of Asklepios, Aphrodite, Apollo, Zeus—all sorts of gods and goddesses.

In addition, Smyrna was a center of emperor worship. In about 195 BC, the city built a huge temple to the goddess of Rome, called Dea Roma—the first city in the world to do so. Rome marveled at such allegiance to emperor worship that when six cities competed to build a huge temple to Tiberius Caesar, Smyrna won the competition. For many years it was the center in the eastern Roman Empire for worshiping Caesar. Once a year, every Roman citizen would stand before a bust of Caesar, and with a pinch of incense tossed into a sacrificial fire, would say, "Caesar is the lord." Christians would not say this; if anything, they would say, "No, Jesus Christ is Lord." And for that they were marked as traitors and political insurrectionists.

Jesus also noted the poverty of the Christians in Smyrna. The social and economic life of Greek cities was tied to their pagan worship. Each set of workers had its own guild, and each guild had its own patron god or goddess. Workers began each week by expressing some kind of allegiance to the gods of the Greek pantheon. Because Christians refused to adopt this practice, they were cut off from the right to make a living—and that meant abject poverty.

Jesus never offered these Christians—or anyone else—an insipid form of painless Christianity. Faith does not mean walking through life from victory to victory. Victory means you've made it through the battle. You've won, but you've been in the fight.

Next, Jesus mentions religious persecution. The first Roman emperor to persecute Christians was Nero. He liked tying up Christians to poles, putting pitch on their bodies, and igniting them as living torches to light his gardens at night. He also sewed Christians inside the skins of dead animals and then tossed them to wild beasts to eat them alive.

Jesus gives these poor, persecuted Christians some important counsel (v. 10). He offers no solution to their pain, but simply says, "Don't be afraid; rather, remain faithful. You are about to be cast into prison and face death." Being faithful won't alleviate the problem of persecution; it only makes it worse. So if you want to stop the persecution, then stop being a good witness. Jesus doesn't tell the Smyrnans to stop being faithful, however. Rather, He counsels them to not be afraid.

In our day, a Christian pastor speaking in Nicaragua about persecution and the future once said, "It's the strangest thing. But where the war has been the bloodiest, where the needs are the most desperate, this is where the church has grown the most. Yes, brethren, become martyrs. Yet remember that the heavier the cross, the more powerful the resurrection."

Could it be that our lives don't challenge unbelievers enough? John Stott once said, "We are respectable. We are conventional. We are inoffensive. We are ineffective."[1] We like soft music, soft lights, and soft sermons, which together produce soft Christians. Suppose the Christian church in our culture decided to stand out and say, "Enough of this! We'll raise the standard of righteousness. We will live biblically, we will love biblically, and we will proclaim the exclusive gospel of Jesus Christ without reservation." What would happen? We will be called narrow, unloving, Victorian, bigoted, and worse. In other words, the church will find itself where it belongs: outside of the favor of the world, but firmly in the love of God.

Jesus did give some consolation to the suffering church of Smyrna. To a suffering church facing death, He introduces Himself as the One who already has died and returned to life. In effect He says to them, "I've been there; I know what it's like to be persecuted, to be in poverty. I know what it's like to be slandered. I know what it's like to suffer death. I'm the First, I'm the Last. I'll be there at the beginning, the middle, and the end of what you're going through." Jesus knew their works, tribulation, and poverty—and yet He called them "rich." How different is His valuation from the world's!

Jesus would say, "You can be a wealthy poor man as well as a poor rich man." I'd rather have the world against me than Jesus opposing me! The world can say to me, "You're a loser, man. You're nothing" so long as Jesus says to me, "You're a winner."

Finally, Jesus offers the crown of life and promises that the Smyrnans will not be hurt by the second death—spiritual death. Those who were facing persecution and physical death would die but once. Then they would live forever with Jesus in eternity. Unbelievers have a very different death to face, which is described in Revelation 20. When you live for Jesus the world will not applaud you, but your Father in heaven will.

Pergamos: The Curse of Compromise (vv. 12-17)

I can think of nothing more embarrassing than Jesus handing me a report card saying, "I have something against you." That's exactly what He does to the church in Pergamos. And then He closes His letter to this church as He does the other letters, by saying, "He who has an ear, let him hear what the Spirit says to the churches" (v. 17). Jesus wants to speak to each of us through these words.

The church at Pergamos was on a collision course. Its members suffered from compromise; they were trying desperately to fit in with the world. While compromise is not always bad, there are times when it is not only dangerous, but lethal. There's an Arabian proverb that says, "He who lives all of his life trying to please and appease everyone will die in sadness." The church at Pergamos tried to appease the world by tolerating certain things within its membership.

Pergamos (the modern-day city of Bergama, Turkey) was located north of Smyrna and fifteen miles inland from the Aegean Sea. It was a huge, spectacular city.

Jesus depicts Himself as having a "sharp two-edged sword," which is a reference to the written Word of God, the Bible (see Ephesians 6:17; Hebrews 4:12). This church was having problems with the correct doctrine of Jesus Christ, which led to lewd behavior. In response, Jesus comes to them with the ultimate standard of the truth—the sword of the Spirit, the Word of God. False doctrine is nothing to be toyed with; it can destroy any church, any movement, any person. So Jesus comes to Pergamos wielding the sword of the Spirit.

Jesus recognizes that these people lived in a tough place. They were light in the midst of darkness and they "dwelled" in that place. And unfortunately, Satan's "throne" was located there (v. 13). Satan is not in hell, as some suppose. Peter called him a lion looking for someone to devour (1 Peter 5:8); Jesus called him the god of this world, the prince of this age (2 Corinthians 4:4). He's very active and very mobile.

Temples dotted this ancient city. One particular temple was dedicated to Dionysius, the god of wine, whose upper body was that of a man and lower body was that of a goat. There also was a temple to Asklepios, the god of medicine, who was depicted as a snake. Some think the throne of Satan (called in Genesis 3 the seed of the serpent) refers to the temple of Asklepios. Others think it refers to the altar of Zeus, which was located high atop the Acropolis. This huge altar to Zeus, the largest in the area—forty feet tall, ninety feet square—looked like a throne from afar. The city was a tough place for Christian ministry. Yet this church remained loyal to Jesus. Its members did not deny Him. Tradition says that the martyr Antipas was placed in a hollow brass bowl and roasted alive until death. Despite such horrific persecution, these believers remained loyal to Jesus.

But they also had a big problem. It started with wrong belief, and led to wrong behavior. Make no mistake: What you believe eventually will determine how you behave. And these believers had allowed all sorts of false doctrine to seep into their church.

The New Testament mentions the word "doctrine" thirty-seven times. We're told, for example, that the church in Jerusalem continued steadfastly in "the apostles' doctrine" (Acts 2:42). Paul wrote, "Till I come, give attendance to...doctrine" (1 Timothy 4:13). To Titus he said, "Speak the things which are proper for sound doctrine" (Titus 2:1).

Following Bible doctrine is crucially important, but the church at Pergamos had welcomed both "the doctrine of Balaam" and "the doctrine of the Nicolaitans" (vv. 14-15). Both groups apparently taught that it didn't matter how believers in Christ behaved, and Jesus opposed both of them.

The Old Testament figure of Balaam (see Numbers 22–24) represents greed, covetousness, and compromise. Many temples in Pergamos had prostitutes for the purpose of "worship," and perhaps some church members attended not only Sunday services with fellow Christians, but also pagan temple services during the week. Evidently their compromise caused others to slip, resulting in mutual destruction.

It's interesting that "Pergamos" means "a mixed marriage." This church was trying to marry both Christ and pagan deities. It had lowered its standard of holiness and had begun flirting with the things of the world. Jesus had a simple correction for the problem: "Repent, or else" (v. 16). This might be translated, "Stop right now and turn around. Reroute your life. And do it *now*." And if the church refused? Jesus promised to fight against it with the sword of His mouth.

To whom much is given, much is required, Jesus says. We are responsible for the amount of truth that goes into our ears and minds. An inscription found in a cathedral in Lubeck, Germany, reads,

> Thus speaketh Christ our Lord to us: You call Me Master and obey Me not. You call Me Light and you see Me not. You call Me the Way and you walk Me not. You call Me Life and you live Me not. You call Me Wise yet you follow Me not. You call Me Fair but you love Me not. You call Me Rich yet you ask Me not. You call Me Eternal yet you seek Me not. And if I condemn thee, then blame Me not.

Likewise, Jesus says to the church at Pergamos—and to us— "Enough compromise! Enough false teaching! Enough of your false lifestyles!"

To "him who overcomes," Jesus promises to "give some of the hidden manna to eat" (v. 17). When ancient Israel wandered for forty years in the desert, God gave them manna, a food that nourished the people. I think the hidden message here is this: "Overcome this tolerance of false teaching, and I will provide for you."

Jesus also promises to give them a "white stone." Some say this may refer to a stone of acquittal. At the time, Athenians who were being judged for a crime faced many judges, each of whom held two stones, a white one and a black one. At the end of the trial, each judge would walk by an urn and place one of the two stones inside it. A majority of black stones meant "You're toast." White, on the other hand, meant "You are acquitted." Jesus may be saying, "I'm voting for you. I will come against sin and error, but if you overcome, I will acquit you."

But I think Jesus' reference to a white stone probably means something else. I believe the white stone has an Old Testament context. When the high priest came before God, he had a little pouch in which he kept two stones, the Urim and the Thummim. The white Urim was used to discover the will of God. If this indeed is what Jesus had in mind, then Jesus is saying, "I am representing you before the Father, and as you overcome, I will reveal Myself and My will more and more to you."

In both cases, the counsel is to overcome.

Years ago a mountain climber died in Switzerland and was buried with these words on his tombstone: "He died climbing." Don't you want that? I do. I don't want my tombstone to read, "He died sliding" or "He died vegging in the Spirit." Let's reach new heights and move further along in our walk of faith. Let's grow in pleasing God, not in compromising.

Thyatira: Corruption Without Discernment (vv. 18-29)

The letter to the Christians in Thyatira is the longest of the seven letters Jesus writes, although Thyatira was the smallest of the seven cities. This letter also has a stronger opening. Jesus begins with judgment and severe words, and yet He speaks out of His relationship with the church. The church at Thyatira was tolerating some false doctrine taught by a woman in their midst, and somehow, no one seemed disturbed by her immoral teaching.

Thyatira was a commercial city with numerous guilds, each with its own temple and god. A woman known as a chief prophetess presided over one temple for fortune-tellers. Thyatira also produced the most expensive garments in that part of the world; workers took a special shellfish from the Mediterranean Sea, known as a murex, and extracted purple dye from it, using the dye to color wool (see Acts 16:14).

This letter reminds us that sometimes God approaches us with warm and upbeat words; but at other times He uses much firmer language. The latter sort of divine love is disciplinary, and it should never shock us (see Hebrews 12:5-11). Jesus introduces Himself to this church as the Son of God—the only time that term is used in Revelation. It speaks of authority. The Son of God comes with eyes of burning fire and feet of brass, both of which suggest judgment. Jesus takes a "sandwich approach" to this church. He first says, "This is what I like about you," and He closes by saying, "You don't have to keep going the way you've been going." And in between the two positive statements He gives His words of judgment.

This church had always been known for its tender care for people. At the time Jesus wrote, it was increasing in good works. The Christians in Thyatira had learned the vital lesson that the Christian life is not static, but dynamic and growing. And yet this church had a problem. It got involved in immorality. How? I can think of only one answer: While the people did many good works, they did not bind themselves completely to the Word. Corruption coexisted with a lack of discernment. The people allowed it to happen; they tolerated it. They had permitted someone in their fellowship to teach that it was okay to be unholy.

We're told in verse 20 this woman is "Jezebel." I believe Jezebel was the woman's spiritual nickname, not her real name. Some commentators identify her with the prophetess from the temple of fortune-tellers, a woman who had some kind of conversion experience. The church evidently allowed her to teach because of her stature in the community. She began seducing members of the church with doctrines that encouraged sexual immorality, much like the Jezebel of the Old Testament (see 1 Kings 16–21; 2 Kings 9). The modern equivalent of Jezebel would be someone who says, "Let's mix other religions with Christianity. Let's put them together and not treat Christianity as an exclusive faith because we all have a part of God. We all have a part of the truth. So let's all worship together."

As Christians, we should pray for the spiritual gift of discernment so that we can distinguish between truth and error. When someone claims, "I'm inspired; I've got divine revelation," we have to learn to discern, to not be gullible. Jesus said, "Beware of false prophets, who come to you in sheep's clothing"—that is, they use the right names and spiritual words and language—"but inwardly they are ravenous wolves" (Matthew 7:15). In fact, there are three easy tests for spotting a wolf in sheep's clothing: the test of character, the test of creed, and the test of converts. Does their teaching foster holiness? Do they speak of Jesus as the Son of God who came to die for sinners? Do their followers bear godly fruit?

In the case of Thyatira, this woman's teaching led others to commit sexual immorality. Jesus called both her and her followers to repent, but they refused; and that meant *big* trouble. Jesus doesn't like to come in judgment; He'd rather that erring people repent. God is not willing that any should perish but that all should come to repentance (see 2 Peter 3:9). When sinners refuse to turn to God, however, the consequences can be both painful and deadly.

When Jesus speaks of "tribulation" in verse 22, He could be referring to persecution by the Roman government, or He could mean that certain consequences can follow sexual immorality (such as disease or suffering). Or perhaps He has in mind the Great Tribulation, the seven-year period of divine judgment coming upon the earth in the last days. He might even mean that this corrupt church system will last all the way until the end. Whatever His meaning, He is saying to them and to us, "Don't get involved in immorality. Avoid it at all costs."

To those who follow His counsel, Jesus promises authority (see verses 26-27; Jesus was quoting from Psalm 2). During the Millennium, a 1000-year period of peace and justice described in Revelation 20, Jesus will rule the earth as with a rod of iron—and He says to His obedient followers, "You will rule with Me for 1000 years."

He also tells the overcomers that He will give them "the morning star" (v. 28). If we look ahead to Revelation 22, we see Jesus calling Himself "the Bright and Morning Star" (v. 16). The context of the phrase "the morning star" in Revelation 2:28 helps us to unlock what Jesus meant when He spoke about giving them the morning star. In verse 24 He referred to some who claimed to know the "depths of Satan." Many false religious groups of that era spoke of knowing the deep things of God. Jesus corrected them: "You mean the deep things of Satan." Jesus was saying that when we have Him, we need nothing else.

We all need discernment. Where does discernment fit into *your* scale of important Christian attributes to cultivate? Jesus commended the church at Ephesus for being intolerant of evil and false teaching, but He rebuked the church at Thyatira for its desperate lack of discernment.

Let us train ourselves to discern good from evil. And then let us encourage each other with the knowledge that Jesus has promised to give *Himself* to us without reservation. How much more encouragement could we need?

3

The Churches of Revelation, Part 2
Revelation 3

SUMMARY

In His brief letters to Sardis, Philadelphia, and Laodicea, Jesus addresses two "problem" churches and one congregation that labors under heavy persecution and yet remains faithful to spreading the gospel. Both the challenges and the opportunities faced by these ancient congregations can stimulate our own faith and help us to get busy with the things that Christ Himself deems most important.

RELATED SCRIPTURES FOR STUDY
Genesis 45:7; Acts 2:42; 1 Corinthians 16:9; 2 Corinthians 11:3-4; Colossians 4:3

One of my favorite movies has earned a reputation as a modern classic. *The Princess Bride* is a fairy tale about a hero, the good guy against the bad guys, and the girl he gets at the end. But at one point the hero is captured, tortured, and presumed dead. Two of his friends take his body to Miracle Max and lay it on the table in front of him.

In despair they plead for Miracle Max to help their friend, whom they say is dead.

Max, however, looks at the body and says their friend isn't dead. Rather, he is *mostly* dead.

They then ask Max what he means. Max replies that there's a

difference between *mostly* dead and *all* dead. Then he goes on to revive the hero.

I bring this up because the fifth church addressed in the book of Revelation has much in common with the hero from *The Princess Bride*.

Sardis: The Church of the Living Dead (3:1-6)

The church at Sardis was dead; the divine coroner, Jesus Christ, pronounced it so. But even in that congregation not all had died (although even they were mostly dead). Sardis still had a chance for revival. A miracle could happen! But for the most part, this church amounted to a morgue with a steeple.

Jesus had harsh words to say to the church at Thyatira, but at least He had a few good things to say to the people there. Not so with the church at Sardis. And so He jumps right in with a warning and an exhortation.

Sardis was among the most important and wealthy cities in ancient Asia Minor. It sat at the junction of the imperial highway that connected Ephesus and Smyrna and Pergamos with the inland cities of Asia Minor. Two features of this city made it different from all others. First, it had an acropolis that functioned as a necropolis—a graveyard called the Cemetery of One Thousand Hills. From seven miles away you could see not only the temple of Diana (or Artemis) atop the acropolis, but also this cemetery filled with hundreds of burial mounds and tombstones. The city was preoccupied with death.

It's significant, then, that Jesus tells this church, "You're dead." In other words, Sardis was a church full of hypocrites. In the words of Paul, the people had a form of godliness but had denied its power (see 2 Timothy 3:5). The church of Sardis lacked the one thing it needed the most, which is the Holy Spirit. So Jesus introduces Himself as "He who has the seven Spirits of God" (v. 1). I believe He's using an idiom borrowed from Isaiah 11:2, which denotes the fullness of the Holy Spirit. A dead church *needs* the infusion of the sevenfold Spirit of God, just as a dead individual does.

The church at Sardis had become so much like the world around it that it could no longer confront its society. That's what "spiritually dead" means. Three factors had contributed to this sobering assessment; let's look at the spiritual autopsy Jesus conducted.

First, the church died because its members relied on their past successes. A sure sign of death is when a church worships its past, its history, and its traditions.

Second, this church lived on the surface of things. Its members cared more about their reputation than the reality that was taking place around them. While they had "a few names even in Sardis who have not defiled their garments" (v. 4), there were many people who *had* defiled their garments. So while the church at Sardis had a great exterior and a supposedly wonderful reputation, filth and spiritual death lay underneath. Quite simply, the church wore a beautiful burial garment.

According to the historian Herodotus, eventually the church in Sardis became lax in its moral standards and open in licentiousness. In other words, it became very much like the world. The members of this church became so concerned with their reputation—with what others thought about them—that they lost all of their character. Reputation is how you are perceived; character is how you are really living. Sardis was a church filled with nominal Christians who were living superficially for God.

Third, the congregation at Sardis became satisfied with aimless activity. Jesus told the people their works were imperfect or incomplete. They did empty labor with no life in it. They spent their time on aimless, dead activity. While men saw them as great—they had the reputation—God saw them as an empty, lifeless shell. The church of Sardis had many irons in the fire, but none were hot.

And what is the antidote to such a serious spiritual malaise?

The first step toward spiritual renewal is to realize something is wrong. So Jesus tells those who still had a little life in them, "Wake up! Recognize that something is wrong" (see v. 2).

Second, He says, "Strengthen what is weak" (see v. 2). The Greek word used here means "stabilize that which is frail." Paul used the same term while on his third missionary journey through Galatia when he said, "I will go and strengthen the brothers" (see Acts 18:23). He wanted to return to these Christians and strengthen them lest they fall away.

Third, they were to call to memory the basics. We can only assume that they had received core things of the faith, such as the gospel and the Holy Spirit. Jesus instructed the church members to look to their past and get in touch with their heritage—the things that once made them great. Yet He urged them to use those things as a guidepost, not as a hitching post.

Philadelphia: Body Building, God's Way (3:7-13)

While the church at Philadelphia was not perfect, it was both strong and noteworthy. It bore the marks of a faithful church and built itself up God's way, so Jesus had nothing scathing to say to it. What made these people such a commendable congregation?

First, the people in the church had placed themselves under the authority of God. Jesus introduces Himself as One who is faithful and true and holds the keys—always a mark of authority in Scripture. In the Old Testament, God often introduced Himself as the Holy One of Israel. That name was given only to God, but Jesus uses it here. Jesus also called Himself "true," or more literally, "genuine" or "authentic." Jesus commended the church at Philadelphia because the people lived under the authority of the genuine, true, and authentic Jesus Christ.

Tragically, people often concoct "a different Jesus" from the one revealed in the Bible. Many teachers even today proclaim the name of Jesus but attach attributes and ideologies to His name that do not at all represent the biblical Jesus. Cults do this regularly, such as the Jehovah's Witnesses or the Christian Scientists or the Mormons. A true church has to remain under the authority of the authentic Jesus Christ.

Second, Philadelphia was a church in revival. Jesus says, "See, I have set before you an open door, and no one can shut it; for you have a little strength, have kept My word, and have not denied My name" (v. 8). The word translated "strength" comes from the Greek term *dunamis*, which means "power." Sometimes the term was used of weak people who were getting stronger or were reviving. This church was undergoing a revival and returning to its New Testament roots. And as the people returned to the Lord, they gained strength. Because they were weak, they were perfectly suited to be the objects of God's strength.

A prerequisite for revival is to say, "I am weak; I need God's strength." People in revival know they need God's power. Revival usually begins with small numbers of people who recognize they need help and who desire God's strength so much that they seek Him with all of their hearts. Charles Finney once said, "Revival begins when God points His finger at you."[1] And Gipsy Smith said, "If you want revival, go inside your room, close the door, lock it, get on the floor and draw a circle around yourself and pray that God would revive everything inside the circle—not outside."[2] True revival is contagious.

The church in Philadelphia enjoyed revival because it was a church of the Word. In the Amplified version of the Bible Jesus says, "I know that you have but a little strength, but you have kept My word and you have guarded My message." This church loved the Word. At the heart of every true revival you find the priorities listed in Acts 2:42, and at the top of that list is the Word of God.

Think of all the things that *aren't* on that list. Love isn't mentioned, for example, and yet Jesus says love is the mark of a true church. Why doesn't Jesus mention love to the Christians in Philadephia? Because the Word teaches us how to love. All of our cues, even in love, are found in the Word of God.

Jesus also commends the Philadelphian church for its loyalty. Jesus says to the people, "You…have not denied My name" (v. 8). They held fast to the name of Jesus Christ. He had commanded them (and us) to persevere, and they did so, all the way until the time of this letter. Despite persecution, the Philadelphian Christians remained loyal to Jesus.

This was also a church of opportunity. Jesus introduces Himself as the One who opens the door—a door no one can shut. What is this door? It could be the door of salvation. Earlier Jesus had said, "I am the door. If anyone enters by Me, he will will be saved" (John 10:9). Or He could be talking about the door of safety, of rescue from "the hour of trial which shall come upon the earth" (v. 10).

But I think it's most likely that Jesus is speaking about the door of opportunity for service. Often in the New Testament, a door represents an opportunity to serve God (see 1 Corinthians 16:9; 2 Corinthians

2:12; Colossians 4:3). Philadelphia was strategically located so that the people who lived there could reach out to many cities. Great Roman armies marched through Philadelphia via a famous highway, and merchant roads also wound through the city. Looking out from Philadelphia, one could see the kingdoms of Lydia, Mysia, and Pergia. The Philadelphia church therefore had great opportunities for service.

Finally, this church had a future. Jesus tells the people that their enemies would be humbled, that they would be kept from the time of trial, and that He would make them into a pillar in the house of His God so that they would "go out no more" (v. 12). Now, a pillar was used to strengthen a building, to uphold a roof. So a pillar is a symbol of strength and security. Earthquakes periodically hit Philadelphia, and whenever they did, people would run out of the city. And Jesus was telling them, "I will strengthen you, I will honor you, and I will be your security. You won't have to go out anymore. And I, the true God, will honor you by erecting a pillar in your name." What a beautiful promise!

Just as the people in the ancient church in Philadelphia walked through the doors of opportunity that Jesus presented to them, so let us do the same.

Laodicea: A Problem with Spiritual Temperature (3:14-22)

The church in Laodicea thought it was far better off than it really was. Its members had an elevated sense of self-esteem and thought they needed nothing, but Jesus approached them with the sobering truth.

A man named Antiochus II founded Laodicea and named it after his wife. The church there eventually became wealthy, prosperous, and active. Yet these Christians had a spiritual disease; they had become complacent, apathetic, and halfhearted in their commitment.

Jesus introduces Himself as "the Amen, the Faithful and True Witness, the Beginning of the creation of God" (v. 14). The Bible uses the word "amen," a transliteration of a Hebrew term, some seventy-seven times. In the Old Testament, God's people sometimes used the word to express agreement with a statement from the Lord. In the New Testament, Jesus uses the term to endorse His own words. Interestingly, He never says amen at the end of a statement, but always at the beginning, as if to say, "What I am about to say is the absolute truth."

We don't normally think of "amen" as a proper name, but Jesus uses it that way here. He speaks the truth because He is the truth, and to fortify His claim, He describes Himself as "the Faithful and True Witness." That's important because Jesus' patient has misdiagnosed himself; he thinks he's fine, but he's not. In fact, he's very sick, and Jesus comes to him with an accurate, reliable diagnosis. He speaks the absolute truth as the Amen, the Faithful and True Witness.

Jesus also calls Himself "the Beginning of the creation of God." This title has confused some readers, who take this to mean that Jesus is part of God's creation. But the Greek term translated "beginning" is *archae*, which means "chief" or "source." So an *arch*angel is the chief of the angels. Jesus is the *archae* of creation, the source and chief of it all. The implication of what He is saying is profound: "Not only do I know everything about you, not only is My evaluation about your condition accurate, but as the source of God's creation, I can do something about it."

Laodicea lay in the great Lycus Valley, some forty miles east and inland of the church at Ephesus. The city sat astride the main trade route from east to west that brought together the two major empires of the world. Because Laodicea was on the main drag—the Route 66 of the ancient world—it became a great commercial and banking city boasting great wealth. The city was famous for two products: black, shiny wool used in garments, and a school of ophthalmology. The residents boasted of having a cure for eye problems; they made a salve of clay and rubbed it in patients' eyes.

The residents of Laodicea had one major problem: They had a very poor water supply. Two other cities nearby had better water sources, and the Laodiceans tried to make use of them. Colosse sat at the foot of some huge mountains that supplied the city with an abundant runoff of snowmelt. This meant the water in Colosse was cold and refreshing. The other city, Hierapolis, boasted of hot springs, with steaming hot water for baths. The Laodiceans built one aqueduct to bring water from Colosse and another to bring water from Hierapolis, but by the time the water from Colosse arrived it had gone from ice cold to luke-warm, and by the time the water from Hierapolis arrived it had gone from steaming hot to tepid. Jesus played off that dilemma and when He rebuked the Laodiceans, He said they had become spiritually luke-warm, just like their insipid water.

To be spiritually lukewarm is to be complacent, halfhearted, and unable to recognize the depth of one's spiritual need. The lukewarm person straddles the fence and is halfhearted about spiritual things. Conviction never affects his or her conscious level; the conscience remains untouched. Lukewarm people don't take either Jesus or the Bible seriously. They wink at sin and have no concern for a lost world; hence they have no viable witness. What could be worse?

G. Campbell Morgan wrote, "Lukewarmness is the worst form of all blasphemy."[3] A lukewarm person names the name of Christ but lives as though God doesn't exist. This kind of a person has been inoculated with an insipid form of Christianity that makes him or her immune to the real thing.

While the Laodiceans said, in essence, "We're rich, we're fine, we don't need anything," Jesus basically responded, "You're lost, you are miserable, you are poor, you are blind, you are naked" (see v. 17). The misguided self-esteem of the Laodiceans blinded them to their true condition. They were wretched because they remained in their sin. They were miserable and to be pitied because they were unaccept-able to God. They were dirt poor but didn't know it because of their blindness. Finally, they were naked because the garments they draped around themselves were of their own making. They were like the king in the Hans Christian Andersen story *The Emperor's New Clothes*—though he was naked, he felt certain he was wearing a beautiful outfit.

Jesus counseled the Laodiceans to buy from Him gold, white gar-ments, and eye salve—things they thought they already had but didn't. Jesus basically told them, "You are *desperately* needy—and I have what you need. You can't do without it."

Augustine once said to God, "You have made us for Yourself, and we are restless until we find our rest in You." No other solution to the things we experience in life exists except for what Jesus Christ wants to give you. You will remain a restless person until you rest in Him.

Even though Jesus rebuked the Laodiceans for their lukewarmness, He still loved them. In fact, that's *why* He rebuked them (see Hebrews 12:5-11). If you're engaging in all sorts of sin while claiming to be a Christian and you have not been rebuked, it could be that you're not of your Father in heaven but of your father the devil. Jesus says that *every* child of God receives rebuke and discipline. God loves you, and He will do whatever is necessary to get you back on the right track. Sometimes that means a sharp rebuke.

Jesus also tells the Laodiceans to be "zealous" and to "repent" (v. 19). The Greek word translated "zealous" means "be on fire, be hot." The Greek rendering of this text is very telling. Literally it goes something like this: "Stop once and for all this action, and turn around once and for all, but continue to be zealous for Me." Note that the first command speaks of finishing an action, and the second speaks of a continuous action. So Jesus is saying, "Continually, progressively be on fire and be hot. Be fervent in spirit for your Lord, Jesus Christ."

If you are holding on to something in your life that shouldn't be there, spit it out. That's a far better option than having God spit *you* out! Jesus tells the Laodiceans, "You nauseate Me so much that I'm going to vomit you out of My mouth" (see v. 16). Jesus *hates* lukewarmness.

But Jesus also gives these lukewarm Christians a gracious invitation (v. 20), one of the most famous in all of Scripture: "Behold, I stand at the door and knock; if anyone hears My voice and opens the door, I will come in to him and dine with him, and he with Me." In the Middle East, eating is considered a sacred activity. If you and I sit down at a table together, and you eat what I eat, then the food we both consume becomes part of each of us. We're nourished by the same common element, and so we become one with each other. So in essence Jesus is saying, "I want to enjoy intimate fellowship with you. I will come and share My secrets with you so that we can be one." What a great offer!

The Doorknob Is on the Inside

Years ago an English artist named Holman Hunt painted Revelation

3:20 on canvas. He pictured Jesus standing in a nice little glen at the end of a roadway, knocking on the door of a cottage. When Hunt finished the painting, he invited his artist buddies to critique his work. One of them said, "Holman, there is a problem with the door itself. There's no doorknob on the outside."

"I did that on purpose," Hunt replied, "because the door is the opening to the heart, and it can open only from the inside." Hunt understood that Jesus will never force Himself on anyone. He gently knocks; He won't impose. Whether the door remains closed or opens is completely up to the person on the inside.

Long ago Jesus spoke His words of encouragement, rebuke, and counsel to the seven churches of Asia Minor. Now He's speaking to you and me. What is He saying? And how will we respond? The future awaits…and it is up to us whether we look forward to good news or bad.

4
Peeking into the Portals of Heaven
Revelation 4

SUMMARY

Immediately after John records Jesus' letters to the seven churches, a heavenly voice summons him to heaven. He then describes both his entrance into heaven and his experience of heaven. It is striking that the church is not mentioned again in Revelation until chapter 22, which suggests that John's experience here is a picture of the rapture of the church. That is, the church is not present on earth during this time.

RELATED SCRIPTURES FOR STUDY

Isaiah 6:1-7; 1 Corinthians 15:52-57; 1 Thessalonians 4:13-18; 2 Thessalonians 2:1-7

A few years ago during a long flight I began paging through an airline magazine. Soon I saw an advertisement for a new hotel in Seattle: "Great views, great location, great rates" trumpeted the ad, seeking to attract the attention of wealthy executives. *That's really what people want in a home, isn't it?* I thought. *They want a lovely view, a convenient location, and great rates.*

I believe we will enjoy those features in our eternal home. We'll be blessed with a great location: the new heaven and the new earth. We'll have a great view: the throne of God, the tree of life, and a river that flows from the Lord's throne, as pure as crystal. And we'll enjoy great rates: it's *free*! God will give all of this, without cost, to everyone who gladly follows His Son. Can you imagine the happiness overflowing from a place like that?

I'm reminded of some parents who took their little boy to the pet shop for his birthday. They allowed him to pick any dog he wanted. The shop owner showed the boy every type of dog imaginable, but the boy picked the one who wagged its tail nonstop. "Why'd you pick that dog?" everyone asked. "Because I want the one with the happy ending," the boy replied.

That's a wise little boy! When God lays out all of the possible paths for us into eternity, we need to make sure we choose the one with the happy ending. And that's what the fourth chapter of Revelation is about.

John's Entrance into Heaven

At the beginning of the chapter, John sees a door standing open in heaven. Notice it's not a gate; we don't find Saint Peter standing there and telling dumb jokes. In fact, Peter has *nothing* to do with your getting into heaven. Only Jesus determines your eternal destiny. Jesus Himself said, "I am the door. If anyone enters by Me, he will be saved" (John 10:9).

Recall that in Revelation 3, Jesus spoke to the church in Philadelphia about another door, this one on the earth: "See, I have set before you an open door, and no one can shut it" (v. 8). God has opened a door of opportunity for all of us, a door of service. But the time will come when that door on earth will close forever and the one in heaven will open. At some point, *every* opportunity on earth will vanish and eternity will begin. So Jesus declared, "I must work the works of Him who sent Me while it is day; the night is coming when no one can work" (John 9:4). *Now* is the day of opportunity. *Today* we have an open door of service; and when that door closes—with our deaths or the rapture—another door will open in heaven. And at that moment we'll hear Jesus say, "Well done, good and faithful servant; you have been faithful over a few things, I will make you ruler over many things. Enter into the joy of your lord" (Matthew 25:23).

Let's recognize that this earth is not our goal. Earth is merely our gateway to heaven. The Bible repeatedly reminds us that we will live on earth for only a short time; that is why it calls us pilgrims, travelers, sojourners. We're on our way to another destination, a heavenly one. Remember that Jesus said, "My kingdom is not of this world" (John 18:36).

What about *your* kingdom? Is it of this world, or of the next? Does your own little happiness now and your own small world here consume you? Jesus advised us to "lay up for yourselves treasure in heaven" (Matthew 6:20). And the apostle Peter declared, "We, according to His promise, look for new heavens and a new earth in which righteousness dwells" (2 Peter 3:13). Our English word "heaven" comes from the old Anglo-Saxon term "heave on," which simply means "to be lifted up." The word normally described a place or a condition *above* the common condition of the earth. Therefore heaven is up, beyond, above the common condition of the earth.

The Bible uses the word "heaven" to describe three distinct areas. The "first heaven" refers to the terrestrial heavens—what we'd call our atmosphere. The "second heaven" refers to the celestial heaven, where we find the moon and the sun and the stars. And the "third heaven," the ultimate heaven, is the holy place where God dwells. In Hebrew this is called the heaven of heavens (Deuteronomy 10:14). It is this third heaven that John has in mind in Revelation 4.

Immediately after John arrives in heaven, he hears a trumpet "speaking with me" (Revelation 4:1). Likewise, 1 Thessalonians 4:16-17 speaks of the "trumpet of God" calling believers to join the Lord in the air through the rapture. Revelation 4:1-2 thus provides us with a picture-prophecy of the rapture of the church. John illustrates what will happen to God's people at the end of the church age, when we are caught up together in the clouds to be with Jesus forever.

Notice the words "come up here" (v. 1). John had been on the earth, writing about the church—and suddenly he finds himself in heaven. In the rest of the book he writes about the events taking place on earth from a bird's-eye view, or from a heavenly perspective before the throne of God. As we noted earlier, the key verse to the whole book is Revelation 1:19, which gives us the divine outline of the book's message. Jesus tells John, "Write the things [a] which you have seen, [b] and the things which are, and [c] the things which will take place after this" (the Greek word used here means "after these things"). The "things which are" refer to the letters to the seven churches in chapters 2 and 3. After Jesus gives His messages to those churches, John is told to write what happens "after these things."

Chapter 4 opens with exactly the same Greek wording. John wrote, "*After these things* I looked, and behold, a door." After what things? After the things he described in chapters 2 and 3—namely, the age of the church. For John, this experience of being caught up to heaven was instantaneous. He found himself instantly in the presence of God—which is exactly what we will experience at the rapture. Paul writes in 1 Corinthians 15:51-52, "We shall all be changed—in a moment, in the twinkling of an eye, at the last trumpet. For the trumpet will sound, and the dead will be raised incorruptible, and we shall be changed."

And let's not forget the main theme of chapters 2 and 3: the church. The word "church" appears nineteen times in chapters 1 through 3—but from Revelation chapter 4 until Revelation 22:16, the church is not mentioned even once. That means that chapter 4 marks the third division of the book of Revelation ("after these things").

Over the years people have asked me, "How can you talk about the rapture? It's not even in the Bible!" On the contrary, the teaching of the rapture is all over the New Testament. The word "rapture" comes from 1 Thessalonians 4:17. The phrase translated "caught up" comes from the Greek word *harpazo*, which appears thirteen times in the New Testament. Four times it's translated "catch up," three times it's translated "to take by force," twice it means "to catch away," twice "to pluck," one time "to catch," and another time "to pull."

When Jerome, in the fourth century, translated this passage from the original Greek text into Latin, the word he used for "to catch up in the air" was the Latin term *raptus*, which means "to rapture." Scholar Kenneth Wuest translated 1 Thessalonians 4:17 like this: "We shall be snatched away forcibly in masses of saints, having the appearance of clouds for a welcome meeting with the Lord in the lower atmosphere."

Do you see how this describes the same phenomenon that John experienced? He wrote, "Immediately I was in the Spirit" (Revelation 4:2)—just as will happen in the rapture.

People tend to confuse two distinct events: (1) the rapture of the church, and (2) the second coming of Jesus Christ. In fact, they are two separate events, and the Bible always presents them as distinct. At the rapture, Jesus comes *for* His church. He does not descend all the way to earth, but instead we ascend to meet Him in the air. This event is sudden, unannounced, and totally unanticipated. Jesus said, "Therefore you also be ready, for the Son of Man is coming at an hour you do not expect Him" (Matthew 24:43). In fact, we should think, *Jesus could return for His church before this light turns green. He could come before I take the big test at school today. He could rapture me into the air before I finish reading this sentence.* Thinking like this could alter forever the way you live on earth!

Revelation 4 does not give us a picture of the second coming; we don't see *that* staggering event until Revelation 19. And at that point, heaven opens and Jesus descends all the way to the surface of the earth, accompanied by multitudes of His saints. Jesus described His second coming as a very predictable event that will occur immediately after the seven-year-long Tribulation: "For as the lightning comes from east and flashes to the west, so also will the coming of the Son of Man be" (Matthew 24:27). At the second coming, "every eye will see Him, even they who pierced Him" (Revelation 1:7).

At the rapture, Jesus comes *for* His church—unexpectedly, without notice. At the second coming, He comes *with* the church, and the whole world—everyone, every person, every eye—will see it happen. If we don't get this crucial distinction clearly in mind, much of Bible prophecy will seem incomprehensible.

What Is Heaven Like?

What will heaven be like? We should admit at the outset that we don't know a lot about it. Even Paul said, "I was caught up into the third heaven and I heard things that were inexpressible" (see 2 Corinthians 12:2-4), or as it says in the King James Version, Paul saw things that were "not lawful for a man to utter." In other words, Paul might say to us, "If I tried to describe to you what I saw and heard in heaven, it would be a crime." Still, the Bible gives us some interesting snapshots of heaven. While we lack a full, complete description of the place of God's majestic throne—I doubt very much whether we could handle it— Scripture does gives us some important clues about what heaven is like.

When John first arrives in heaven, he sees "a throne," and "One sat on the throne" (v. 2). The word "throne" is the key term in chapter 4, appearing a dozen times (and thirty times elsewhere in Revelation). This fact alone should signal to us that *heaven is a real place*. It is not a figment of our imagination, nor is it a fantasyland. The writer of Hebrews describes heaven as a place with solid foundations, "whose builder and maker is God" (Hebrews 11:10). It is real, stable, and permanent.

Also, heaven is *huge*. If you have placed your faith in Christ, not only will you be there with millions of other Christians; not only will you see twenty-four elders and four living creatures buzzing around God's throne; but think of all of the people throughout history who have followed God's plan and obeyed Jesus Christ—they'll *all* be there (see Revelation 5:11)! Think of it—millions, even billions of angelic creatures will join with the saints of all ages and sing with full and joyful voices the anthems of heaven.

Heaven might even be a place of many cities. Jesus said, "In my Father's house are many mansions" (John 14:2). The book of Revelation tells us of at least one of these places; chapter 21 describes the New Jerusalem. The New Jerusalem is a tangible, measurable, corporate city in the shape of a gargantuan cube that descends from heaven toward the earth. Can you imagine?

But despite heaven's immensity, it is God's throne that captures John's attention as the central piece of heavenly furniture. And why is the throne so important? It's not that the throne itself is so spectacular, although it is magnificent. It's because *God* sits on that throne. What makes heaven heaven is not the presence of angels or the streets of gold or even the happy reunions we will enjoy with loved ones. What makes heaven so heavenly is that the God we love and serve will be there for us *forever*. We'll see Him in person. David said, "As for me, I will see Your face in righteousness; I shall be satisfied when I awake in Your likeness" (Psalm 17:15).

John tries to picture God by describing at least three kinds of brilliant stones. He mentions a jasper, which is a clear, diamond-like gem with spectacular brilliance. He also speaks of a sardius stone, a gem something like a ruby, with a reddish hue. As he gazes upon the throne, he sees a brilliant white light exploding outward, all colored with a reddish hue—perhaps reminding the heavenly inhabitants of the blood of Christ shed on the cross. Whenever they look toward the throne, they recall the Savior's departure from heaven and the crimson stain that followed, which bought their salvation.

John also saw a rainbow, "in appearance like an emerald" (v. 3)—the third gemstone. He sees this rainbow not after the storm of divine judgment, but before it—as if to remind him that God always keeps His promises. Only when God's patience has come to an end will He judge. And even after that future judgment, we can rest assured that the rainbow, as a promise of God's commitment to keeping His word, will remain throughout all eternity.

Next we see twenty-four elders and other living creatures (vv. 4,6). Who are the elders? The Old Testament speaks of twenty-four courses of priests who served in the temple in Jerusalem near the Ark of the Covenant (the earthly symbol of God's throne). That's the only other time in the Bible we see this number in a similar context. The twenty-four courses of priests represented the nation of Israel before God; so I think it's safe to say that the twenty-four elders represent the church before God.

John then says, "From the throne proceeded lightnings, thunderings, and voices" (v. 5). These things are probably meant to remind us that God will judge the earth. The first mention of thunder and lightning and voices in the Bible comes in the context of the giving of the law at Mount Sinai. Four times in the book of Revelation we'll read of thunder and lightning and voices, and each time they come from the throne of God.

God's throne has served as a place of grace for many centuries, yet there will come a time when God prepares His throne for judgment. It's as though He says, "I love the earth and I've been patient. I've given My Son; I've sent My Christian witnesses throughout the earth. But now I'm fed up. I'm tired of rebellion and unrepentant wickedness and arrogance. The time has come for judgment." Judgment is a divine necessity—and at just the right time, God will judge.

In verses 5 and 6, John sees seven lamps of fire and a sea of glass before the throne. Again we get some clues about the text's meaning by looking back to the Old Testament. The writer of Hebrews plainly says that the tabernacle—the big tentlike, portable temple that Israel used during its wilderness experience—was a model of something in heaven (Hebrews 9:23). The wilderness tabernacle featured a seven-branched candlestick; and here in heaven we see seven lamps of fire. Similarly, the tabernacle served as the "home" for the ark of the covenant, which had two golden cherubim with two wings apiece covering its lid, hovering over what was called the mercy seat.

John tells us in verse 6 that he sees four living creatures hovering around God's throne, and a "sea of glass, like crystal" in front of the throne. In front of the Old Testament tabernacle was a bronze laver full of water, in which the priest would wash his hands before offering a sacrifice. And here in Revelation we see a huge sea of glass, like crystal. It's solid now, no longer liquid, because in heaven there will be no need for cleansing. Jesus died on the cross, paying the price for our sins. And in heaven, we'll stand on the finished work of Jesus Christ.

The chapter closes with a vision of worship before the throne of God (vv. 8-11). And in this, our first peek into God's throne room, we see *lots* of worship. Remember this, because it will be a significant theme throughout the rest of the book. The throne room of God overflows with praise and worship! And notice that it's all *corporate* worship. The people and angels of God all worship Him together, in unity, each voice adding its strength to the next. That being the case, why not get little practice in corporate worship while we're still down here?

Follow Me?

God will never force anyone to spend eternity with Him. He gives us all a choice as to where and with whom we will live forever. If you don't want God in your life, rest assured that He will honor your choice.

A famous tombstone on the East Coast of the United States features this clever little poem:

> Pause, stranger, as you pass me by;
> as you are now, so once was I.
> As I am now, so you will be;
> so prepare for death and follow me.

A visitor to the cemetery read the words on the tombstone and used chalk to add these words:

> To follow you I'm not content,
> until I know which way you went.

Which way are *you* going? Consider your current path and understand that only one door to heaven lies open—and His name is Jesus. When you trust Him, He will lead you to a great location with great views and great rates. And best of all, He promises to stay with you there forever.

That's why we call it heaven.

History's Greatest Real Estate

Revelation 5

SUMMARY

A deed to the earth is presented; it's in the hand of Him who sits on the throne (vv. 1-2). But a problem with the transaction reveals a great dilemma (vv. 3-4). John weeps, but the Deliverer prevails (vv. 5-7). His triumph leads to a threefold heavenly praise chorus, lauding Jesus for His sacrifice, His rulership, and His holy relationship to His Father (vv. 8-14).

RELATED SCRIPTURES FOR STUDY

Exodus 15; Ruth; 1 Chronicles 15; 25; Psalm 95; Jeremiah 32; Matthew 13; John 5:23

M y father was a real-estate broker and something of an entrepreneur. He bought property, developed roads, and subdivided lots on which he built model homes. His claim to fame is that he once subdivided a piece of property for Roy Rogers.

Dad once had an interesting opportunity to buy a piece of property in Orange County, California, called Lemon Heights. Back then it was simply a hilly area filled with lemon groves. He wanted to build homes there, and so he approached the local authorities for permission to proceed. When he told them his plans, they replied, "You'll devalue the land if you build homes on it." And they refused to give him permission.

Of course, things have changed since then. If you visit Lemon

Heights today, you'll see a beautiful area filled with homes that my dad never developed. And their value has vastly increased over the years.

Modern history is filled with real-estate opportunities. Walt Disney, for instance, purchased property twenty-five miles from civilization, where cows mooed and wandered among a few little shacks in a field. Eventually that property became Anaheim and Disneyland. Or we think of Manhattan, a little island in New York that Peter Minuit, the general director of the Dutch Colony of New Netherlands, purchased from Native Americans for goods valued at $24. Or we think of the Louisiana Purchase, in which Thomas Jefferson bought 800,000 square miles of land west of the Mississippi River for $15 million from Napoleon Bonaparte. That purchase, which took place in 1803, changed the course of America's future.

But hands down, the greatest real-estate deal in history is recorded in Revelation 5, where the real estate at stake is the entire earth.

A Property Reclaimed (5:1-7)

John saw an invaluable scroll in God's hand, written on both the inside and outside. Seals kept it shut. Normally a scroll was sealed in sections with wax, either on the very edges of the scroll or on the inside. When a scribe had completed one section, he'd roll it up to conceal the writing, seal it, and then continue on to the next section. By this process he would assure that whoever read the scroll would do so in a predetermined order, and that only the person who would read the document was someone who had the authority to break the seals. Anybody from the early church who read John's account about this scroll would instantly think of real-estate transactions. Title deeds to a piece of property were often written on a scroll and sealed with seven seals.

In Old Testament days, something called the redemption clause allowed a former owner to buy back his land; the land could never be sold permanently. So if someone had lost a piece of land but later could fulfill the requirements to buy it back, he had the authority to take the scroll, break its seals, and read the words inside. It then became his property. If he could not fulfill the conditions, a close relative could "redeem" the property instead. The Bible calls him the *ga'al*, the "kinsmen redeemer." Every kinsmen redeemer had to meet three qualifications. First, he had to be related to the original owner; second, he had to be able to fulfill the requirements for purchasing the property; and third, he had to be willing to buy back the property.

We know the scroll in Revelation 5 is highly significant because, first, we see it in God's right hand, which, in the Bible, is the hand of authority. Second, it appears to involve the fate of the whole earth (vv. 3-4); that is why observers weep and wail when no one is found worthy to open the scroll. When finally someone comes forward who *is* worthy to take and break the seals, exuberant worship breaks out (v. 8). It seems, then, that this scroll is nothing less than the title deed to the earth— the earth that God created, the earth that God sustains and maintains. But it is also the earth that God must reclaim by redemption, and so the Lamb steps forward to fulfill those obligations. The idea here is, "I can redeem or reclaim this land that was lost."

Someone might object, "But if God is the Creator and the maintainer of the earth, then why does He need to reclaim what's already His? After all, doesn't the Bible say, 'The earth is the LORD's and the fullness thereof'?" (Psalm 24:1 KJV). But remember that God gave Adam dominion over the earth. When Adam fell into sin, the earth came under a divine curse (Romans 8:20-22), and it will remain under that curse until the time arrives for God to remove it.

In the garden, Adam gave dominion over the earth to Satan; that makes the devil a usurper. The earth isn't his. But while Satan does not "own" this earth, the New Testament does give him the title "the god of this age" (2 Corinthians 4:4). Note that when the devil tempted Jesus, he showed the Lord all the kingdoms of the earth in a moment of time and said, "All this authority I will give You, and their glory; for this has been delivered to me, and I give it to whomever I wish. Therefore, if you will worship before me, all will be Yours" (Luke 4:6-7). Satan apparently knew that Jesus had come to shed His blood to buy people back to God, and he tried to convince the Lord that He didn't have to go to the cross. Of course, Jesus spurned that temptation. He did go to the cross, and He did shed His blood for our redemption.

In Revelation 5, a dilemma momentarily puts a hold on the

festivities around opening the scroll: Sadly, no one could be found who met the criteria for claiming and opening the document. John sees this as an utter catastrophe, and so he weeps uncontrollably (v. 4). And who can blame him? The earth is left burdened with the curse, and hopelessness overwhelms him. Dr. W.A. Criswell said,

> John's tears represent the tears of all of God's people through all the centuries. They're the tears of Adam and Eve as they view the still form of their dead son Abel and sense the awful consequence of their disobedience. These are the tears of all of the children of Israel in bondage as they cried to God for deliverance from affliction and slavery. They are the sobs and the tears wrung from the heart and soul of God's people as they've stood beside graves of loved ones and experienced the indescribable heartaches and disappointments of life. Such is the curse that sin has laid upon God's beautiful creation. No wonder John wept so fervently. If no redeemer could be found to remove the curse, it meant that God's creation was forever consigned to remain in the hands of Satan.[1]

But suddenly, everything changes. A Deliverer steps forward! He is called by other names. First, He is called the Lion of the tribe of Judah. This would lead Jewish readers to immediately think back to Genesis 49:9, where the future ruler of the world, God's Messiah/King, was prophesied to come from the tribe of Judah. The symbol used to represent the tribe of Judah was the lion. Second, He is called the Root of David, which points back to Isaiah 11:1—again, a prophecy of the coming Messiah.

When John turns, looking for a lion, instead He sees "a Lamb as though it had been slain" (v. 6). Immediately we think of Jesus Christ, of whom John the Baptist said, "Behold! The Lamb of God who takes away the sin of the world!" (John 1:29). In the Old Testament, Jews who wanted their sins atoned for would bring a lamb to the temple, lay their hands on it, and confess their sins over it. The priest would then slit the lamb's throat and drain its blood while the worshipers watched. The ritual meant that their sins had been transferred to the lamb, so to speak, and their guilt would land upon this innocent, sacrificed animal. That's the image of Jesus as the Lamb of God, a name used twenty-nine times in the book of Revelation to speak of Jesus.

But the Lamb in John's vision is no ordinary lamb, for He has seven horns. In the Bible, a horn is a symbol of authority, so the image here in verse 6 speaks of Jesus' complete and perfect authority. He is omnipotent. He is also said to have seven eyes, which speaks of His perfect omniscience; He has complete insight into everything. John further says the horns are the "seven Spirits of God" moving through all the earth, which speaks of His perfect presence; He is omnipresent.

John sees Jesus as "a Lamb as though it had been slain." Now, don't forget where John is—he's in heaven, not on earth. He's just seen the brilliance of the throne of God and a rainbow around that throne and heavenly creatures surrounding it. Yet even in heaven, the Lamb bears the marks of His crucifixion. When Jesus rose from the dead, He still bore scars on His hands, feet, side, and brow. In that state, He ascended into heaven and sat down at the right hand of God. So John sees Jesus in heaven, still bearing the tokens of His sacrificial love—for all eternity. We'll always have a reminder that God's grace alone brought us safely to heaven!

Finally the exciting moment arrives when Jesus takes the title deed from His Father. Rejoicing instantly overtakes weeping, for the kinsman-redeemer, the *ga'al*, will reclaim the lost property forfeited in the garden and will redeem the cursed earth with His own blood. And so He will fulfill the redemption clause, for He meets all the criteria.

As a human, Jesus is related to us by blood. He stepped out of eternity and into time to be placed inside of the womb of a peasant girl from Nazareth, who would give birth to Him in Bethlehem. Second, He paid our debt with His own blood. And third, He willingly paid that debt; He laid down His life for us by His own choosing (see John 10:18). Can you therefore grasp why every creature erupts in jubilant praise and worship as the Lamb takes the scroll out of the right hand of Him who sits on the throne? The first time Jesus came, He did so as a Lamb. But the second time He will come as a Lion—as One in charge, in authority.

A Worship Service to Remember (5:8-14)

Revelation 5 records history's greatest worship service, especially with regard to its size. Of course we can worship God anyplace, anytime. As Jesus told the Samaritan woman at the well, God is looking for people who will worship Him in Spirit and in truth, no matter where their location (John 4:23).

But worship will have its climactic fulfillment once you and I get to heaven. We'll see God face-to-face and celebrate for all eternity the person and work of His Son.

How important is worship to you? Certainly, worship is a priority with God. Everything in the Christian life—both outreach and inreach—stems from our relationship to the Lord in upreach—that is, in worship. All our work, all our evangelism, all our Bible studies and training must flow out of our worship of God.

In Revelation chapter 5 are featured three distinctive songs. In the first song, worship comes in response to the action of the Lamb, reminding us that true worship is a response to God. It should be the natural response of every redeemed person. Note that the living creatures and the twenty-four elders, who represent the church, fall down before the Lamb (v. 8). They are awestruck and grateful that the earth can be fully redeemed and bought back to God.

In ancient times, perhaps the greatest demonstration of veneration was to bow low. The idea is humility: "I'm in God's presence, I am grateful, and I humble myself before Him." The very act of worship requires the absence of self-absorption. William Temple, the Archbishop of Canterbury, once wrote, "Worship is the most selfless emotion of which our nature is capable and therefore the chief remedy for that self-centeredness which is our original sin and the source of actual sin."[2] In other words, the cure to self-centeredness is to put all of our focus upon Christ.

When the elders and living creatures fall down before the Lamb, they don't do so empty-handed. Each of the elders has a harp (v. 8). This may be why some people assume that those who go to heaven will sit on clouds and play harps. The harp here is more accurately a lyre, an ancient instrument that was rectangular or trapezoidal in shape and lined with strings that were plucked to make music. Musicians would often accompany a song or poem by plucking or strumming the strings on this instrument.

But the elders have more than harps; they also have "golden bowls full of incense, which are the prayers of the saints." In the outer courtyard of the temple in Jerusalem, the people of Israel prayed as they offered incense to God. David had something like this in mind when he wrote, "Let my prayer be set before You as incense, the lifting up of my hands as the evening sacrifice" (Psalm 141:2). God loves hearing from His children! Even when you pour out a plea—"O Lord, I need this!"—it is an act of worship because you are voicing your dependence upon God. You are expressing your trust and your faith by bringing your concern to the Lord in prayer.

These elders and creatures also raise their voices in song, and that's important because worship usually involves singing. And theirs is not merely "a" song, but "a new song," a frequently cited concept in worship, especially in the book of Psalms. They sing about what Jesus had done: "You are worthy to take the scroll, and to open its seals; for You were slain, and have redeemed us to God by Your blood out of every tribe and tongue and people and nation" (v. 9). If you want to be assured of having an anointed worship song, then fill its stanzas with praise directed toward Christ, and make sure His sacrifice at the cross is your focal point. Only the church can sing this new song: "You have redeemed us out of every tribe, tongue, people, and nation."

These elders sing not only about what Jesus had done on the cross, but also about what He would do presently and in the future (v. 10). Worship ought to catapult us into the future to remind us of our future state. Worship balances us out. It's like the great counterweight to the Christian life. It keeps us from going headlong into self-absorption.

The second and third eruptions of praise come from the angels. They first praise Jesus for His rulership—He reigns over all. And then they shout their praise to the Lamb for His intimate relationship with His Father.

While the redeemed thank Jesus for what He has done for them— namely, His work on the cross—the angels praise the Lamb for who

He is. They ascribe worth, strength, blessing, and honor to the Person of Jesus Christ. Notice that the angels are described not as singing, but as "saying." While the twenty-four elders who represent the church sing, the angels merely speak. And while the elders sing directly to the Lamb, the angels speak indirectly about what He has done. Why? One reason may be that the elders have personally experienced their redemption and being washed clean by the blood of Jesus Christ. The angels, however, know nothing of this. No angel knows what it is like to experience redemption from sin.

The angels declare God's worth by saying, "Worthy is the Lamb who was slain." Earlier in verse 9, the elders sang to the Lamb, "You are worthy to take the scroll." Both groups use the word "worthy" in connection with their worship. In English, the terms "worship" and "worthy" have the same root. The idea behind these terms is that we ascribe value or worship what we deem worthy. We worship God, then, for no other reason than He is worth it. He is worthy of praise. A.W. Tozer put it this way: "Whoever seeks God as a means toward a desired end, will not find God. For God will not be used."[3]

In verse 14, the Greek word John uses for "worshiped" is the term *proskuneo*, literally "to kiss toward," or to kiss the hand in reverence. It's an intimate, loving term, a term that describes a close relationship. Reverence is involved, but it's more intimate than that; it means to direct affection to somebody whom you love. Does that make you feel uncomfortable? After all, He's God and we are His servants! But we need to remember that Jesus told His disciples, "No longer do I call you servants, but friends" (see John 15:15). It was Jesus who initiated that kind of intimacy.

Note that the angels ascribe seven things to Jesus: power, riches, wisdom, strength, honor, glory, and blessing. All are things that Jesus profoundly deserves but didn't receive when He first came to earth. At His incarnation He laid aside His glory, but in heaven He receives again all that He laid aside.

By the third song, all creation worships the Lamb for His relationship with His Father (v. 13). This is the grand finale, the fortissimo that wraps everything up. This is where the classic biblical prediction comes to pass: "Every knee will bow…and…every tongue will confess that Jesus Christ is Lord, to the glory of God the Father" (Philippians 2:9-11 NIV, cf. Isaiah 45:23). Note that *every* creature in heaven, on earth, on the sea, and under the sea—in other words, everyone—worships God and confesses His worth. Note too that this worship is directed to both Him who sits on the throne *and* to the Lamb. This is worship of the Son and the Father together.

Worship, to be accepted by God, must praise the only true God and His Son, Jesus Christ. He will accept no other worship. Jesus bought us with His blood, which makes Him worthy of our worship. And the One who sits on the throne is worthy of creation's worship and praise. No one else is. True and valid worship must have the right object, which means it must center on the one true God and His Son.

To someone who might say, "I believe in God; it's Jesus whom I'm not too certain about," the apostle John would reply, "Whoever denies the Son does not have the Father either" (1 John 2:23). God didn't tolerate the mixing of worship in the Old Testament, and He tolerates it no better now. The first commandment tells us to worship and serve the Lord and Him only; we are to have no other gods before Him.

All roads do *not* lead to God, except in the sense that every road we choose eventually ends up at the throne of God for eternal judgment. God accepts only the worship He prescribes, and the only worship He prescribes is worship of Himself and His Son.

Remember, we worship what we see as worthy. What do you consider worthy in your life? Where do your thoughts and motivations go when nobody's around?

Some Don't Worship

A very simple Christian farmer lived out in the country. God took care of him, and he trusted God. One day the farmer invited a sophisticated relative out to the farm. When everyone sat down for dinner, the simple farmer grabbed the hands of those next to him and said, "Let's pray. O God, we worship You and give You thanks for this food. In Jesus' name, Amen."

His sophisticated relative said, "That's so outdated and old-fashioned!

Anybody with an education knows that you don't pray anymore, especially in public."

"Well," the farmer replied, "I acknowledge that it's old-fashioned. And I have to admit that on my farm some don't do this. They refuse to do it. Many don't either worship or pray."

"Really?" asked the sophisticated relative. "I'm so glad to see enlightenment finally come to the farm. Who are the wise ones?"

"My pigs," answered the farmer as he grabbed a roll.

God's people, humans, were created in His likeness for intimate fellowship with Him and for wholehearted worship of Him. And the question for every believer is this: How do we show the universe His infinite worth?

Four Riders with Bad News

Revelation 6

SUMMARY

From Revelation chapter 6 all the way through chapter 19, we see the wrath of the Lamb poured out on an unrepentant earth. Seven seals are broken—six of them in chapter 6—each broken seal signifying the pouring out of a new judgment. As the judgments unfold, we see them intensify in a progressive fashion.

RELATED SCRIPTURES FOR STUDY

Isaiah 13:6-13; Matthew 24; Romans 12:1-2; 2 Thessalonians 2:1-12

Chapter 6 begins what we might call the action part of the book of Revelation. And at the opening, it's as if we are taken into a massively dark Western. Four mysterious riders and their ghoulish steeds gallop through town, bringing with them evil tidings that shake the earth. Picture grizzled cowboys riding a devastated range. We're entering some scary territory! But there's a purpose behind all of this, as we'll soon see.

A cowboy applying for insurance once walked into an insurance agent's office to answer some routine questions. "Have you had any accidents?" the agent asked.

"No," replied the cowboy, "I haven't had any accidents—though a steer kicked me in the ribs once and broke two of them, and a rattle-snake bit me on the ankle."

"Well, wouldn't you consider *those* accidents?" demanded the agent.

"No," answered the cowboy, "I think they did it on purpose."

As we prepare to look into a period of world history during which life becomes very, very dark, remember that a divine purpose underlies all that takes place. The divine judgments that God pours out upon the earth will culminate in Jesus Christ taking over the globe. The calamities we'll read about may seem haphazard, as if they were random accidents, but be assured that God has a definite purpose behind everything that will occur.

An Overview of What Lies Ahead

As we begin looking at the judgment cycles in Revelation, it might help us to first get our bearings. Chapter 6 describes six "seal judgments" that are followed by a brief interlude before the opening of the seventh seal. This will usher in seven more judgments, called "trumpet judgments." The seventh trumpet judgment will then usher in seven final judgments, called "bowl judgments," in which God will continue to pour out His wrath upon the earth.

Only when all of these judgments run their course will the end come. Only then will the chaos cease. Only then will God finish judging the earth. And that's when Jesus Christ will return and usher in the millennial kingdom, during which we will experience 1000 years of peace upon the earth.

The Tribulation Begins (6:1-8)

Consider all the dark periods that have occurred in human history. One particularly difficult time was the Dark Ages, when enlightenment and progress seemed to come to a halt. Those in America know about the Civil War, and the entire globe knows about World Wars I and II. Some will also remind us how tough things were during the Great Depression. But by far the worst period in human history is yet future. The Bible calls it "the wrath of the Lamb" (Revelation 6:16-17), "the day of the Lord" (1 Thessalonians 5:2), "the time of Jacob's trouble" (Jeremiah 30:7)—or the Tribulation.

Jeremiah predicted it: "Alas! For that day is great, so that none is like it; and it is the time of Jacob's trouble" (Jeremiah 30:7). Daniel said, "There shall be a time of trouble, such as never was since there was a nation, even to that time" (12:1). Jesus predicted, "There will be great tribulation, such as has not been since the beginning of the world until this time, no, nor ever shall be" (Matthew 24:21).

Of all dark times, this will be the darkest. If you're a believer in Christ, however, you don't have to be afraid of it. In the same way that John was caught up into heaven, we will be too. And just as John saw God's fearful judgments from the vantage point of heaven, so will we.

After the first of the seven seals is opened, a potent counterfeit of Jesus Christ comes galloping into view, riding a white horse (v. 2). He will appear as though he is Christ, but Jesus will not return to earth on a white horse until chapter 19. There, we see Him with many diadems on His head, or many crowns, which speak of His authority as a sovereign ruler. The impostor in Revelation 6:2, however, wears a *stephanos*—the kind of crown that a marathon winner would receive. His crown is that of a laurel wreath, that of a temporary victor.

This rider, in fact, is the Antichrist. He will come in peace, carrying a bow but no arrows. He will ride a white horse, which will cause people to think, *The hero has come—the Messiah has arrived! He will bring us peace.* And for a short while, he will indeed bring world peace, which no ruler has ever been able to deliver. He will help the Jews rebuild their temple. He will put together a confederation of ten nations (or geopolitical units) that will give him unprecedented power. And he will manage this semblance of peace for three-and-a-half years—until the middle of the Tribulation, at which point he will take off his mask and everybody will recognize him as a wolf in sheep's clothing.

One commentator said the Antichrist will have the oratorical skill of a John Kennedy, the inspirational power of a Winston Churchill, the determination of a Joseph Stalin, and the vision of a Karl Marx. He will have the respectability of a Gandhi, the military prowess of a Douglas MacArthur, the charm of a Will Rogers, and the genius of a King Solomon. Even so, he will be nothing but a counterfeit Messiah who attempts to manufacture a counterfeit second coming. He will attempt to replace Jesus Christ.

Jesus made a frightening prediction. He said to the Jews of His time, "I have come in My Father's name, and you do not receive Me; if another comes in his own name, him you will receive" (John 5:43). I believe He was speaking of this future world ruler, the Antichrist, who will sway the nations and especially the nation of Israel. They will say, "Messiah has finally come! We always knew the Jesus of the New Testament wasn't him. *This* is our Messiah!"

A few years ago *The Wall Street Journal* interviewed Moshe Schlass in Jerusalem. Schlass told the reporter, "What's going on now is like labor pains. It looks pretty messy, but in the end what will come out is a new and a living light. The Messiah may be just an eye-blink away."[1] That rabbi used an interesting phrase reminiscent of one the apostle Paul employed: "When they say, 'Peace and safety!' then sudden destruction comes upon them, as labor pains upon a pregnant woman. And they shall not escape" (1 Thessalonians 5:3).

Just as the magicians in Pharaoh's ancient court could duplicate some of the miracles Moses performed, so the Antichrist will stand on the world stage and perform his own lying wonders. Paul wrote that these counterfeit miracles will be "according to the working of Satan, with all power, signs, and lying wonders" (2 Thessalonians 2:9). Eventually the Antichrist will demand that people worship him.

The supposed peace brought by the Antichrist won't last, however. After him are three more riders, who will bring war, famine, and widespread death. The citizens of earth will take the Antichrist to themselves as ruler, but swift destruction will overtake them all.

That destruction will begin with the appearance of a second horse, a red one (vv. 3-4). In Revelation, the color red is associated with terror and carnage. We see a red horse here, a red dragon in chapter 12, and a red beast in chapter 17. This red horse and its lethal rider will engulf the world in global warfare.

Famine will soon follow upon the arrival of a rider on a black horse (v. 5), and war and famine usually go together. When war breaks out, food supplies get contaminated and fields get burned and ravaged. We are told that people will pay a denarius for "a quart of wheat" and "three quarts of barley" (v. 6). A denarius amounted to a day's wage in John's time, so at this point in the Tribulation, it will take a working man a full day's wage to buy a little more than a loaf of bread. But notice that there will be no scarcity of oil and wine, or goods that are consumed by the rich. The rich will get richer, the poor will get poorer, and the middle class will become impoverished. The Tribulation will exacerbate the already bad conditions on the earth.

To get some idea of how severe this famine will be, consider that it took from the beginning of history until 1850 for the world population to reach one billion people. From 1850 to 1930 the earth grew to two billion people. From 1930 to 1960 the population grew to three billion. Then it took only fifteen more years to reach four billion. Today nearly seven billion people live on earth. So you can imagine the effect a worldwide famine would have.

And thundering into the deadly mix of war and famine will come the fourth horse, a pale one who brings death and Hades with it (v. 8). One-fourth of the world's population—currently almost two billion people—will die in the carnage. Things will go quickly from very bad to ghastly. Four elements will work together to produce this staggering loss of life: sword, hunger, death, and beasts (v. 8). With war comes famine; with famine comes malnutrition; with malnutrition comes the breakdown of the immune system. And hungry beasts deprived of their natural food sources will look for people to eat.

Although Satan will bring about all of this carnage, remember that God, who is our sovereign Lord, will oversee all that takes place. He will use these calamities to purge and judge the earth, making it ready for the reign of Christ. I take comfort in knowing that the word "Antichrist" means "instead of" or "against" Christ. Everything the Antichrist is, Jesus is not. And everything the Antichrist is not, Jesus is. The Antichrist is a fake, an impostor, while Jesus is called faithful and true. The Antichrist will bring a false peace followed by war and destruction. Jesus Christ, the Prince of Peace, will give you peace even when circumstances around you grow chaotic. In the wake of the Antichrist comes famine and death. By contrast, Jesus said, "I am the bread of life. He who comes to Me shall never hunger" (John 6:35). The Antichrist will be everything the world says it wants. Yet Jesus Christ is everything the world truly needs.

The good news is that those of us who know Jesus Christ not only have His peace, we will also be saved from the wrath to come. For God has not appointed us to wrath, but to obtain salvation (see 1 Thessalonians 5:9).

The Cries of Heaven and Earth (6:9-17)

Great persecution is often the result of obeying the Great Commission. Believers who are on earth during the time of the Tribulation will not believe the lies and tricks of the Antichrist, and many of them will pay with their lives for their faithfulness to Jesus (v. 9). John sees the souls of these martyrs under the altar in heaven.

In the Old Testament, priests killed sacrificial animals and poured out their blood at the base of the altar. In the courtyard of the tabernacle/temple stood a brass altar of sacrifice, and at its base the animal's lifeblood was drained. This pouring out of blood, in Old Testament imagery, symbolized the pouring out of life. As Leviticus says, "the life of the flesh is in the blood" (17:11).

While the souls of these persecuted saints are under the heavenly altar, their bodies lie on the earth, their blood pooling in city streets. They pour out their lives unto death. Our testimony of service to Christ lasts through life and, if need be, through death; that's what it means to be a true witness (see 2 Timothy 4:6). The Greek word translated "testimony" is *marturia*, referring to someone who gives a testimony, a witness—someone who is a martyr.

These souls are "the Tribulation saints." Before the Tribulation occurs, all those on the earth who are part of the church will be raptured. And during the Tribulation, many more people will come to faith in Christ. Now, there are some who ask, "But how could anyone come to faith in Christ during the Tribulation if all the Christians have left the earth? How will those who are lost hear the gospel?" God has many ways to deliver His message! In chapter 7 we'll read about 144,000 Jewish evangelists who spread the gospel; in chapter 11 we'll read of about two witnesses who will gain a worldwide audience; in chapter 14 we'll even read about an angel tasked with delivering the "everlasting gospel" to every person on earth. And don't discount the "silent witness" of Christians who went before. Even after these Christians vanish, their books will remain. Bibles, Christian books and magazines, video and audio recordings, MP3 files and YouTube clips, and portions of Scripture translated into virtually every language will still be available. There will be many ways for people to hear about how they can place their faith in Jesus.

We should not forget that martyrdom, which will be incredibly widespread during the Tribulation period, has been around since the beginning of the church. From the inception of church history, men and women have stood tall to pour out their lives, even to the point of death, for the gospel. And martyrdom is still commonplace even in our day. Kent Hill, the executive director of the Institute of Religion and Democracy in Washington, D.C., says there were more martyrs produced in the twentieth century than in every other century combined since the time of Christ. The Manila Conference on World Evangelism estimated that since 1950, at least ten million believers have been put to death for their faith.

The Tribulation martyrs in Revelation 6:9-10 are heard crying out to know when their Lord will judge their persecutors. That has been the cry of God's children for a long time, especially among Old Testament saints—which is a key reason I don't think these martyrs represent the church. In our age of grace and mercy, we're told to pray for those who persecute us and to love them. But the Tribulation is a time of vengeance and wrath, and that's why these saints wonder when God will judge their murderers.

How does God answer? He presents each of them with a white robe and tells them to rest a little while longer, until the full number of martyrs has been reached (v. 11). This reminds me of a crucial question Jesus once asked: "What profit is it to a man if he gains the whole world, and loses his own soul?" (Matthew 16:26). The soul is the most important part of us; it's the part that will live on. God counts as precious the deaths of His children (Psalm 116:15), for in dying they cross forever from death to life.

While the martyrs in heaven cry out to God, "Avenge us," humankind on earth cries out to the mountains, "Hide us from the face of Him who sits on the throne and from the wrath of the Lamb!" (v. 16). They scream after a horrific earthquake rocks the earth upon the opening of the sixth seal (v. 12). After this earthquake hits, the sun will become "black as sackcloth" and the moon will become "like blood" (see also Joel 2:30-31; 3:15-16). You might imagine that after such terrifying events, everybody would turn and repent. But not so. Callousness will reign instead of repentance (vv. 15-17). While God intends these judgments to shake men awake, men will refuse to repent. In fact, their hearts will grow harder and harder (see Revelation 9:20; 16:9).

The extraordinary thing is that these people appear to know who is ultimately behind these judgments. They call for the rocks to fall on them so that they may hide from God and the Lamb (see v. 16). They recognize that God and His Son—the Lamb who was slain—are judging the world, and that the divine judgment involves wrath. And yet they do not repent.

Do you struggle with the fact of God's wrath? If so, recognize that God's holy response to sin is wrath; it's part of His nature. He is truth, He loves justice, and His love requires that He does what most benefits His creatures. God's attributes and His character are complementary, not contradictory. God hates sin and He can't ignore it. At the same time, He gave His Son to die for sin so that its penalty would fall upon Jesus. If people say, "I reject Christ," then they reject their only lifeline and sentence themselves to judgment. If someone asks, "How can a loving God judge?" I would reply, "How could a loving God *not* judge?" To be truly loving is to desire the best for others, and judgment is sometimes the only tool left for bringing sinners back from the precipice.

In his book *The Cross of Christ*, John Stott quotes a playlet titled "The Long Silence":

> At the end of time, billions of people were scattered on a great plain before God's throne.
>
> Most shrank back from the brilliant light before them. But

some groups near the front talked heatedly—not with cringing shame, but with belligerence.

"Can God judge us? How can he know about suffering?" snapped a pert young brunette. She ripped open a sleeve to reveal a tattooed number from a Nazi concentration camp. "We endured terror… beatings… torture… death!"

In another group a Negro boy lowered his collar. "What about this?" he demanded, showing an ugly rope burn. "Lynched… for no crime but being black!"

In another crowd, a pregnant schoolgirl with sullen eyes. "Why should I suffer?" she murmured. "It wasn't my fault."

Far out across the plain there were hundreds of such groups. Each had a complaint against God for the evil and suffering he permitted in his world. How lucky God was to live in heaven where all was sweetness and light, where there was no weeping or fear, no hunger or hatred. What did God know of all that man had been forced to endure in this world? For God leads a pretty sheltered life, they said.

So each of these groups sent forth their leader, chosen because he had suffered the most. A Jew, a negro, a person from Hiroshima, a horribly deformed arthritic, a thalidomide child. In the centre of the plain they consulted with each other. At last they were ready to present their case. It was rather clever.

Before God could be qualified to be their judge, he must endure what they had endured. Their decision was that God should be sentenced to live on earth—as a man!

"Let him be born a Jew. Let the legitimacy of his birth be doubted. Give him a work so difficult that even his family will think him out of his mind when he tries to do it. Let him be betrayed by his closest friends. Let him face false charges, be tried by a prejudiced jury and convicted by a cowardly judge. Let him be tortured.

> "At the last, let him see what it means to be terribly alone. Then let him die. Let him die so that there can be no doubt that he died. Let there be a great host of witnesses to verify it."
>
> As each leader announced his portion of the sentence, loud murmurs of approval went up from the throng of people assembled.
>
> And when the last had finished pronouncing sentence, there was a long silence. No one uttered another word. No one moved. For suddenly all knew that God had already served his sentence.[2]

That's the life of Jesus Christ, who came as a sacrificial Lamb and endured all of those things. He will return with wrath for those who reject the gentle Jesus, meek and mild, the One who saves from sin. And He will say, "You have spoken. Now you will experience the consequences—you have sentenced yourself."

Jesus freely took judgment upon Himself in order to receive us as His children so that we don't have to face His future wrath. Yes, people will be saved even during the terrible judgments of the Tribulation—in fact, "a great multitude which no one could number, of all nations, tribes, peoples, and tongues" (Revelation 7:9). That's the extent of the mercy and the grace of God.

Does the Lord Have Your Attention?

As I noted earlier, God inspired the book of Revelation not only to speak to believers of long ago, but also to speak to us today and to those who will follow us. Do you sense that He is trying to get your attention? Has all the shaking captured your interest? Can you say, "Lord, I'm all ears! What do You want from my life? Is my relationship with You less than what it could be? I'm not going to run away from You because of what I'm hearing; rather, I'm going to run to You. What are You wanting to tell me?"

Now that we've seen the judgments begin—the judgments of the last days—I urge you to ask yourself: "What does God have to say to *me*?"

7

A Blessed Interruption in a Tough Time

Revelation 7

SUMMARY

John's account of divine judgment is briefly interrupted in order to focus on two groups of believers who come to faith in Christ after the rapture of the church. These two groups, one Jewish and one Gentile, demonstrate the grace and mercy of God even in the midst of a very dark time.

RELATED SCRIPTURES FOR STUDY

Ezekiel 9; Daniel 9:24-27; Matthew 25; Romans 9–11

When times get especially grim, most of us long for a break from the gloom. During the Great Depression, for example, a majority of ordinary Americans struggled to find enough money to live—but that didn't stop more than 100 million of them each week from streaming to the movies. Even if the cost of admission was steep, they paid it anyway so they could escape for a while from their financial woes. So they piled into the theaters by the multitudes to see the Marx Brothers in yet another zany adventure, or Shirley Temple in some sweet comedy, or the newest Busby Berkeley star-spangled musical.

And if they couldn't afford to go to the movies, they would stay home and listen to the radio as Little Orphan Annie and her chums solved another spine-tingling mystery. Or maybe they would put on some hot jazz or swing music and play cards. Duke Ellington, anyone?

When you find yourself in the middle of an especially tough situation, it's helpful sometimes to exit the madness—if even for a brief, brief moment—and take a break. Ah, to drift somewhere else for a while as you catch your breath!

Perhaps the apostle John felt something like that by the time he reached the end of Revelation 6. Think of it: Broken seals, blaring trumpets, bowls of divine wrath, famine, death, man-eating beasts, plagues and war and pestilence and smoke and blood—he needed a break! And so chapter 7 brings a pause in the action, a parenthesis from the deepening gloom.

Think for a moment of Revelation as a movie. The action builds, divine judgment boils, wave after angry wave of wrath crashes upon the shore. Then another wave, a massive one, swells on the horizon. It peaks, ready to crash and to destroy everything in its path—and just then the projector stops. The scene hangs in midair. You hear a muffled cough, and then someone in official-looking attire steps to the front of the theater and announces, "We interrupt our film to bring you a special message."

Why the interruption? In this case, it's because an important question had been asked at the very end of Revelation chapter 6: "The great day of His wrath has come...who is able to stand?" (v. 17). Well, who *will* be able to stand during that ghastly time? Chapter 7 answers the question.

In fact, two groups will stand. One group numbers 144,000 and is made up of 12,000 individuals from each of the 12 tribes of Israel. The second group is so enormous that no one can count its members. While the two groups are related, they differ markedly from each other. But God enables both to stand during a very difficult and heart-stopping time.

The First Group (7:1-8)

The first group is Jewish, "sealed...on their foreheads," and comprised of a specific number of individuals (vv. 3-4). God deals differently with these Jews than He does with the Gentiles. These are Messianic Jews, 144,000 Jews who will proclaim the gospel during the great Tribulation period. God deals specially with them because the

Jewish people have been chosen by God for some specific purposes. He has plans for them.

The Jewish people are special for several reasons. First, they gave us the Scriptures. Our God-breathed Bible came through the Jewish nation. They also preserved the Scriptures, meticulously handing them down from father to son. The Hebrew scribes would copy every word of the sacred text letter by letter, page by page—and they did it very accurately for thousands of years. Perhaps the best example of this is found in the Dead Sea Scrolls. Those scrolls were written around 200 BC, and when scholars compared them with what were then the most ancient Hebrew Bible manuscripts (from around AD 900), they found the texts to be virtually identical. So the greatest thing they found in the Dead Sea Scrolls is what they *didn't* find: mistakes.

Second, our Savior came through the Jewish nation. He was born into the tribe of Judah, born of a woman, born under the law (see Galatians 4:4). The first disciples were all Jewish and they took the gospel of the Messiah to all corners of the known world. Paul summed it up when he said that to the Israelites belong "the adoption, the glory, the covenants, the giving of the law, the service of God, and the promises; of whom are the fathers and from whom, according to the flesh, Christ came, who is over all, the eternally blessed God" (Romans 9:4-5).

Did you know that God keeps a calendar? He revealed a portion of that calendar to Daniel. He said, in effect, "Daniel, there will come a time when your exiled people will return to Jerusalem. And when they do, those who pay attention will be able to count out a certain number of years and days from a specific event until the time the Messiah rides into your capital city."

The Lord also let Daniel know that seventy "weeks" (of years, or 490 years) had been set aside for the Jewish nation "to finish the transgression, to make an end of sins, to make reconciliation for iniquity, to bring in everlasting righteousness, to seal up vision and prophecy, and to anoint the Most Holy" (Daniel 9:24). Seven years of that 490-year period has not yet been fulfilled, which corresponds to the forthcoming seven-year Tribulation period described in Revelation. (You can find this portion of the divine calendar in Daniel 9:24-27.)

Historically, Jesus made His triumphal entry into Jerusalem exactly 483 years after the Persian king Artaxerxes issued a royal decree allowing the Jews to return to and rebuild Jerusalem, which had been devastated by the Babylonians. That brings us to 483 years out of the 490 that were prophesied by Daniel. We know that the Jewish religious leaders of Jesus' time rejected Him as the Messiah; and so seven years of Daniel's prophecy remain to be fulfilled. Those seven years will unfold during the Tribulation, a time during which God will focus on the Jewish people. In the future God will begin His timetable again, but until then, we live in a parenthesis, a break, called the church age. And eventually God will fulfill His promises—all of them—to the Jewish people.

Romans 9–11 develops the theme that God has not yet finished with Israel. Chapter 9 describes God's election of the Jewish nation, chapter 10 explains God's temporary rejection of Israel, and chapter 11 predicts the divine restoration of the nation. Paul wrote that "blindness in part has happened to Israel until the fullness of the Gentiles has come in" (Romans 11:25). When Israel rejected Jesus as the Messiah, a "national blindness" swept over the nation. Of course, there is a remnant of Jewish people in every generation who receives Christ as Messiah, but until God refocuses His attention on Israel, His plan will center on the church, which is comprised of both Jews and Gentiles.

Eventually God's focus will shift back to the Jewish people—that will happen when the full number of Gentiles has come in, or come to salvation. God alone knows how many Gentiles—people from all the *other* tribes, nations, kindred, and tongues—will be saved. When the last one comes to faith in Christ, He will remove the church from the earth through the rapture. At that point the seventieth week of Daniel will unfold—the Tribulation period—and God will once again focus His attention on the holy city and His covenant people. He has a plan for the future!

Part of that plan involves judgment. God will send angels to alter the world's wind patterns, but before that judgment falls, He will task an angel with the job of sealing the 144,000 on their foreheads (v. 3). For years people have focused on a different mark mentioned later in the book of Revelation—the 666 mark that the Antichrist will put on the foreheads of deceived men and women (Revelation 13:16-18), but in doing so, they have missed the really important mark, which is found here. The "mark of the beast," or 666, is simply a counterfeit of the seal mentioned in Revelation 7:3. Satan has never had an original thought. When he sees God do something, he says, "I can do that." In response to Christ, Satan will have an Antichrist. In response to a true prophet, Satan will produce a false prophet. And because God will place a true mark on the foreheads of His own, Satan will produce a false mark to lead the world astray.

In the ancient world, people made a seal by forming an imprint in soft wax. If you owned something, you dripped some hot wax on it, pressed your signet ring into the wax, and thereby left your seal. The seal meant you owned that commodity and that your authority protected it. God does something similar here with His people, although not with wax. By sealing them, He declares that they belong to Him and that He will protect them during this horrific time.

Scripture gives many examples of God sealing various groups to protect them during times of judgment. For example, when God sent the great flood, He "sealed" Noah and his family in the ark. When the time of the exodus arrived, Hebrew families were instructed to put blood on the doorposts and lintels of their homes so that the destroying angel would pass over them. The blood was their "seal." When God later judged the city of Jericho, Rahab the harlot (who had hidden two Hebrew spies and by her courageous action saved their lives) followed instructions that she was to hang a scarlet thread from her window. This was the "seal" that indicated she belonged to God and lived by faith. By following the spies' instructions, Rahab preserved her whole family from harm when the nation of Israel came against Jericho. And the most noteworthy example of a biblical seal appears in Ezekiel 9:4; I believe it provides the model for the seal described in Revelation 7.

In Ezekiel 9, as God prepared to judge the people of ancient Jerusalem, He sent a servant throughout the city with an inkhorn to place a mark on the forehead of every person who detested the evil ravaging the nation. God promised to protect all those who displayed a heart of repentance and who had therefore received the mark; but all other

Israelites He intended to utterly destroy. Interestingly, the term translated "mark" in Ezekiel 9:4 is the Hebrew word *tav*, the last letter of the Hebrew alphabet. In the ancient Greek alphabet, this letter looks like a cross. This might have foreshadowed the divine protection of the cross, which will be given to the 144,000 Jewish servants in Revelation 7.

And what is the purpose of these 144,000 individuals? Why will they have to endure the Tribulation? God will send them out to serve as witnesses for Him. He promises to preserve them and make them essentially indestructible so that they can give a strong gospel witness to the world. Every one of these people will say, "I believe in Jesus Christ. I've turned my life over to Him. And now I intend to tell others about Him." Think about how incredible this is. Here we have 144,000 Jewish representatives who not only accept Jesus Christ as their Messiah, but who also become bold evangelists for Him—during a time of great divine wrath in which the nation of Israel will suffer tremendously. Amazing!

These 144,000 Jewish witnesses will help fulfill a prophecy Jesus made shortly before His crucifixion. When the Savior spoke about the events of the Tribulation and the awesome judgments to come, He said, "This gospel of the kingdom will be preached in all the world as witness to all the nations, and then the end will come" (Matthew 24:14). I believe these 144,000 Jewish witnesses will spread the news about Jesus all over the world—and not until they're finished will the end come.

The Second Group (7:9-17)

The second group is an unnumbered multitude, a group vastly larger than the 144,000. These people are not sealed, and they are Gentiles from all the nations (v. 9). They are not the church, for John doesn't even know who they are. When one of the twenty-four elders asks John to identify them, he's stumped. The elder then informs John that "these are the ones who come out of the great tribulation, and washed their robes and made them white in the blood of the Lamb" (v. 14). All of them will have placed their faith in Jesus Christ and suffered immensely for it. No doubt we are to understand that they committed their lives to Christ largely through the witness of the 144,000. So even though the Tribulation will be a very dark time of fearful judgment, God will continue to show His grace and mercy and bring untold millions of people to faith in Jesus.

In every age, God preserves a remnant. God always maintains a believing witness. When the depressed prophet Elijah complained to God that he was the only faithful person left in Israel, God replied, "No, you're not. I have 7000 others just like you" (see 1 Kings 19:18). God always has a witness. In Revelation 7 we see that the Tribulation witnesses will bear a staggering amount of fruit for the Lord's kingdom.

And where do these redeemed men and women come from? John notes that they are from "all nations, tribes, peoples, and tongues" (v. 9). In other words, the gospel is for *everybody*. *Every* nation on earth has a stake in Jesus the Messiah.

God gladly accepts this gargantuan group. They stand before the throne, clothed with white robes that symbolize victory (v. 9). They stand triumphantly, waving palm branches in their hands. Although the world had rejected them—they suffered hunger, thirst, and brutal persecution for standing up for a message fiercely unpopular during the time of the Antichrist's lies—heaven wholeheartedly accepts them.

It's possible that you might be facing some tough peer pressure right now. Your friends want you to conform; they are pressuring you to take those drugs or run with that group or quit being such a geek and carrying your Bible around. "Be like us!" they taunt—and you feel the pressure. Whenever that happens, remember that the time will come when you'll stand before God and all those memories will fade away. At that future moment, all their sentiments and pressure will be utterly unimportant. That's why Jesus said, "Do not fear those who kill the body but cannot kill the soul. But rather fear Him who is able to destroy both soul and body in hell" (Matthew 10:28). These who endure the Tribulation willing to stand up for the truth of the gospel instead of trying to find safety in mere social acceptance will be rewarded by God.

In heaven, these men and women joyfully cry out with a loud voice, "Salvation belongs to our God who sits on the throne, and to the Lamb!" (v. 10). They fill their worship with such great intensity that the angels, elders, and four living creatures around God's throne all immediately fall on their faces and worship God (v. 11). Their exuberance has a radical effect on those around them. Recall that Jesus said, "There is joy in the presence of the angels of God over one sinner who repents" (Luke 15:10). Imagine the thundering celebration that will take place in heaven when *this* group of saints comes marching in!

While they live on earth, the members of this group will suffer in excruciating ways. During the Tribulation, anyone who refuses to take the mark of the Antichrist will be unable to buy or sell and thus won't be able to get food—resulting in severe hunger. In addition, the world's water sources will be polluted and undrinkable—resulting in severe thirst (see Revelation 8:10-11). Later in the Tribulation, the sun will become unbearably hot for a time (see Revelation 16:8). So it is very significant that God promises these believers that they will never hunger again, they will never thirst again, and the blazing sun will never beat down on them again (v. 16). And best of all, "the Lamb who is in the midst of the throne will shepherd them and lead them to living fountains of waters" (v. 17).

With such great promises, it only seems right that still another is given: "And God will wipe away every tear from their eyes" (v. 17). In ancient times, people kept little glass bottles called lachrymatories, in which they collected the tears of mourners. These bottles were placed on the graves and in the tombs of departed loved ones. David, thinking of this practice, once said to God, "Put my tears into Your bottle; are they not in Your book?" (Psalm 56:8). In other words, God knows every detail of my life and God cares about every tear I shed. And in Revelation 7:17 we see that there is coming a day when those tears will be wiped away. Only God's handkerchief can, once and for all, remove tears of rejection, of persecution, of depression! This is such a spectacular and potent promise that later in Revelation the blessing of no more tears will be extended to the redeemed of all ages (21:4).

The happy throng of Gentiles in Revelation 7 are before God's throne and serve Him day and night, which means they dwell eternally in His majestic presence (v. 15). That's a big part of their reward. Jesus said that one day He will say to His faithful followers, "Well done, good and faithful servant; you were faithful over a few things, I will make you ruler over many things. Enter into the joy of your lord" (Matthew 25:21).

And what joy there will be in heaven! We'll have new bodies, strong and incorruptible, and we'll be able to serve God perfectly. We'll never get tired. All of us will remember for eternity that the Lord is the One who made it all possible, for we'll all wear robes washed white and clean in the blood of the Lamb (v. 14). The lives of these Tribulation believers, and our own, will have been made pure by the sacrifice of Christ, through the power of the gospel. Other messages on earth might make you feel good, but only the gospel of Jesus Christ can remove the stain of sin.

Many Voices, but Only One Savior

A man fell into a pit and couldn't get himself out. A subjective person came along and said, "I feel for you down there." An objective person came along and said, "It's logical that someone would fall down there." A Christian Scientist came along and said, "You only *think* that you're in that pit." A Pharisee said, "Only bad people fall into pits." A mathematician calculated how the man fell into the pit. A news reporter wanted the exclusive story on his fall into the pit. A legalistic Christian said, "You deserve that pit." Confucius said, "If you had listened to me, you wouldn't be in that pit." Buddha said, "Your pit is only a state of mind." A realist said, "That is a pit." A scientist calculated the pressure necessary in pounds per square inch to get the man out of the pit. A geologist told him to appreciate the rock strata in the pit. An evolutionist said, "You are a rejected mutant destined to be removed from the evolutionary cycle—you'll die in that pit so that you cannot produce any pit-falling offspring."

The county inspector asked the man if he had a permit for digging the pit. A professor gave him a lecture on the elementary principles of the pit. An evasive person avoided the subject of the pit altogether. A self-pitying person said, "You haven't seen anything until you've seen *my* pit." A charismatic from the Faith movement said, "Just confess it and you'll not be in that pit any longer." An optimist said, "Things could be worse." A pessimist said, "Things will get worse."

But Jesus, seeing the man, took him by the hand and lifted him out of the pit.

There's only one Savior who saves Jew and Gentile alike, both in this age of grace and in the time of judgment to come. In His great grace and mercy, untold millions will find eternal life in Him. God has at least one great revival still on His divine calendar. In the meanwhile—in this parenthetical age of grace—we have the privilege of leading others to faith in Him, and celebrating what He does through believing hearts.

8

Trumpets of Doom

Revelation 8

SUMMARY

The opening of the seventh seal causes all of heaven to grow utterly quiet in anticipation of increasingly traumatic and horrific judgments to come upon the earth. Seven angels blowing seven trumpets signal the approach of unprecedented destruction and death; in chapter 8, we hear from the first four of them. The chapter ends with a warning that what is to come will overshadow the devastation that has already engulfed a third of the earth.

RELATED SCRIPTURES FOR STUDY

Genesis 19; Amos 4:6-12; Luke 21

More and more people today seem either obsessed with knowing about how the world will end or sick of hearing about it.

But in fact, people have wondered about the end of the world since the beginning of the world. In theology, it's a section of study all to itself. The Greek word *eschata* means "end things." And nearly every theology course or textbook has a whole section devoted to eschatology, or the study of the end times.

Ten times the prophet Daniel used the phrase "the time of the end" in his book, while four times Jesus spoke of "the end of the world." In the Gospel of Matthew the Lord said, "Heaven and earth will pass away, but My words will by no means pass away" (24:35). And later, Peter wrote, "The end of all things is at hand; therefore be serious and watchful in your prayers" (1 Peter 4:7).

By the time we reach Revelation 8, the end is well in sight. The opening of the seventh seal portends such momentous developments that all of heaven falls silent. What could make even the angels go deathly quiet? That becomes apparent all too quickly.

Calm Before the Storm (8:1-2)

To this point in Revelation, we've seen a lot of activity and heard a lot of noise, so verse 1 stands in stark contrast to everything that has preceded it. All of a sudden the noise and commotion and activity we have witnessed comes to a screeching halt (without the sound). John tells us that when Jesus opened the seventh seal, "there was silence in heaven for about half an hour" (v. 1). I've heard more than one joke about this silence in heaven, but it's no joke, and it's certainly no laughing matter. The phrase is *intended* to be ominous.

This eerie silence brings a brief and momentary calm before the major storm of divine judgment slams into the planet. A hush falls over heaven just before the opening of the seventh seal releases utter chaos. Many times the prophets spoke about this earth-shattering period. "Be silent in the presence of the Lord GOD, for the day of the LORD is at hand" (Zephaniah 1:7). And Zechariah proclaimed, "Be still before the LORD all mankind, because he has roused himself from his holy dwelling" (2:13 NIV). As the seventh seal is opened, God rouses Himself from His dwelling—and it is a sobering, awesome, overpowering moment.

As Jesus breaks the seventh seal and unrolls the scroll, apparently everyone in heaven can see what is written. They respond with utter, total silence. All of the exaltation stops; all of the alleluias cease; all the music is put on pause. No one says a word. This is a silence of awe, a stillness of solemn anticipation as the citizens of heaven gaze upon the opened scroll and see the calamities to come upon the earth. They know what is about to happen.

And yet they do not dread it. This is a serious yet joyous silence. The day has finally come! At last the time has arrived for the saints to be vindicated, Satan to be defeated, sin to be vanquished, and Jesus Christ to reign forever! They have good reason for falling silent. I believe these heavenly residents have been anticipating this moment ever since the Fall. All of God's creation had a hunch that one day God would finally take it all back. And as He readies Himself to do exactly that, a deep silence falls over everyone.

And soon the silence gives way to blaring trumpets. Seven angels who "stand before God" are given a trumpet apiece (v. 2). It's like a silent movie: Nobody says anything, we hear no noise, but silently seven mighty angels take hold of brass instruments that will make a *lot* of noise. And they know how to blow them.

The text says "the" seven angels, using the definite article, which seems to indicate these are special angels. Some theologians call them "the presence angels." Perhaps a text out of Luke's Gospel may help us to identify one of them.

In Luke 1:19, an angel appears to an old priest named Zechariah and declares to him, "I am Gabriel, who stands in the presence of God." It may well be that Gabriel is one of these seven angels who stand in God's presence; perhaps one day he will take a heavenly trumpet given to him and blow with all his might. The angels sound their respective horns in Revelation 8:7,8,10,12; 9:1,13; and 11:15.

John would have been very familiar with the use of the trumpet in Israel's history. The trumpet was the most significant of all the Hebrew musical instruments. It is mentioned in the Bible twice as often as the harp and it played a key role in the nation's meetings. In Numbers 10 it was used to call the people of Israel together. Designated men would sound the trumpet, making a certain sound, and the people would know they were to congregate. A different kind of blast on the trumpet would mean war. Still other trumpet sounds indicated special feast times or festivals. What happened at Mount Sinai when God gave His people the Law? A loud trumpet was sounded. At Jericho, when the Hebrew army marched around the city and then the walls were leveled, trumpets were sounded. In 1 Kings, trumpets are blown when a king is anointed and elevated to rule.

By this point in Revelation, John has twice heard the sound of a trumpet. In the first chapter, he heard the voice of Jesus, which sounded like a trumpet. In chapter 4, the voice of a trumpet called him heavenward. But these seven trumpets are different—they have an ominous sound because they herald severe judgment. Some commentators have suggested that the half hour of silence in heaven—just before the trumpets blow—represents God's final thirty minutes of grace and signal His final chance: "I'm about to pour out judgment, but before I do so I'm going to wait for just another moment, just half an hour."

God is never in a hurry to judge anyone. One of the Lord's main attributes is His longsuffering, patient nature. He is not anxious to judge, not willing that any should perish (see 2 Peter 3:9). The prophet Ezekiel insisted that the Lord takes no pleasure in the death of the wicked (Ezekiel 18:32; 33:11). In fact, God has waited for thousands of years to bring this judgment, issuing warning after warning to a world that has consistently rejected the gospel message.

But now, finally, the long wait is over. God's patience and longsuffering have come to an end. The time for judgment has arrived.

Cries Before the Throne (8:3-6)

Back in the days when Israel worshiped God in the wilderness with the help of the tabernacle, two altars served separate purposes in Israel's system of worship. In the outer court stood a brass altar at which animals were killed and sacrifices were burned. A much smaller golden altar stood inside the temple, in the Holy Place, in front of the veil of the Holy of Holies. The priest would take a coal from the brass altar of sacrifice, put it in a little incense burner—a censer with a small bowl attached to a rope or a chain—and walk from the outer court into the Holy Place, where he approached the golden altar of incense. He would put the coal on that altar and sprinkle incense on it. From that would rise up a sweet aroma that pleased God. This provided a graphic picture for the people of how their prayers rose up to God.

In Revelation 8:3 we see an angel mix "much incense" with the prayers of the saints, giving us a clear image that God is about to answer the prayers of His beloved people. In fact, God *always* answers the prayers of His children. He never loses a single prayer. If you are a child of God, walking in fellowship with Him and obeying Him, then rest assured that He answers all your prayers.

But now things turn violent. The angel takes the censer, fills it with fire from the altar of incense, and throws it to the earth. Immediately "noises, thunderings, lightnings, and an earthquake" shake the planet (v. 5). This apparently is the signal for the seven angels to get ready to sound their horns of judgment. Don't miss the symbolism here: God's final judgment on the earth comes as a direct response to the prayers of His people. Remember, Jesus told His disciples, "When you pray, say, 'Our Father in heaven, hallowed be Your name. Your kingdom come. Your will be done on earth as it is in heaven'" (Luke 11:2). One day that prayer will be answered; in fact, *here* that prayer is answered. That's why we see utter silence in heaven for half an hour. God is about to judge this earth, take it over, vindicate the saints, eradicate sin, defeat Satan, and exalt Jesus Christ.

Paul spoke about this time when he wrote,

> It is a righteous thing with God to repay with tribulation those who trouble you, and to give you who are troubled rest with us when the Lord Jesus is revealed from heaven with His mighty angels, in flaming fire taking vengeance on those who do not know God, and on those who do not obey the gospel of our Lord Jesus Christ (2 Thessalonians 1:6-8).

Earlier we saw the Tribulation saints praying, "How long, O Lord?" God told them, "Wait." But now the time for waiting has ended, and the time for answering their prayers has come.

These Tribulation saints had been greatly injured and abused by their ungodly neighbors, and it's worth remembering that when you hurt one of the members of the body of Christ, you strike the head of the church—Jesus Christ—Himself. And one day, though He is patient and longsuffering, He will intervene…and in a *big* way.

Catastrophes Before the End (8:7-13)

The earthly catastrophes about to ravage the earth come in response to the trumpet blasts of the seven angels. The first four are natural—meaning they deal with things in nature, such as green plants, the sea, springs of water, and heavenly bodies. And the subsequent two are supernatural. That is, the latter judgments are more profound and involve things such as demonic forces.

The first of the seven trumpet judgments brings upon the earth hail and fire mingled with blood (v. 7). Immediately a third of the world's trees burn up, and all of its green grass burns up. The prophet Joel had seen some of this coming. When he peered ahead to the Day of the Lord, or the Tribulation, he wrote that the Lord would declare, "I will show wonders in the heavens and in the earth: Blood and fire and pillars of smoke" (Joel 2:30).

How did God destroy Sodom and Gomorrah? With fire from the sky. What about the plagues of Egypt? One of them involved hail falling from the sky that destroyed Egypt's crops. Here in Revelation 8:5 we see mention of an earthquake, and it's possible that a massive quake could trigger volcanic eruptions all over the globe—eruptions that spew lava and hot ash all around the planet. The target of this judgment is the earth's vegetation—one-third of the trees and all of the grass. Imagine how the massive loss of all this vegetation will upset the balance of nature. Pasturelands will be devastated, which will seriously affect livestock. The ruin of farmland will greatly reduce the availability of grains and vegetables and fruit worldwide. The cost of housing construction will skyrocket because lumber production will plummet. In essence, God will trash the world's ecology—and all this will take place under just the *first* of the trumpet judgments.

There is an environmental atheism today that essentially worships Mother Nature. It says that nature is God and God is nature—but the real God will judge their god. If you think we've trashed the planet so far, just wait until God begins pouring out His judgments. This planet belongs to Him—He made it. And He also made humankind. In a later chapter we'll learn about other ways God will destroy the earth. We'll read about the sun scorching men, and the depletion of the ozone layer. God will get very involved in global warming.

So much for the first trumpet!

When the second trumpet sounds, John sees "something like a great mountain burning with fire" thrown into the sea, turning a third of the oceans into blood. A third of all the sea creatures die, and a third of oceangoing vessels are destroyed (vv. 8-9). The text doesn't say an actual mountain burns with fire, but rather "something like" a mountain—an asteroid, perhaps?

Whatever it is that is thrown into the sea, we read that a third of the world's oceans and ships will be affected. According to the U.S. Department of Commerce, some 25,364 merchant ships are on the high seas right now. Imagine over 8000 ships being destroyed simultaneously in a moment! An asteroid or a small comet will enter the atmosphere, and as it falls to the earth, friction with the atmosphere will ignite it so that it appears to be a big, flaming mountain. It will smash into the ocean and kill a third of its creatures. This, of course, will play havoc with the fishing industry and worldwide seafood production. This event will have the same impact as dozens of thermonuclear warheads going off all at once, and the shock wave from the collision will send huge tsunamis rippling over the globe's seas, smashing a large portion of the world's navies and commercial ocean vessels.

Again, many Old Testament prophets had foreseen bits and pieces of this devastation. Hosea wrote, "The land will mourn; and everyone who dwells there will waste away with the beasts of the field and the birds of the air; even the fish of the sea will be taken away" (4:3). And the Lord said through Zephaniah, "I will sweep away both men and animals; I will sweep away the birds of the air and the fish of the sea" (1:3 NIV).

For the third trumpet judgment, the action will move inland. John sees a "great star" fall from heaven, burning like a torch. It will fall "on a third of the rivers and on the springs of water." John gives this falling object a name: Wormwood. And as happened with the second trumpet judgment, the consequences will affect a third of the earth. In this case, a third of the world's fresh water will become poisoned, and many people will die from drinking the polluted water, which "was made bitter" (v. 11).

Whatever this "star" is—the Greek term here is *aster*, from which we get the word "asteroid"—it falls into our atmosphere from outer space, apparently disintegrates, and spreads debris over the whole earth, almost like a kind of chemical warfare. It fouls a third of the earth's fresh water supplies, whether rivers or springs or reservoirs. The name of the star, Wormwood, simply means "bitter." It refers to a plant with a root that exudes a dark, green oil. The Greek term is *apsinthos*, from which we get the word "absinthe," a very strong liqueur favored by many as an after-dinner drink. But in this context the word conveys something that is undrinkable, or poisonous. And a third of the world will instantly lack the fresh water its people need to survive.

When the fourth angel sounds his trumpet, divine judgment will come to the skies (v. 12). A third of the light from the sun, moon, and stars will somehow be darkened. Here the world's attention will turn away from the earth and focus skyward. Perhaps some sort of massive eclipse will affect not only the sun and moon, but everything humans can see in the sky.

This is just what one might expect after the earth collides with at least two enormous space rocks. Huge amounts of dust and debris created by such collisions would get lifted into the upper atmosphere and quickly disperse around the world, blocking out a sizeable portion of the light coming from the sun, moon, and stars. Temperatures would drop and travel would become dangerous. Remember what happened in early 2010 when a single volcano in Iceland began erupting, sending ash into the upper atmosphere and severely curtailing air travel throughout Europe? This event here in Revelation 8:12 will be far greater, causing pandemonium to erupt and become the worldwide course of the day.

No doubt Jesus had this in mind when He looked into the future and prophesied about what will take place during the Tribulation: "There will be signs in the sun, in the moon, and in the stars; and on the earth distress of nations, with perplexity, the sea and the waves roaring; men's hearts failing them from fear and the expectation of those things which are coming on the earth, for the powers of the heavens will be shaken" (Luke 21:25-26). That sounds a lot like what would happen if large asteroids were to strike the earth. We would experience massive tsunamis, darkened skies, and a colossal loss of both animal and human life. And that's after only four of the trumpet judgments; three more angels have yet to sound their trumpets.

Suddenly another angel—not one of the seven who are blowing trumpets—will fly around the world crying out, "Woe, woe, woe to the inhabitants of the earth, because of the remaining blasts of the trumpet of the three angels who are about to sound!" (v. 13). This angel refers not to what has already happened, but to what's yet to come—as if to say, "You haven't seen anything yet! If you think it's bad now, just wait. Three woes are rushing your way, and quickly."

That sounds grim, doesn't it? And all of this will happen because the world will have pushed away Christ and rejected the gospel for so long. God has been so very, very patient. But there is coming a day when His patience will run out.

No Mystery Here

If you ever visit San Jose, California, you might consider taking the time to visit a fascinating attraction called the Winchester Mystery House. It's an odd building because it has stairways going nowhere and doors that lead to nothing. The structure rambles all over the place. Why build a house like that?

The story goes that Sarah Winchester, married to the man who made the Winchester rifle famous, inherited all his money when he died in 1918 from influenza. She moved to San Jose, California, where she continued her involvement in spiritism. At a séance it was conveyed to her that she would remain alive so long as she continued to build a house. Fearful of death, she went to work right away.

She spent $5 million on her home—back in the days when the going wage was 50 cents an hour for an accomplished contractor and homebuilder. Her huge house has 150 rooms, 13 bathrooms, 2000 doors, and 10,000 windows. When she died—which she did, despite her perpetually active construction project—she left enough materials behind to continue the project for another 80 years.

What a picture of humankind on the earth! Countless people are busily running here and there, getting wrapped up in projects that momentarily take their minds off of eternity yet have no real or lasting value. That was Sarah Winchester, and too often, that's us. But no matter what we build and where we put our stocks in the here and now, there's no real mystery ahead for us, just as the Winchester Mystery House doesn't really present a mystery. Sarah died despite all her frantic activity and regardless of what some medium told her. Likewise, all of us will one day leave this earth, ready or not.

Jesus declared that heaven and earth will one day pass away. And if we place all of our hope in this earth, in this kingdom—in this house— then what a sad day is coming for us. The four trumpet-blowing angels of Revelation 8 warn us to wake up and give our lives wholeheartedly to Christ. He is at the center of this book, and only He can give us any kind of lasting hope.

Life has its mysteries, but your ultimate purpose and destiny does not have to be one of them.

When All Hell Breaks Loose

Revelation 9

SUMMARY

With the fifth trumpet judgment, a shift of focus occurs—off of heaven and onto hell. All that heaven left undone in the previous devastations, Satan will now do. The time is coming when hell will visit the earth, bringing about a period of unprecedented terror.

RELATED SCRIPTURES FOR STUDY
Luke 21:25-33; 2 Peter 2:4; Jude 5-7

A few years ago a clothing company made apparel under the label No Fear, and their products became very popular. One day when I was walking through a terminal at Dallas/Fort Worth International Airport to catch a plane back home I saw someone wearing a T-shirt with the No Fear slogan on the front. On the back I read the words, "Absolutely, Definitely, Positively, without a Doubt No Fear." And then, underneath in parentheses, I read, "No, not even just a little bit."

I thought about that slogan in light of these chapters in Revelation and realized that is one T-shirt that will *not* sell during the Tribulation. Such a slogan just won't go over well because at that dark time, people's hearts will fail them from the fear of anticipating ever more horrific things to come on the earth. These upcoming chapters of Revelation are not for the faint of heart!

The Emergence of Four Terrors (9:1-12)

In Revelation 9:1 we see a "star" unfixed and fallen to earth, and subsequently given the key to the bottomless pit. This star differs from the ones in the previous chapter; this one has personality. The text calls it "him." He's like the stars mentioned in Job 38:7, which we identify as angels. This individual, however, is a fallen star; the phrase is written in the Greek perfect tense, which means it fell in the past, but with lingering results. So most likely this star is Satan (whom Scripture elsewhere calls a star—see Isaiah 14:12-15).

Satan lost his residence in heaven after his rebellion, and Revelation 12:9 indicates that a time is coming when he will be cast out of heaven permanently. Apparently he still has some access to heaven as a visitor, where he accuses the saints before God (see Job 1–2). But during the Tribulation, probably around the midpoint, Michael and the other angels who have not fallen will evict Satan permanently—and likely that is why the second half of the Tribulation will be far worse than the first half. Satan will be angry, and he will know he has only a little more time to practice his evil before the Lord pronounces a final sentence on him.

In verse 1 the devil is given "the key to the bottomless pit," which he will put to use very quickly. For generations, Satan has remained a largely invisible enemy on earth, and an enemy is never so dangerous as when nobody sees him or even believes in him. But it seems that in the last days Satan will want visibility, and the key to the abyss will give him the spotlight as never before.

In verse 2 we read that Satan will use the key to unlock the pit. Immediately smoke will rise out of the darkness, "like the smoke of a great furnace." Out of the pit will billow a cloud of ugly, black pollution as hell belches out its corruption. A strange blackness will darken whatever light is left from the sun and the moon and the stars. The Greek term *abussos*, or pit, is used seven times in Revelation, each time referring to the abode of fallen spirits—the Bible indicates that in times past God incarcerated certain demon spirits (Luke 8:30-31; 2 Peter 2:4; Jude 5-7). During this time, Satan will unleash hordes of demonic spirits to run rampant on planet Earth.

Thank God for the Holy Spirit, who restrains evil on the earth! Paul called the Holy Spirit "He who now restrains," and the Spirit will continue to hinder the swarm of evil until He is taken out of the way (2 Thessalonians 2:7). That removal will happen at the rapture, when the church is taken up from the earth. Because the Holy Spirit dwells in Christians, when they go, He goes. The Spirit will still be active in the world, of course, but He'll be "taken out of the way" in the sense that the true church won't be around to help stop the spread of evil. And so the world will have its way. It'll quickly become a festering sore, or rotting meat. You think the world is bad now? Wait until God removes the church from its midst and lets the enemy have his heyday.

The opening of the bottomless pit will unleash a demonic horde. These wicked spirits have power "as the scorpions of the earth have power" (v. 3) and are commanded not to harm vegetation, but only those individuals who lack the seal of God on their foreheads. They will torment men for five months. John says they have a horrific appearance: "The shape of the locusts was like horses prepared for battle. On their heads were crowns...and their faces were like the faces of men."

For several reasons, I don't believe these creatures are ordinary insects. First, Proverbs 30:27 says that locusts have no king, and the creatures in Revelation 9 have a king called "Abaddon" (v. 11—Hebrew, meaning "ruin" or "destruction"), or "Apollyon" (Greek, meaning "exterminator" or "destroyer").

Second, locusts normally eat vegetation, but these beasts do not (v. 4). I think they symbolize a very real plague, albeit not a natural one, that will hit the earth. The prophet Joel saw this: "A nation has come up against My land, strong, and without number. His teeth are the teeth of a lion, and he has the fangs of a fierce lion...Their appearance is like the appearance of horses; and like swift steeds, so they run" (Joel 1:6; 2:4). They appear to be "designer locusts" of some kind, perhaps genetic mutations. And they are possessed by demons of hell. Revelation 9:3-5 speaks of their scorpion-like power to torment men for five months. The poison of ordinary scorpions affects a victim's nervous system, causing him to feel as though the whole body had been set on fire. Someone who takes the full brunt of a scorpion's sting writhes on the ground, foams at the mouth, and grinds his teeth in agony. Remember, these evil spirits have been imprisoned for a long time, and now they seek to cause as much pain as possible.

So is this enough to get humankind to repent? While some individuals no doubt will have a change of heart, the vast majority will not (v. 20). They will continue to worship demons and their idols of gold, silver, brass, stone, and wood. Although they will have seen the collapse of world peace, the destruction of the earth, the fall of heavenly bodies, and now demonic tormentors, they will stiffen their necks once again. Dr. Henry Morris said God will allow them to experience a little direct fellowship with their future cohabitants in the lake of fire.[1]

Despite the ghastly nature of the fifth trumpet judgment, don't forget that God will remain in control of all that takes place. Martin Luther once said that the devil often appeared to him, and on one occasion Satan said, "Let me come into your heart. I want to discuss some very important matters with you." Luther classically answered, "I don't have the keys to the door. Ask God—He's got them." Luther knew that God remained sovereign and that He continued to exercise a restraining control over what He allowed the enemy to do.

But all of this supernatural activity will unnerve the inhabitants of earth (v. 6). Men will seek to die, but won't be able to. They will see no future, no hope. They will want to end it all—but death will take a holiday. I can't imagine anything worse—when death would seem like a blessing, not a curse. That gives us some idea of how horrific all this will be.

The sounding of the fifth trumpet will, in a sense, bring hell upon earth. It will bring people a little foretaste of eternal damnation. And if the inhabitants of earth are so terribly miserable during those five months, imagine what hell will be like for eternity! And, still, people will refuse to repent. Why? The answer is plain. Jesus once said, "This is the condemnation, that the light has come into the world, and men loved darkness rather than light, because their deeds were evil" (John 3:19).

God does everything He can to bring people to the light. When at the end of Revelation 8 He sends an angel to shout, "Woe, woe, woe!" to the world, He does it out of mercy, to give people another opportunity to say, "I'm turning my life over to Jesus Christ." Perhaps that is why the Bible gives some 600 warnings about hell. Perhaps that is why Jesus Christ spoke more about hell than anyone else in Scripture. And perhaps that is why Paul wrote, "Knowing, therefore, the terror of the Lord, we persuade men" (2 Corinthians 5:11). It all makes me want to get on the ball and tell people about the love of God, lest they face the wrath of God.

Angels of Mass Destruction (9:13-21)

The sixth trumpet judgment (or the second woe) has four focal points: an altar, angels, an army, and an audience. The devastation now begins to reach a crescendo.

The altar is a strange one—we are told that it talks (it reminds me of the burning bush of Exodus 3:2). In the earthly temple in Jerusalem, incense was offered on the golden altar near the Holy of Holies, representing the prayers of God's people ascending to heaven. Then in Revelation 8 we saw the heavenly golden altar in connection with judgment. And now we see this altar mentioned again.

In Old Testament days, God instructed the high priest to make atonement for the Jewish people on the horns of the golden altar. This took place once a year (Exodus 30) on what is now known as Yom Kippur. The priest was to go to the outer altar, gather blood spilled from a sacrificial animal, then take that blood and smear it on the four horns (or corners) of the golden altar, and finally take incense and offer it before God. God was thereby telling the people, "I will hear your prayers, but only on the basis of blood sacrifice." That principle has never changed. So when we cry out to God and plead our case before Him, we do so only on the basis of the blood of Christ, which was shed for us on Calvary. His sacrifice alone is what opened our access to God.

But Revelation 9:13 records the voice of judgment from the altar, not mercy. In the Old Testament era, guilty people sometimes grabbed hold of the horns of the altar and said, "If I hold tight to this altar, there will be mercy." But by this time in world history, there will be no mercy left.

The voice from the altar will call out for the release of four wicked angels who until then had been held captive near the Euphrates River

(v. 14). These four spirits, "who had been prepared for the hour and day and month and year," will be released to kill a third of humankind (v. 15). This text reminds me that it is *God* who binds angels and demons; we do not. Some believers feel empowered when they say, "I bind you, Satan!" But their "binding" must use very flimsy ropes or defective chains, because it never seems to last for long.

The Euphrates was the great river that formed the eastern boundary to the Promised Land. The Euphrates also marked the uttermost eastern boundary for the Roman Empire. From the very beginning, this region of the world has served as the fountainhead of all sorts of weirdness and wickedness. Somewhere in this area, in the delta formed by the Tigris and Euphrates rivers, the Garden of Eden once stood. Into that garden came the evil usurper, Satan; and in that garden the first sin was committed and the first lie told. Near that garden the first murder was committed and the first grave was dug.

Also, it was near the Euphrates that a man named Nimrod defied God and started a world religion against the Lord, culminating in the building of the Tower of Babel. The Euphrates region gave birth to ancient Israel's most oppressive enemies, including the Assyrians, the Babylonians, and the Medo-Persians. And it is by the Euphrates River that Israel remained captive for seventy years.

The area also is the fountainhead of world idolatry: Weird spirituality, pantheism, polytheism, naturalistic religions, and more all came from Babylon. Revelation uses that name to speak of "mystery, Babylon," which it calls "the mother of harlots and of the abominations of the earth" (Revelation 17:5). Here human history began, and here it will end.

These four wicked angels, chained for millennia, had been prepared "for the hour and day and month and year." That testifies to us that God is always right on time. I take comfort in the fact God is sovereign and my life and my times are in His hands. God knows my months and years and days and hours, and He restrains even these powerful spirits who will kill large numbers of human beings.

God is in ultimate control of history. His releasing of these malevolent spirits to kill a third of mankind will come on the heels of an earlier devastation in which a fourth of the world's population will be destroyed. When you combine those figures, you learn that a staggering half of all the humans alive at the start of the Tribulation will be dead long before it ends.

These four evil spirits won't come alone. John says an army of 200 million horsemen will accompany them (v. 16). Together, these wicked forces will kill a third of humanity, through fire and smoke and brimstone. Who are these millions of horsemen? Scholars disagree. Some say they comprise a human army under the command of the "kings from the east" (Revelation 16:12)—nations like China and Japan—which would make for an enormous force. Others say that the description John gives defies ordinary identification, and therefore this has to be some sort of demonic army.

But put yourself in John's sandals for a moment. What would it be like for a first-century man to get a vision of the distant future? Let's say the vision involved tanks and planes and nuclear warfare and missiles falling out of the sky. When all you know is spears and swords and shields and arrows, how would you comprehend all the future weapons, let alone describe them? John mentions horses; could he have in mind what these people sit on (or in) for warfare? He says they had heads like those of lions; could he mean they were fierce and determined, advancing in their attack like a lion? It's impossible to say for sure.

At the height of World War II, American forces numbered 12 million—and John speaks here of *200* million troops. Understand that when John wrote Revelation, there weren't even 200 million people living on earth! A few decades ago, Mao Tse-tung said that in the battle for the world, China could field an army of 200 million soldiers, and today 1.2 *billion* people live in China. Some recall Mao's boast and think of Revelation 16:12, where we are told the Euphrates River will dry up so the kings of the east can march across it. Who knows?

Though the specifics of such details are debated, we need to keep in mind that one of the focal points of this chapter is the audience. How will the planet's residents respond to all that has happened so far? Verse 20 reports, "The rest of mankind, who were not killed by these plagues, did not repent of the works of their hands." Nor did they "repent of their murders or their sorceries or their sexual immorality or their thefts" (v. 21).

The world of that time—and I would say, our world as well—is marked by five categories of sin. First is idolatry (v. 20). Men and women are always driven to worship *something*. We all want some spiritual experience beyond ourselves. Many today borrow a little bit of Jesus' love and use it to create a New Age faith, a pick-and-choose smorgasbord of the top ten hits of the world's religions. One day the Antichrist will erect an animated image of himself for the world to worship. But ultimately, idol worship is demon worship (1 Corinthians 10:20). Already we're seeing trends in this direction, with fashion magazines promoting as chic the wearing of amulets, skulls, and all sorts of occultic jewelry around the neck and wrist and ankle.

These unrepentant people will also refuse to turn from murder. During this time they will kill Christians, Jews, and one another. They will have acquired the taste for blood and they won't want to quit. The Tribulation will simply be a massive proliferation of what we're already seeing today. In 2009, there were 15,241 murders. This comes out to approximately 42 murders per day in the United States.[2] Jesus said that as it was in the days of Noah, so will it be at the coming of the Son of Man (Matthew 24:37). If you look back at the days of Noah, you'll find that violence covered the face of the earth (Genesis 6).

These people will also refuse to give up their "sorceries," which literally refers to "druggings." In both ancient and modern times, sorcery and witchcraft are always connected to drug usage, for drugs intertwine fantasy with reality. Dr. Henry Morris said, "Stupefying and hallucinatory drugs have been associated with sorcery and witchcraft for ages, yielding to their users strange visions and hallucinations which they could interpret as oracles for the guidance of their clients. Also, they divested their users of the control of their own minds, making them easily available for possession and control by evil spirits."[3] A strong link exists between drug use and the occult.

These people also won't give up their sexual immorality. Consider the immorality that is currently portrayed on prime-time television today, and then imagine what it will be like when the church is removed—how the portrayal of fornication, adultery, homosexuality, bestiality, and pedophilia will explode. Malcolm Muggeridge, the late English writer and critic, looked at Western culture many years ago and said, "The orgasm has replaced the cross as the focus of our longing and the image of fulfillment."[4]

Finally, theft will become rampant. Honesty will vanish, and all without reprisal. Revelation 9:20-21 describes unbridled crime without just retribution; there will be no justice system in place in order to take corrective action. Some have said that capital punishment will be eliminated during the Great Tribulation for all crimes except one: that of being a Christian.

A Missionary Mandate

Does Revelation 9 have a message for Christians today? Most certainly it does. In fact, we see a missionary mandate running all through Revelation 9.

Paul spoke of this mandate when he wrote, "Knowing, therefore, the terror of the Lord, we persuade men" (2 Corinthians 5:11). The late Vance Havner agreed with the apostle when he said, "The real test of how much we believe prophetic truth is what we're doing to warn people to flee from the wrath to come. To believe the solemn truths of prophecy and then make our way complacently through a world of sin and shame is not merely unfortunate; it is criminal."[5]

Perhaps you have already heard the following statement before, but in light of what we've just studied in Revelation 9, it's well worth considering again: "Any Christian who does not evangelize will fossilize." It's true. Without getting involved somehow in telling others about Jesus, you'll dry up. Through the harsh message of Revelation 9, Jesus is asking you to represent Him to the world.

"But I'm not an extrovert," you may say. Well, that's okay; you don't have to be an extrovert to witness effectively. In order to represent Jesus to others, you simply have to care for them. That's all.

And who among us can't do that?

A Big Angel with a Little Book

Revelation 10

SUMMARY

The book of Revelation reveals a pattern in God's judgments. Six judgments unfold, then there is a pause, and then a seventh judgment comes. So six seals are broken on a closed scroll, followed by six judgments, and then there is an interlude. Six trumpets are blown, signaling six judgments, and then there is another interlude. Chapter 10 records the interlude that follows the sounding of the sixth trumpet.

RELATED SCRIPTURES FOR STUDY

Deuteronomy 29:29; 2 Peter 3:8-9

One of the big questions people have debated through the centuries is this: Why does God allow evil to continue? Why does He permit Satan to run wild, seemingly unchecked? If there is a God and He is holy, then why doesn't He intervene? Why doesn't He just stop all of the carnage and confusion? And if God loves His own people, as He claims, then why does He let them suffer, as so often happens?

As World War II loomed on the horizon, the Nazis deported Elie Wiesel, a Jew, and his whole family to the Auschwitz death camp. Later they transferred Wiesel to Buchenwald, another notorious concentration camp, where he spent part of his teenage years. While in the camps, both of his parents and his younger sister died.

One biographer wrote that for Wiesel,

> Nietzsche's cry was expressed in almost physical reality—
> God is dead. The God of love, the God of gentleness, the
> God of comfort, has vanished forevermore. And how many
> pious Jews have experienced this death? On that day, horri-
> ble even among those days of horror, when a child watched
> the hanging of another child who, he tells us, had the face of
> a sad angel, he heard someone behind him groan, "Where
> is God? Where is He? Where can God be now?"[1]

All of those questions find their ultimate answers in the book of Revelation. And all of them are tied to what the Old Testament prophets called
the Day of the Lord. Everything comes to resolution at the sounding of
the seventh trumpet. Before the seventh trumpet even blows (it does not
sound until Revelation 11:15), John writes, "In the days of the sounding of the seventh angel, when he is about to sound, the mystery of God
would be finished, as He declared to His servants the prophets" (10:7).

God is not filled solely with vengeance, as some think. He always
tempers His judgment with mercy, so we always see a mixture of both
when He acts. The prophet Habakkuk saw God pour out His judgments upon the nation of Israel as well as upon the surrounding pagan
nations. And he prayed, "O Lord, revive Your work in the midst of
years!...In wrath remember mercy" (Habakkuk 3:2).

It's a pattern that God follows. Even when part of His work involves
judgment, He always mingles it with mercy.

A Description of the Messenger (10:1-4)

Verse 1 introduces us to an angel, a huge one who has set one foot
on the land and his other foot on the sea. Clearly he is a mighty angel,
although not one of the trumpeting angels. John's description of him
so closely resembles the picture of our Savior painted in chapter 1 that
many scholars have thought this could be Jesus Christ. And it is true that
in the Old Testament, Jesus often shows up as "the Angel of the Lord"
(see, for example, Genesis 16:7; 22:11; Exodus 3:2; Numbers 22:22).

John sees the angel "coming down from heaven, clothed with a cloud" (v. 1). In the Gospels Jesus Himself said, "They will see the Son of Man coming on the clouds of heaven with power and great glory" (Matthew 24:30; see also Luke 21:27). And at the beginning of Revelation, John sees Jesus as the Alpha and the Omega and writes of Him, "Behold, He is coming with clouds" (Revelation 1:7).

In Revelation 4:3, John describes a heavenly throne surrounded by a rainbow. The rainbow, you'll remember, was originally given to humankind after the Great Flood as a visual reminder that God had promised never again to destroy the world through a flood (Genesis 9:13-15). John certainly knew the Old Testament story (confirmed by his scores of references and allusions to passages in the Hebrew Bible), so when he saw this vision of a rainbow, it must have brought him comfort. No doubt we should consider the rainbow around the angel's head as a symbol of the authority of God, who sits on a rainbow-framed throne. This angel, therefore, comes as a messenger of God, and with all His authority.

In addition, John says the angel's face looked like the sun, and his feet like pillars of fire. In chapter 1, John wrote that Jesus' countenance was like the sun shining in its strength, and that His feet were like fine brass, as if refined in a furnace. Moreover, in verse 3 John says the angel cried with a loud voice, "as when a lion roars," while in Revelation 5:5 John calls Jesus the Lion of the tribe of Judah. In addition, the prophet Hosea predicted that the Lord "will roar like a lion. When He roars, then His sons shall come trembling from the west" (11:10).

So this angel really could be Jesus. But it also could be the archangel Michael, whose name means "who is like God." I think the text contains a big clue that indicates this angel is *not* Jesus Christ; namely, the use of the Greek term *allos* to mean "another," as in "I saw *another* angel." The term *allos* means "another of the same kind," which indicates that John wants us to think of another angel of the same kind as the angels we have just observed. Had he meant Jesus, John probably would have chosen the Greek term *heteros*, which means "another of an entirely different sort."

Whatever the case, a mighty angel puts his feet down. And through him, God is putting His own foot down, so to speak. Satan is having his heyday, the earth is going haywire, and for millennia God has been patient. But now this mighty angel, in anticipation of the sounding of the seventh trumpet, steps forward to announce the end.

We get yet another feel for the gravity of this moment in verse 4, when seven thunders utter their "voices." John is about to write down what he heard, but a heavenly voice instructs him, "Seal up the things which the seven thunders uttered, and do not write them." We don't know what they said because God chose not to reveal it. But the very mention of the incident heightens the mystery and intrigue of the passage and adds to the momentousness of the occasion. There is an Old Testament text that helps to tie all of this together: "The secret things belong to the LORD our God, but those things which are revealed belong to us and our children forever, that we may do all the words of this law" (Deuteronomy 29:29).

Remember that Jesus once said to His disciples, "I still have many things to say to you, but you cannot bear them now" (John 16:12). Because He loved His followers, He refused to give them more than they could handle. Later, through the Holy Spirit, He would tell them the things He now held back; but at that moment, they did not have the resources to assimilate His words. So He shelved them for a time. As J.I. Packer observed, "We should not pry into God's secrets. We are to be content to live with what He has told us. Reverence excludes speculation about things that God has not mentioned in His Word. We must be content not to know what the Scripture does not tell us."[2]

The Declaration of the Messenger (10:5-7)

John sees this mighty angel raise his hand to heaven, probably his right hand, and take a solemn oath that there should no longer be any delay (vv. 5-6). In doing so, the angel simply affirms the certainty of the message he had heard in heaven. He emphasizes the character of God—"Him who lives forever and ever, who created heaven and the things that are in it, the earth and the things that are in it, and the sea and the things that are in it"—in order to call attention to the certainty of the prophecy. This will surely happen because as the Creator, God is not bound by time or space.

Remember that by this time, a lot of the environment has been trashed. And now the mighty angel plants one foot on the land and one foot on the sea—God's creation—and swears by the Creator of the sea and the land and the sky, as if to say, "This is *God's* creation. You foolish humans have been worshiping God's earth, God's creation, instead of God—and now God is taking it over because He is the Creator."

At this point, many unbelievers may say, "Sorry, but I have to part company with you. I can sort of believe in a god who used evolution to wind things up, but I absolutely don't believe in the kind of special creation that you say makes us unique." The origin of the universe has been the object of dispute for generations. How did we get here? Evolution provides the basis for many philosophies, including atheism. In fact, evolutionary thought underlies many secular ideologies, including Hitler's Nazism and Marx's communism. But the theory of evolution is only a theory, and the Bible upholds creation, not evolution.

When I look at this universe, it's clear to me that it reflects incredible design. And yet many people say it "just happened." It's merely a fortuitous occurrence of accidental circumstance. It just so happened that the earth orbits 93 million miles from the sun. It just so happens that the sun has a surface temperature of 12,000 degrees Fahrenheit—and if we were a little closer we'd burn up, or if we were a little further away we would freeze to death. It just so happens that the earth is tilted on its axis 23 1/3 degrees so that we enjoy a beautiful balance of four seasons; and it just so happens that if the earth were tilted a little differently masses of vapors would travel north and south, creating huge continents of ice. It just so happens that we have the optimal mix in our atmosphere of carbon dioxide and oxygen, and if the mix were just a bit thinner, the asteroids and meteors that now disintegrate in our atmosphere would instead plummet all the way to our planet's surface. It just so happens that the moon is precisely the right size and at exactly the right distance from earth to create the tides necessary to sustain ocean life. If the moon were any bigger or closer, those same tides would inundate the land.

So why, then, do many bright people look at verse 6 and say, "There is no Creator, and creation is a myth"? I think perhaps it's because they assume other intelligent people believe in it. And it's also politically correct. In our day, it's become intellectually chic to believe in evolution.

There is a second and more profound explanation for why many people endorse evolution and deny creation. Once you acknowledge the possibility that evolution is wrong, then you also acknowledge the possibility that you were created. And once you open that door, you allow a Creator into the room; and if a Creator exists, then you are accountable to Him. Oops—don't like that! Better come up with another theory.

And there's a third and even more profound reason some people reject creation (and the Creator) in favor of evolution. The Bible says that sin blinds the minds of those who do not believe. And if you don't believe, then you have to search for alternate explanations. No doubt that is the main reason individuals who are on earth during the Tribulation period will so consistently reject God and refuse to repent. Their unbelief will so harden their hearts that they *cannot* believe. Jesus asked a group of men who opposed His message, "How can you believe, who receive honor from one another, and do not seek the honor that comes from the only God?" (John 5:44; see also 2 Corinthians 4:4).

But regardless of sin and unbelief—in fact, because of it—the Creator acts during the Tribulation to set right what went wrong so long ago. And verse 6 reminds us that, by this point in the story, "there should be delay no longer." The word "delay" is the Greek term *chronos*, or time, and so some translations render the phrase "that there would be no longer time." In other words, God is saying, "Time's up! I've been patient. I have delayed…and now your time has run out. There will be no more delay."

All of this is tied to verse 7: "In the days of the sounding of the seventh angel, when he is about to sound, the mystery of God would be finished, as He declared to His servants the prophets." Do you remember the prayers of the martyred souls under the heavenly altar? They cried out, "How long, O Lord…until You judge and avenge our blood on those who dwell on the earth?" (Revelation 6:10). Now they get their answer: "The time has come. It's here. There will be no more delay. The mystery is finished."

What "mystery of God" did the prophets speak about? (10:7). I believe this refers to the mystery of God's silence. Why does God allow evil to prosper? Why doesn't He stop the wicked from harming the innocent? With one voice, the prophets all declare that one day God will speak from heaven. In fact, He will roar from heaven. He will send a day of darkness, a day of cataclysm, a day of catastrophic and holy judgment. God *will* intervene in human history and God *will* judge the earth. And when that time comes, there will be no more delay.

Walter Scott, the statesman poet of England, said,

> Does it not seem strange that Satan has been allowed for 6,000 years to wrap and twist his coils around the world and to work evil and spoil and mar the work of God? Is it not a mystery why God, the God of righteousness and holiness, allows evil to go unpunished and His own people to be crushed and broken on every hand? Truly this is the mystery of God. God bears with evil until the hour of judgment arrives, when He will avenge the cry of His elect and come out of His place to punish the wicked. Evil now tolerated and allowed will be openly punished. The mystery is at an end. Christ is about to reign.[3]

Right now we live in the time of delay. But somewhere beyond the starry host there waits a mighty angel holding a special musical instrument. And one day, at just the right moment, he will blow that seventh trumpet and God will say, "It's over." He will turn to the devil and say, "It's over for you. This is your destruction." And the Lord will say to the demons, "Your dominion is over." And God almighty will say to the unbelievers, "This is your last chance." And the God of all comfort will say to believers, "This is your final suffering."

The apostle Paul looked ahead to that day and said, in essence, "You know, the way I figure it, the glory that we're going to receive is so much greater than the suffering—so infinitely greater—that our sufferings aren't even worthy to be compared with the glory that will be revealed in us" (see Romans 8:18).

That day is coming. But for now, we still live in the time of the Long Pause.

The Directions of the Messenger (10:8-11)

In verse 8 John is told, by a voice which he heard from heaven, to take a little scroll held by the mighty angel. Apparently this little book contains the rest of the message that John will write regarding the future. It's not the same scroll that had been in the hand of Him who sits on the throne (Revelation 5:1). In the original Greek text, that book was called *biblion*. But here in Revelation 10:8, this book is called *biblaridion*, a small book or a little scroll. It seems to contain the rest of what John is going to prophesy in the book of Revelation. When John asks for the little scroll, the angel tells him to eat it and warns him that "it will make your stomach bitter, but it will be as sweet as honey in your mouth" (v. 9).

This is not the first time in Scripture that God's people "ate" some special scrolls. Jeremiah wrote, "Your words were found, and I ate them, and Your word was to me the joy and rejoicing of my heart" (Jeremiah 15:16). David said in Psalm 119, "How sweet are Your words to my taste, sweeter than honey to my mouth!" (v. 103). Jesus likened the Scriptures to bread and said, "Man shall not live by bread alone, but every word that proceeds from the mouth of God" (Matthew 4:4). Peter compared the Scriptures to milk and recommended that his readers crave it like newborn babies hunger after their mother's milk (1 Peter 2:2). This reminds us of our responsibility not just to read the Bible, but to feed on the Bible. Not just to underline a verse or even memorize a verse, but to "eat" it. That is, to take it into you and let it become a part of your life. The Word of God is to become a part of us.

When John ate this little scroll, at first it tasted sweet. But once he digested the message, it became bitter. The words gave him a sour stomach. That sounds somewhat similar to Ezekiel's experience. In a vision, God gave Ezekiel a scroll and told him to eat it. Written on the scroll were lamentations, mourning, and woe. At God's instruction, the prophet ate the scroll, and he reported that "it was in my mouth like honey in sweetness" (Ezekiel 3:3). Unlike John, however, Ezekiel does not report that he got heartburn.

So what does John mean when he says that at first the little scroll tasted sweet, but in his stomach it turned bitter? The sweetness was the news that Jesus Christ would reign when this time of judgment came to an end. He will take over the earth, and that's sweet. The bitter part was all of the darkness and death that would overtake the world until the time of the restoration. But how sweet it was to know that Jesus would reign in the end, and that evil would be done away with!

John's experience is our own. The Word of God always has both a sweet and a bitter flavor. The apostle Paul said that the gospel is the aroma of life to some, and the aroma of death to others (2 Corinthians 2:15-16). The same gospel that brings some individuals to heaven also brings others to hell. So it's both bitter and sweet.

Love Honors the Choice

Periodically I get the question thrown at me, "Why does God allow Satan to reign and sin to abound? Why the delay?"

The answer, of course, is that God is incredibly patient and long-suffering. He doesn't want anybody to perish, but all to come to repentance (see 2 Peter 3:9). If He so chose, God could instantly destroy every wicked person who caused suffering. In fact, He could obliterate a person the moment an evil thought occurred to him.

Or, He could patiently wait for sinners to turn to Him. Where would any of us be without that divine patience?

God created us with the ability to make a choice. And for God to give us a choice, He must honor that choice. That's part of love. So for God to stop us from doing anything wicked would not be love. In love, He *has* to allow those choices to continue—up to a point. And that includes the freedom even to defy God and to reject His love.

God could have made us into automatons. He could have made us so all He has to do is push a button and we'd have no choice but to say, "Praise the Lord. I love Jesus." But if He had done that, we'd simply be responding to Him mechanically and not out of love. So God says to all of us, "You can choose to love Me, or you can choose to reject My love. I will honor either choice. And know this: I will allow plenty of time and be longsuffering before I act in judgment. One day, however, I will put My foot down on both the sea and on the land and I'll say, 'It's over. My patience has run out, and there are bitter things to come.'"

I think God would add one more thing. I'm pretty sure He would say, "But I'd much rather you chose to join Me in the ultimate, sweet ending. What do you say?"

11

Two Powerful Preachers

Revelation 11

SUMMARY

God never leaves Himself without a witness. Even in the Tribulation period, He will raise up two remarkable witnesses who will tell the world that the calamities upon the earth come in response to its unrepentant wickedness. As the judgments grow ever more severe, Jesus' kingdom approaches ever nearer—to the great delight of heaven's citizens.

RELATED SCRIPTURES FOR STUDY

Exodus 7:15–12:32; 1 Kings 17:1; 2 Kings 1:10-12; Zechariah 4; Malachi 4:5-6; Acts 20:24

After the rapture of the church, some of the greatest evangelism this world has ever seen will bless planet Earth. It will come primarily in the form of two witnesses who preach the gospel from their headquarters in Jerusalem. As a result of their ministry, in cooperation with others, millions of men and women will come to faith in Jesus Christ.

Why will they know such great success? It's largely because they will understand that witnessing isn't just something you *do*; a witness is something you *are*. And they are something else.

Jesus once told His disciples, "You shall be witnesses to Me in Jerusalem, and in all Judea and Samaria, and to the end of the earth" (Acts 1:8). When you combine someone who has the right message with someone who is living the right lifestyle, then you can expect to see an extremely powerful dynamic at work. And that's true both in the future as well as today.

The Setting of Their Ministry (11:1-2)

Verse 1 appears to place the setting of the ministry of these two witnesses in Jerusalem, for the mention of "the temple of God" strongly suggests that city. In addition, verse 8 names "the great city which spiritually is called Sodom and Egypt, where also our Lord was crucified," which clearly is Jerusalem.

The temple is the very heart and center of Judaism. Solomon built the first temple in Jerusalem. After that temple was destroyed by the Babylonians, a second temple was later built when the Jewish people returned from exile in Babylon. Then hundreds of years later Herod expanded the building and its courtyards for his Jewish subjects. That temple was demolished by the Romans in AD 70. John saw his vision and wrote the book of Revelation about AD 95, a quarter of a century after the Romans razed the temple. And because his vision is about the future, he's clearly looking at a future temple, and he's told to measure it. This tells us there will be a temple in Jerusalem at some point in the future.

Jesus talked about a future event that would take place in "the holy place" of the temple, which meant He was referring to a future temple (Matthew 24:15), for the structure of His day was destroyed. Daniel likewise spoke about a future temple that a pagan leader would defile (Daniel 9:26-27). And Paul the apostle foretold that the "man of sin," the Antichrist, would sit in the temple and declare himself to be God (2 Thessalonians 2:4).

Ever since the Romans destroyed the temple in AD 70, the Jewish people have never been able to rebuild it due to a host of geopolitical difficulties. They didn't even have sovereignty over the city of Jerusalem until June of 1967, and even after that, building a new temple on the ancient site has posed a number of insuperable political problems (so far). One of the biggest is that on the spot where many believe the temple once stood, there is now a structure called the Al Aqsa Mosque, which is the third holiest site for Islam. Muslims believe that from a rock under a nearby dome the prophet Mohammed ascended into heaven, received the Koran, and came back to the earth and gave it to man.

On the other hand, there are scholars who doubt the temple ever stood there. In fact, Asher Kaufman, a professor of physics at the Hebrew University, has researched this problem extensively and says the archeological evidence puts the original temple about twenty-six meters to the north. He says the temple lined up with the East Gate, and if he is right, then the temple could be built on that spot, leaving the Dome of the Rock completely outside the temple compound. In fact, the Dome of the Rock would sit in what was called, in ancient times, the Court of the Gentiles.

In verse 2 John is called to measure the temple area, but is instructed to avoid the court "which is outside the temple…for it has been given to the Gentiles. And they will tread the holy city underfoot for forty-two months." Now, why would the Lord tell John to measure the temple area? It's one thing to see a vision; but what does it mean that he was to measure the site?

A few times in the Bible, men are instructed to measure the temple or the city. Ezekiel is told to measure the future millennial temple (Ezekiel 40). Zechariah was called to measure the city (Zechariah 2:2). In Revelation 20, the city of Jerusalem is measured (since there will be no temple there). In the Bible, measurement appears to speak of ownership and evaluation.

But John is to measure not just the temple, but also the altar and those who worship at it (v. 1). God observes and measures the worship of man! The Gospel of Mark reports how one day Jesus sat across from the temple treasury and observed how people put money into it (Mark 12:41-43). God is always our observer, and He sees everything. It's very important to Him. Moreover, He watches our attitudes, not just our actions. God *notices*.

The Significance of Their Ministry (11:3-6)

The two witnesses in Revelation 11 will prophesy with power (v. 3). They will both declare God's words and display God's works, and they will do that for 1260 days, or three-and-a-half years (based on a calendar using thirty-day months, a "prophetic calendar" that most scholars accept). So these men will have a prophetic ministry, centered around Jerusalem, that will last for three-and-a-half years, or during the first half of the Tribulation. They will be witnesses for God, and they will deliver a potent message.

John calls them "the two olive trees and the two lampstands standing before the God of the earth" (v. 4). In an earlier vision, the prophet Zechariah saw two olive trees, and from the trees came pipes that emptied into a receptacle where oil was collected. Other pipes came from the trees to feed the menorah, where oil was burned to provide light in the tabernacle—almost an automated menorah. Oil came automatically, without crushing olives, supplying light for this lampstand. What did this portray? God explained, "Not by might nor by power, but by My Spirit, says the LORD of hosts" (Zechariah 4:6). In other words, "Everything you've wanted to do in coming back to the land, Zechariah and Zerubbabel and Joshua, will be accomplished. You will build this city and you will build the temple; but it will not be done by human strength. Instead, I will empower two witnesses to do the work." At that time, the two witnesses happened to be Joshua, the high priest, and Zerubbabel, the governor of Jerusalem. These two men became witnesses for God by being filled with the Holy Spirit, who supernaturally enabled them to carry on their ministry. They supply us with something of a model for the two witnesses of Revelation 11.

Who are these two witnesses? Most likely they are none other than Moses and Elijah come back to earth. There are four reasons for thinking so. First, notice their works. They destroy their enemies by calling fire down from heaven, as Elijah did (2 Kings 1:10-12). They call for drought, as Elijah did (1 Kings 17:1). And they have the power to turn water into blood and to strike the earth with various plagues, as Moses did (Exodus 7:15–12:32).

Second, the last prophet of the Old Testament, Malachi, predicted that Elijah would return before "the great and dreadful day of the LORD" (Malachi 4:5-6). When John the Baptist came on the scene, the Jewish religious leaders asked him if he was Elijah; they wondered about this because they expected Elijah to return before the Messiah arrived (John 1:21). John denied that he was Elijah. In addition, many Jews through-out history have believed that Moses would come before the Messiah arrives, because in Deuteronomy 18:15 Moses said, "God will raise up for you a Prophet like me from your midst, from your brethren. Him you shall hear." This led many to infer that Moses would come again.

Precedent supplies a third reason: Moses and Elijah have *already* come back as a pair. On the Mount of Transfiguration, Moses and Elijah appeared to Jesus and spoke with Him about His approaching cru-cifixion (Matthew 17:3).

Fourth, both Moses and Elijah left this world in an unusual way. Eli-jah never died, but was taken up into heaven in a chariot of fire (2 Kings 2:11). And although Moses died, God Himself had him buried in an unknown grave; and apparently Michael the archangel and the devil had an argument about Moses' body (Jude 9). Why all the argument over a corpse unless God wanted to retain that body for His own pur-poses in the future?

And ponder this: What two men would have more of an impact on the Jewish nation than Moses, who represents the Law, and Elijah, recognized as the greatest prophet? These two men are the embodi-ment of the Law and the Prophets. Who better to herald the coming of the King?

The Suppression of Their Ministry (11:7-10)

We see the first mention of the Antichrist in verse 7, where he is called "the beast that ascends out of the bottomless pit." He comes to destroy, and we'll see him mentioned thirty-six more times in the book. And the two witnesses will oppose him face-to-face.

For three-and-a-half years the witnesses will interpret for the world all of the cataclysms, destruction, hordes of demons, the heavens fall-ing, and destruction of the sea. They will say, "This is God's judgment on wicked people." And do you think anyone will like their message? A righteous person is always a torment to a wicked person. A righ-teous person living in God's light shines that light upon those living in darkness and makes them feel deeply agitated. So the vast majority of the people of the world will hate these two witnesses and will want to destroy them. One day their wish will be granted, as the Antichrist will be allowed to kill them.

But let me draw your attention to a crucial phrase that should bring great comfort to you. These two witnesses can't be killed *until* they "finish their testimony" (v. 7). They are indestructible until God completes His purposes for them on earth. In a similar way, *every* child of God doing the work of God in the will of God is invincible—until God is finished with them. I don't believe in untimely deaths for Christians. When God is done, it's over. And not until then.

The unrepentant people of this world will hate these men so much that they will let their dead bodies rot in the streets of Jerusalem instead of burying them (v. 9). In fact, people will celebrate the witnesses' deaths by giving presents to one another, as in a satanic Christmas (v. 10). And mark this: This is the *only* rejoicing that will take place during the entire Tribulation period.

The Summit of Their Ministry (11:11-13)

God will use even the deaths of His two witnesses for His purposes. Three-and-a-half days after their murders, He will resurrect them, and they will stand on their feet as the whole world watches in "great fear" (v. 11). Think of the fear and the dread as this miracle happens! And then this holy pair will rise into heaven (v. 12).

You might think that after seeing such an astounding miracle, the people of the world would repent and come to faith. Not so. Remember that Jesus said, "If they do not hear Moses and the prophets, neither will they be persuaded though one rise from the dead" (Luke 16:31). Only the Holy Spirit allows faith to grow in an individual's heart.

While these two witnesses lived on earth, they were faithful. That's really the only way for you as a Christian to live—as God's witness, so that you don't reach the end of your life and find yourself to be an old person full of regrets. The good news is that you don't have to become that regretful old person. If you were to ask God to fill you with His Holy Spirit so that you could lead one other person to faith in Christ this year, and then you trained that person to do the same with someone else, in year two you'd multiply to four Christians. The next year, you'd have eight. And in a half a century, the world would be won to Christ.

The Light at the End of the Tunnel (11:14-19)

This section of Revelation describes the middle of the Tribulation; it's not for those afraid of the dark. John tells us that the second of three woes has passed, and the third is rushing onto the scene (v. 14).

When the seventh angel sounds his trumpet—the last one—loud voices from heaven shout, "The kingdoms of this world have become the kingdoms of our Lord and of His Christ, and He shall reign forever and ever!" (v. 15). Chronologically, the seventh trumpet brings us to the end of the Tribulation. It encompasses everything up to the reign of Jesus Christ.

The seventh trumpet blast brings on seven final plagues, and "in them the wrath of God is complete" (15:1). Ever since the Fall of man, when sin marred the earth and scarred God's creation, people have wondered, *When is God going to take over and rule the earth?* The announcement here says, "It's happening now."

During His earthly ministry, Jesus loved to speak about His coming kingdom. His very first message was this: "Repent, for the kingdom of heaven is at hand" (Matthew 4:17). Matthew chapters 5, 6, and 7 proclaim His kingdom manifesto. Matthew 13 features parables in which Jesus tells kingdom stories. And when the Roman governor Pontius Pilate wanted to know whether Jesus claimed to be a king, the Lord essentially said the answer was yes and then added, "My kingdom is not of this world" (John 18:36). Even after His resurrection, Jesus spent forty days teaching His followers "the things pertaining to the kingdom of God" (Acts 1:3). His kingdom was a major theme in His life and teaching.

In all these things Jesus was declaring, "I am the King. I have come in your midst and I have followers who have received Me as King. The kingdom of God is here, in your midst. One day it will come in its fullness, but even now My followers shift their priorities from themselves and their kingdoms to Me and My eternal kingdom."

In heaven, the twenty-four elders, representing the church, worship God for bringing Jesus' kingdom into full flower (vv. 16-17). They thank God for His sovereign power and His willingness to use it. Then verse 18 encompasses the entire Tribulation period and the millennium to follow; in many ways it's a good summary of the whole book of Revelation. Some of what is described here we've seen already; and some of what is revealed we will see in coming chapters.

The chapter closes with a vision of heaven's temple (v. 19). It's like open house in heaven—the curtains are open, and you can see into the Holy of Holies, in which is placed the Ark of the Covenant. Is this a literal temple, or is John using figurative language here? The temple could be literal; the book of Hebrews belabors the point that the tabernacle on earth and the temple in Jerusalem were models of the true tabernacle and temple in heaven (Hebrews 8:5; 9:24). Or John might have been using figurative language to signify that in heaven we will realize God's full covenant, where we will enter into unbroken fellowship with Him.

The Ark of the Covenant, of course, was the main piece of furniture in the tabernacle and in the Jerusalem temple. Once a year the high priest would walk into the Holy of Holies and sprinkle blood on the Ark—and a miraculous transformation would take place. That Ark normally functioned as the throne of judgment because it contained the Law, which the people had broken. But in an instant it was transformed into a mercy seat from which God forgave the people's sin. The shed blood, placed on the Ark, tells us that God is saying, "When you place your faith in My sinless Son, you can come into the very Holy of Holies and enjoy unbroken, intimate fellowship with Me." The Ark of the Covenant finds its fullness in heaven.

Choose Heaven

The great British novelist and scholar C.S. Lewis said, "Aim at heaven and you will get earth thrown in. Aim at earth and you get neither."[1] In his classic fantasy *The Great Divorce*, he expanded a bit on this compelling idea:

> I do not think that all who choose wrong roads perish; but
> their rescue consists in being put back on the right road…

If we insist on keeping Hell (or even earth) we shall not see Heaven: if we accept Heaven we shall not be able to retain even the smallest and most intimate souvenirs of Hell. I believe, to be sure, that any man who reaches Heaven will find that what he abandoned (even in plucking out his right eye) was precisely nothing: that the kernel of what he was really seeking even in his most depraved wishes will be there, beyond expectation, waiting for him in "the High Countries."…I think earth, if chosen instead of Heaven, will turn out to have been, all along, only a region in Hell: and earth, if put second to Heaven, to have been from the beginning a part of Heaven itself.[2]

Purely earthly kingdoms are temporary. Transient. They don't last. And they don't bring either satisfaction or fulfillment. So if that's true, then why don't we invest in our future? If what is coming down the pike is an eternal kingdom, then why not get ready for it? The apostle Peter asked, "Since all these things will be dissolved"—that is, the new car, the home, the investment property; not that they're necessarily bad, but they are all temporary—"what manner of persons ought you to be in holy conduct and godliness, looking for and hastening the coming of the day of God…?" (2 Peter 3:11-12).

Christ's kingdom is coming! So let's get ready for it by knowing and worshiping and serving the King *right now*.

12

The Panorama of Spiritual Warfare

Revelation 12

SUMMARY

In Revelation 12 we travel in time all the way back to the fall of Lucifer, and then over the next few chapters we move forward again to the Great Tribulation. There we meet three main characters: a splendorous woman, a fierce dragon, and a unique male Child. Then we witness war in heaven, followed by wrath on earth. So in effect we view the Tribulation period once again, but this time from the vantage point of evil, not of good.

RELATED SCRIPTURES FOR STUDY

Genesis 37; Isaiah 14; Ezekiel 28; 1 Peter 5:8

In chapter 12 we get an insider's look at a fierce battlefield within the cosmic war that has raged since the beginning of time—and still rages today. Whenever you go into battle, of course, it's important to know your enemy and his strategy; and so John gives us that crucial intelligence.

Satan is the archenemy of God who long ago sparked a mutiny in heaven that led to the fall of a third of the angels (v. 4). He unsuccessfully tried to overthrow the paradise of God in heaven, and when that uprising failed, he attempted to overthrow the garden paradise on earth. God cursed him for the latter, and ever since then Satan has been trying to ruin *everything* in God's order. He has especially tried to stop the arrival of the Lord's eternal kingdom.

The Splendorous Woman (12:1-2)

At the opening of Revelation 12 we are introduced to a woman. John says of this woman that "a great sign appeared in heaven." For the first time in his vision, John sees something "great" or awesome, indicated by his use of the Greek term *mega*. He uses the same word to describe the dragon mentioned in verse 3, the dragon's "wrath" in verse 12, and an eagle in verse 14. Everything John sees in this vision is massive: a mega-woman, a mega-dragon, mega-wrath, and a mega-eagle.

This "great sign" is not a literal woman, but a symbol that points to a larger reality. Revelation describes four symbolic women in addition to this one: Jezebel, who represents paganism (chapter 2); the scarlet whore, who represents apostate religion in the end times (chapter 17); and the wife of the Lamb, who represents the church (chapter 19). This woman in chapter 12, depicted with the sun, the moon, and the twelve stars (v. 1), represents the nation of Israel. Her appearance instantly reminds us of Joseph's dreams in Genesis 37.

The Bible frequently calls Israel a woman, and sometimes refers to her as the wife of God (too often an unfaithful wife). It should not surprise us, then, to find Israel at center stage in all of redemptive history; after all, God promised a Messianic kingdom to the Hebrews. And because they're God's chosen people, they often have become God's hassled people. So we see this woman in pain, in travail, recalling the prophet Jeremiah's name for this turbulent period of world history: "the time of Jacob's trouble" (Jeremiah 30:7).

The woman is pregnant (v. 2) and gives birth to a male child. This helps us to realize she can't symbolize the church, for the church was already raptured before the Tribulation, and at this time is in heaven and not pregnant.

The Scandalous Dragon (12:3-4)

Suddenly a red dragon with seven heads and ten horns appears before the woman, later identified as the devil (v. 9). The woman,

Israel, is about to give birth to her child, the Messiah, when the dragon shows up spewing hate toward both the woman and her child. The dragon also functions as a sign. He is not a literal dragon; rather, the term "dragon" speaks of his personality—that he is fierce, deadly, and wicked. The color red speaks of bloodshed (see Revelation 6 and the second horseman); Jesus called Satan a murderer from the very beginning (John 8:44).

The dragon's seven heads speak of his comprehensive intelligence; he has an IQ that runs off the chart. He also has ten horns, representing strength (and later, ten kingdoms, see chapters 13; 17). Paul calls him "the prince of the power of the air" (Ephesians 2:2).

This dragon attempts to devour the woman's child at the moment of his birth. Apparently Satan figures, "If I can destroy this child, I can destroy the plan of God." In His Word, God has always said that His kingdom will come through the nation Israel. Evidently Satan thought that if he could wipe out this woman and her child, he could outsmart God and make Him into a liar.

Many people wonder, *Why would God make such a wicked being as Satan?* The fact is, He didn't. God created a beautiful being named Lucifer, and He created him with a free will. That powerful and glorious creature freely chose to rebel against God, thus making himself into the devil.

After Lucifer became Satan, he fell to the earth and there deceived Eve, who fell into sin. Unfortunately, Adam quickly followed suit. At that point, God promised the ultimate destruction of Satan (Genesis 3:15), forewarning him that his kingdom would come to an end and that he would be crushed, though in the process he would bruise the heel of the Seed. From that moment on, Satan and his allies have sought to kill this Seed, this Child, this Messiah—as well as the woman who would bear Him. Satan was ultimately behind the murder of Abel, the gross sin that prompted the worldwide flood, the hatred between Jacob and Esau, the Pharaoh's decree to kill all Hebrew male babies, Saul's many attempts to murder David, Haman's plot to eradicate all Jews, and on and on it goes.

The devil failed to corrupt heaven, and then he failed in his many attempts to murder the Messiah. So in great wrath he turns to persecute Israel, for he knows that God has promised that, in the end, He will use Israel to reign from Mount Zion in Jerusalem. In that way the Lord will fulfill all of His promises made to Abraham, Isaac, Jacob, and the twelve tribes. So the devil's last resort is to try to destroy any remnant of Israel so that the promised kingdom can never come.

Note that whatever God loves, Satan hates. Anti-Semitism, therefore, is more than simple prejudice. It is forged in the pit of hell because of Satan's hatred for all that God loves.

Perhaps that helps give you a better understanding of why you get so much grief as a Christian. You belong to Jesus. He purchased you with His blood. And the devil will do everything he can to keep you from the Lord. He always attacks those who love God and want to serve Him. He has attacked in the past, he attacks us even now, and he will continue to attack all through the future.

The Sovereign Male Child (12:5-6)

Despite the devil's attempts to eradicate the woman and her son, she gives birth to "a male Child who was to rule all nations with a rod of iron. And her Child was caught up to God and His throne" (v. 5). This brief text takes us all the way from Jesus' birth to His ascension after His resurrection. John sees Israel as the Messiah's mother, calling to mind Isaiah's prophecy, "Unto us a Child is born, unto us a Son is given" (Isaiah 9:6). Remember, too, that when Simeon received Jesus in the temple at the Lord's dedication, the old man looked at Him and said, "This Child is destined for the fall and rising of many in Israel, and for a sign which will be spoken against" (Luke 2:34).

After giving birth, the woman flees into the wilderness, "where she has a place prepared by God, that they should feed her there one thousand two hundred and sixty days" (v. 6). This period equals three-and-a-half years, which corresponds to the last half of the Tribulation period. Satan couldn't eradicate the Jews in history. Nor could he stop Jesus from being born, from accomplishing His redemption on the cross, from rising from the dead, or from ascending into heaven. And neither will the devil be able to stop Christ from ruling over all the earth.

War in Heaven (12:7-11)

While evil is bad enough, the worst form of evil covers itself with a veneer of goodness. The Bible plainly describes Satan as a deceiver (for example, John 8:44), and John tells us that Satan deceives the whole world (v. 9). The devil raises up false religious systems and tells people to pick one—any one. He lies by telling nominal Christians, "You're fine the way you are. Just come to church every now and then, and when people mention God, nod your head like you agree."

Satan also deceives people through false doctrine. He spreads his lies throughout the world to make people impotent in regard to the truth. He blinds the minds of unbelievers so that they cannot see the light of the gospel or the glory of Christ (2 Corinthians 4:4). He also masquerades as an angel of light (2 Corinthians 11:14), and so we can expect that his demonic and worldly associates will do the same.

This might shock you, but Satan is not in hell; in fact, he has never been in hell, and he won't be there until the end of Revelation. When God finally consigns the devil to hell, Satan won't be its king; but rather, he will be tormented more than anyone else. Today, however, Scripture makes it clear that Satan continues to have some access to heaven, and here in Revelation 12, we learn a few things the devil doesn't want us to know about an important and effective tactic he uses against God's people. It seems that the devil spends most of his efforts before the throne of God, accusing the saints of wrong.

John calls Satan "the accuser of our brethren" who blames the saints day and night before God (v. 10). This tactic has been one of his most effective throughout history; that's why it's vital to go to the Bible for truth and not rely on what your intuition or feelings tell you. Likewise we must learn to distinguish between the conviction of the Holy Spirit and the condemnation of Satan. We all have times when we say or do things that make us feel guilty. Now, guilt itself is not bad; it can be very good if God uses it to bring us back to Him. But guilt can be deadly if we allow the devil to use it to draw us away from God.

When the Holy Spirit convicts you of sin, He lovingly uses the Word of God to bring you back to repentance. The devil, on the other hand, uses your sin in a hateful way to drive a wedge between you and

God. He urges you to think, *I am so unworthy. I'd better not go to church. I'd better not read the Bible*—all of that nonsense. Think about what happened to Judas. When he betrayed Jesus Christ, his guilt drove him to hang himself. Peter also betrayed Jesus, but a single look into Christ's loving face brought conviction to his heart that prompted repentance, not mere regret. There is a massive difference between the two.

The people described in verse 10, "our brethren," are said to overcome the devil. This is probably a reference to the Tribulation saints who suffer martyrdom. And how do they overcome Satan? They do so by "the blood of the Lamb and by the word of their testimony, and they did not love their lives to the death" (v. 11). These believers overcome Satan not through incantations or by some formula or by rebuking him or binding him. Instead, they do the following three things:

First, they overcome Satan through the blood of the Lamb. Their sins and failures and wrongdoing are covered by the blood of Jesus Christ, so no accusation against them can stand. Charles Spurgeon said, "Nothing provokes the devil as much as the cross."[1] When you apply the cross to your life—when you make Jesus Christ your Lord— you're forgiven of your sins. No accusation against you can stand ever again. And so Satan loses his grip on you.

Second, they overcome the devil by the word of their testimony. Your personal testimony intimidates the enemy because it brings conviction of heart! Others see in you the evidence of a changed life. If you're a believer, you have a testimony.

And third, they do not love their lives unto death—that is, they are prepared to die. They do not consider their lives more valuable than loyalty to Jesus Christ, and so they are willing to pay the ultimate price a witness could pay—the martyr's death. Jesus told us that whoever loves his life and seeks to keep it will lose it, but whoever loses his life for His sake will find eternal life (John 12:25).

These believers will overcome Satan because they have a true and genuine faith. They will endure because they have an ongoing testimony to their wholehearted faith in Jesus Christ. When you live that kind of authentic life, based on the blood of Jesus Christ, you overcome the enemy. John said of such a person, "The wicked one does not touch him" (1 John 5:18).

In the rest of this chapter, John gives us a rare, behind-the-scenes look at the invisible world of the supernatural, in which the devil and his host of unholy fallen angels are fighting the angels of God. At some point during the Tribulation, most likely midway through it, a war will erupt in heaven and result in the permanent expulsion of Satan. In this war, Michael and his angels will fight the dragon and his angels. Notice that the fight doesn't involve Satan in person against God in person; rather, it's two created angels battling each other along with their respective forces. Satan is *not* God's opposite; that's one of his biggest lies. Satan is not omnipresent or omniscient; he lacks the divine attributes possessed by God. The devil is merely a created being whose opposite is more closely Michael the archangel.

While the devil is a fearsome enemy, he's far from your worst possible enemy. Your *worst* enemy would be God. The writer of Hebrews tells us it is a fearful thing to fall into the hands of the living God (10:31). To have God as your enemy is the worst fate possible—and apart from faith in Christ, that is everyone's fate.

When Satan and his minions lose the war in heaven, they will be cast to earth (v. 9)—and this is what will make the second half of the Tribulation the *Great* Tribulation. Satan will lose all access to God in heaven and will be confined to the earth for three-and-a-half years, and in response he will pour out great fury upon the tortured planet.

Wrath on the Earth (12:12-17)

While heaven will rejoice at the expulsion of Satan, great woe will come upon the earth, where the devil lands. He will arrive in great wrath because he knows that he has only three-and-a-half years until his final doom is sealed forever. God now confines him to the realm of the earth, and he is livid.

A new wave of anti-Semitism will hit when the devil violently goes after the woman, Israel. Satan has always hated Israel, and he will do everything he can to prevent the establishment of the kingdom. But John says, "The woman was given two wings of a great eagle, that she might fly into the wilderness to her place, where she is nourished for a time and times and half a time, from the presence of the serpent" (v. 14). So during the second half of the Tribulation, God will protect His chosen people from the wrath of Satan.

Some have suggested that this place of divine protection in the wilderness might be the rock city of Petra (located in ancient Edom, or modern-day Jordan), which is southeast of the Dead Sea. In that area is a valley that can provide protection for many thousands of people. The valley has a narrow entrance; in some places, the canyon narrows to about two shoulder widths.

John says the people of Israel will be taken to this place of protection on "two wings of a great eagle." The Bible commonly uses the eagle as a metaphor to speak of the protection God will provide for His people. When God delivered the people of Israel from Egyptian slavery, He told them, "I bore you on eagles' wings and brought you to Myself" (Exodus 19:4). In Deuteronomy 32 Moses wrote, "As an eagle stirs up its nest, hovers over its young, spreading out its wings, taking them up, carrying them on its wings, so the LORD alone" rescued Israel (v. 11). The same imagery was used when God brought the nation back from seventy years of Babylonian captivity; the Lord predicted that the people would "mount up with wings like eagles," making it all the way back to Israel without fainting—a picture of supernatural strength (Isaiah 40:31).

The Long and the Short of It

Satan has waged war against God for eons. After his initial rebellion before the beginning of human history, he and a third of the angels were cast out of their privileged position in heaven. Nevertheless, Satan has continued to enjoy some kind of access before the throne of God, which he uses to rehearse our sins in an attempt to condemn us. During the Tribulation period he will attempt one final coup against God, and the angels loyal to God will cast him permanently to earth. This event will turn the Tribulation into the Great Tribulation, for a furious Satan and his angry demons will quite literally bring hell to earth.

What is the main point of all this? Satan is going down, and he will take as many as possible with him. That's the only satisfaction he can obtain, as meager as it is. He knows what the Bible says and he knows he's going to lose, and he intends to take as many millions of people as he can with him so that he can keep them from Jesus Christ and the gospel. The devil has no friends; all he has are deceived human souls whose eternal destruction will give him some small measure of satisfaction in his ancient rebellion against God. Satan "loves" his human victims in the same way that a lion "loves" his prey. As C.S. Lewis wrote toward the end of *The Screwtape Letters*, the devil thinks of his cohorts as food: "As dainty a morsel as ever I grew fat on."[2]

And during the Great Tribulation, he will grow fat indeed.

SUMMARY

John introduces us to the Antichrist, an evil world leader who is given nearly fifty names in the Bible. John calls him "the Antichrist" in 1 John 2:18, and in Revelation 13 he is called "the beast." He is the second person in Satan's "counterfeit trinity," and the false prophet is the third. The Antichrist will rule the world through deceit and force and will oppose God and His people.

RELATED SCRIPTURES FOR STUDY

Daniel 7; Matthew 24; 2 Thessalonians 2; 1 John 2:18-19; 2 John 7

In 1979, an article in *Time* magazine carried the headline, "Inflation: Who Is Hurt the Worst?" A worried blue collar worker named Arthur Garcia said, "I keep waiting for a miracle, some guy who isn't born yet, and when he comes, we'll follow him like he's John the Baptist."[1] One day, Arthur Garcia's lament will become the cry of the world.

Revelation 13 introduces us to one of the main characters on the stage during the Great Tribulation. We usually call him the Antichrist. Now, when some people hear of the Antichrist, they tend to snicker and grin in a condescending way, as if to say, "Oh, how hopelessly naïve!" They put him on par with Santa Claus or the Easter Bunny.

But make no mistake: This sinister, dark, evil person *will* come on the scene, and people will say of him, "Our savior!" He will deceive and destroy the world.

The Coming World Leader (13:1-10)

Six characteristics will mark this future world leader. The first is *wickedness*. In verse 1 he is called "a beast." As John stands on a beach, he sees this monstrous, weird-looking creature with seven heads, ten horns, and ten crowns. This creature is a hideous combination of three animals: a leopard, a bear, and a lion. This is how God sees the Antichrist—just as he saw Satan as a dragon rather than an angel of light. God is able to peel away the veneer of supposed reputation and reveal the fabric of one's character.

The Greek term for "beast" is *therion*, which speaks of a wild, venomous beast, a monster. Paul calls this character "the man of sin," "the son of perdition," and "the lawless one" (2 Thessalonians 2:3,8). The Antichrist will come on the world scene much like the angels at Christmas, saying, "Peace on earth" and offering a plan for world tranquility. But this will not last long. Midway through the Tribulation he will commit what both Daniel and Jesus called "the abomination of desolation" (Daniel 9:27; Matthew 24:15), thus revealing his true character. This beast, the Antichrist, will serve Satan and will receive both power and authority directly from this malevolent spiritual being.

The second characteristic is *world dominance*. Verse 1 says the Antichrist will have seven heads, ten horns, and ten crowns; verse 2 declares that the devil will give him his power, his throne, and great authority. This man will be granted power to "make war with the saints and to overcome them" and will be given authority over "every tribe, tongue, and nation" (v. 7). This recalls the vision in Daniel 7 of four beasts representing four distinct world powers: a lion (Babylon), a bear (Medo-Persia), a leopard (Greece), and a grotesque and terrifying creature (Rome). Here, John sees a single beast possessing all of the characteristics of the four creatures in Daniel 7. And this final kingdom will have seven heads and ten horns, representing separate governments that at the time of the end will come together in a confederacy.

This ruler will impose a new kind of world order on the planet—a world order with unprecedented influence. Daniel 7:23 says the Antichrist will devour the whole earth, trampling it and breaking it into pieces. If he is to deliver world peace, then he will *need* a global influence.

Part of the Constitution for the Federation of Earth, produced by the Democratic World Federalists, says,

> Realizing that humanity today has come to a turning point in history; that we are on the threshold of a new world order which promises to usher in an era of peace and prosperity and harmony; conscious of the obligation to save humanity from imminent and total annihilation and conscious that humanity is one despite the existence of diverse nations, races, creeds, ideologies, cultures; that the principle of unity in diversity is the basis of a new age when war will be outlawed and peace shall prevail; conscious of the inescapable reality that the greatest hope for the survival of life on earth is the establishment of a democratic one world government; we, the citizens of the world, hereby resolve to establish a world federation to be governed in accordance with the constitution for the federation of the earth.[2]

The framers of this document thought the new federation should be headed up by a "world executive," a presidium of five leaders who represent five continents. They called for one president and four vice presidents who would aid him. This world executive would control everything.

As world conditions decline—and I believe the world will get progressively worse as we approach the rapture—there will grow such a cry for peace that *any* solution, *any* confederation that can promise peace on earth, will gain global support. By promising exactly this, the Antichrist will achieve global dominion.

One key element to gaining world peace, according to the "one world" strategists and planners, is the removal of absolutes. In his classic book *The Closing of the American Mind*, Alan Bloom said the only way globalism can work is by eliminating any system of absolutes. In other words, nothing is right, and if nothing is right, then no one has the right to say, "You're wrong." And *that's* how we're all going to get along. Linda Faulkinstein of the Northwest Regional Educational Laboratory said, "Black and white answers probably never really existed, but the time has long passed when even the myth can endure. Competent world citizens must act in the large zones of grays where absolutes are absent."[3] Planners like her realize that religious beliefs—which tend to divide people—must be eliminated, and that the adherents to those beliefs must be labeled as close-minded, prejudiced, and intolerant. All of this will contribute toward a massive truth vacuum throughout the world.

The Antichrist will accomplish this total control, in part, through the third characteristic, *wonder* (v. 3). The beast will be engineered by the devil, possessed by the devil, controlled by the devil, and empowered by the devil. Apparently he will survive some kind of head wound that appears fatal, causing the world to marvel over him and follow him. The word "marveled" in verse 3 means "to greatly admire, to wonder, to feel stunned by." Marvel is the first step toward worship.

The "return" from a mortal head wound could be a reference to the revived Roman Empire, but in verse 12 we read that the wound seems to be of a more personal kind. There we find a term used that is also used of Jesus Christ, when John sees the Lamb, or Christ, "as though it had been slain" (5:6). Some scholars believe the Antichrist will conjure some kind of fake resurrection. While the devil can never manufacture an actual resurrection, he can create a sign or wonder that could be mistaken for such—a wound that merely appears to be fatal and from which the Antichrist fully recovers, prompting the whole world to marvel after him.

The fourth characteristic is *worship* (vv. 4,8). Marvel and fear will quickly blossom into full-fledged worship of the beast—and through him, worship of the devil. That's what Satan has always wanted. Ever since he tried to usurp God's authority long ago, the devil has wanted to be like the Most High, and that includes receiving the worship only God can receive. Paul said the Antichrist will oppose God and exalt himself above everything that is called God, to the point that he sits in the temple in Jerusalem to proclaim his divinity (2 Thessalonians 2:4). The world will willingly believe this lie, giving him praise that sounds a lot like authentic worship of God: "Who is like the beast?" (v. 4). In the Old Testament, believers often declared, "Who is like our God?" (see, for example, Exodus 15:11; Psalm 35:10; Isaiah 40:18; Micah 7:18). And the unbelievers during the Tribulation period will say to the beast, "You are our God!"

Satan has *always* tried to masquerade as God. Here the dragon will try to masquerade as God the Father, while the Antichrist will masquerade as the Son. At this point in the Tribulation, all the dreams that people have expressed for a one-world religion will be fulfilled—but it will be demonic and blasphemous.

Fifth, the beast will be characterized by many *words* (v. 5). Almost every dictator who has risen to power has done so through the persuasive use of words. They know how to sway a crowd with potent speeches. Perhaps you have seen films of Adolf Hitler mesmerizing throngs in pre-World War II Germany. The Antichrist will be powerfully persuasive, but his enticing speech will eventually turn into blasphemy against God.

Sixth, the beast will become a man of *war* (v. 7). He will "overcome" the saints and slaughter millions of them (see also Daniel 7:25). These saints are not members of the church, of which Jesus said, "The gates of Hades shall not prevail against it" (Matthew 16:18). Rather, they are Tribulation saints. The church will have already been raptured from the earth, and the believers whom the Antichrist persecutes will be Tribulation saints. Large multitudes of them will suffer a martyr's death.

Evil's Right-hand Man (13:11-18)

The Antichrist will not act alone. As a political ruler, he will need the help of a religious leader, whom John calls "another beast" (v. 11). John also calls this character "the false prophet" (Revelation 16:13; 19:20; 20:10).

Five characteristics will mark this false prophet. First, he will take an *authoritative stand* (v. 11). He will exercise all of the authority of the first beast while in his presence. John saw the first beast come up out of the sea; now he sees "another" (Greek, *allos*) beast, one like the first. This second beast will come from "the earth," or more literally, the land. Often in the Bible the term "the land" refers to the land of Israel, so some scholars think this false prophet could be of Jewish heritage.

Notice this second beast has two horns like a lamb, yet speaks like a dragon (v. 11). He's a bit different from the first beast. While he has authority and the same desire to deceive, the first beast is ferocious and ominous, with seven heads and ten horns and ten crowns, all of which speak of political authority. By contrast the second beast is like a docile lamb, which will reinforce his image as a spiritual leader.

So now John has introduced us to all three members of the devil's counterfeit trinity: the dragon (chapter 12), the beast out of the sea (chapter 13), and the false prophet (chapter 13). Even as Jesus always pointed toward the Father, so the Antichrist will always point toward the dragon. And even as the Holy Spirit always points toward Jesus Christ, so the false prophet will always point the world toward the Antichrist.

Second, the false prophet will operate an *apostate system* (v. 12). He will develop a universal religion and deceive the world (v. 14). Jesus warned that as we get closer to the time of the end, there will come a proliferation of false prophets and false Christs (Matthew 24:5,11,24). This trend will culminate in the false prophet, the second beast, who will point people toward the Antichrist. And though he will look like a lamb, he will speak like a dragon; he will give himself away when he talks. Though he will have the appearance of a lamb, he will speak the words of hell.

The false prophet, like his master, will know how to use persuasive words to sway the people of the earth. He will somehow bring together the followers of the various world religions, everything from apostate Christianity to Islam to Hinduism. He will manage to bring them all together and serve as a go-between who breaks down any barriers among them. Even today there are some liberal theological schools that are beginning to prepare students to serve in multiple religions, whether in Christianity, Judaism, Islam, or some other religion. Man's heart longs to worship *something*. Built into the very fabric of human beings is a need and desire for transcendent truth. The false prophet will use this inborn human desire for the transcendent to turn hearts toward the Antichrist.

Third, the false prophet will perform *authenticating signs* (vv. 13-14). He will perform great (Greek, *megala*) signs, or mega-signs. Imagine how vulnerable the earth will be during this terrible time of tribulation. Catastrophe after catastrophe, disaster after disaster, the earth will be scorched, a third of mankind will die, a third of the seas will be destroyed, the freshwater springs will be wiped out, and people will be tormented for five months by hordes of locust-like demonic beings. They will cry out in desperation and will be open to *anything* that might help them.

And then the false prophet will appear, offering some purpose, some meaning, some hope. He will dazzle all of those who have said, "I need to see a miracle before I'll believe in anything." His signs will be so impressive that Jesus said of them, "False christs and false prophets will rise and show signs and wonders to deceive, if possible, even the elect" (Mark 13:22). Paul said, "The coming of the lawless one is according to the working of Satan, with all power, signs, and lying wonders" (2 Thessalonians 2:9). As we saw earlier, Satan will attempt to imitate God. Satan can engineer miracles, and what better way to distribute lies than by engineering a miracle? In this way the undiscerning will be deceived.

Fourth, the false prophet will use an *animated statue* (v. 15). He will have the power to "give breath to the image of the beast" so that it can speak. All those who refuse to worship the image of the beast will be executed. The Bible takes care to say the false prophet is "granted power" to give *breath* to the statue, not *life*. Here, Scripture uses the word *pneuma*, not *bios*. Satan can't give life, but rather only a simulation of it. Still, what he does will be convincing enough that people will say, "Look! It came to life! It talks, it breathes, it moves! It has *power*."

I believe this may be part of the abomination of desolation. Daniel predicted that a future leader will set up an idol in the temple in Jerusalem (Daniel 9:27), and Jesus made it clear this event has not yet occurred (Matthew 24:15). So let me suggest a scenario: Remember that God's two witnesses will have been testifying in Jerusalem with signs and wonders, telling the people to repent and to turn to Jesus Christ. The beast will kill the witnesses, and their bodies will lay in the streets of Jerusalem for three days. Then God will raise them from the dead, and they will ascend into heaven. Perhaps in response to the world's amazed reaction to these dead bodies coming back to life, the beast will animate his own image in the temple's Holy of Holies at the midpoint of the Tribulation—and perhaps this is part of the infamous abomination of desolation.

Finally, the false prophet will have a clear *administrative strategy* (vv. 16-18). He will require that everyone receive a unique mark that identifies them as worshipers of the beast. John says this mark is a number inscribed on either the right hand or the forehead. Other similar markings have been used in past history. For example, some slaves were tattooed with the names or numbers of their masters. Some soldiers were likewise tattooed or marked. Devotees of cults and mystery religions have used such markings. The cult of Cybele, for example, forced worshipers to have an image or mark put on their bodies.

The false prophet's mark, however, will do more than just affirm a person's worship of the Antichrist. The mark will have an economic function as well. No one on earth will be able to buy or sell anything unless he has on his body this mark or the name of the beast or the number of his name. For those who are without this mark, daily commerce will become impossible.

We can get some idea of how powerful such a forced system of compliance would be by listening to a man who wrote the following when Bulgaria was under communist rule:

> You cannot understand, you cannot know that the most terrible instrument of persecution ever devised is an innocent ration card. You cannot buy or sell anything except according to that little card. If they please, you can be starved to death. If they please, you can be disposed, dispossessed of everything you have. You cannot trade, you cannot buy, you cannot sell without it.[4]

The false prophet will devise such a system to give people a compelling

The Coming World Leader   147

reason to follow the Antichrist. In fact, he will force them to live, eat, and drink the Antichrist's blasphemous system—either receive the mark of the beast, or be marked for death.

John identifies this mark as the number 666. What does he mean by that? Ancient peoples understood the concept of the number of a person's name. In the ancient Greek and Hebrew languages, the letters of the alphabet had numerical equivalents. Each letter had a particular number attached to it, which meant that each name had a corresponding numeric equivalent. Now, of what use is that information to us? I'm not sure, and yet John says, "Let him who has understanding calculate the number of the beast, for it is the number of a man" (v. 18). *Somebody* is called to understand what this means.

Before you say, "Hey, I figured it out!" I believe John is predicting that, when the Tribulation period arrives, the people who are alive *at that time* will be able to figure out and understand the meaning of this number. They will recognize the evil system for what it is, and what it means to be involved in it. And those who are believers in Christ will refuse to receive the mark of the beast.

Now, there's a second way to look at the number 666. It could simply mean "the ultimate man." Note that the biblical "number" of man is six: Adam was created on the sixth day. Slaves worked for six years and were set free on the seventh. Farmers were to plow their land for six years and then let it lay fallow during the seventh. Six, then, is the number of mankind, or one short of completeness (note that the biblical number of God is seven). That the number six is repeated three times in reference to the mark of the beast may show an attempt to lift man to divine status—a reference to the three members of the counterfeit trinity, or an echo of God's triune majesty: "Holy, holy, holy, Lord God Almighty" (Revelation 4:8; see Isaiah 6:3).

Whatever 666 means, we at least know that it stands for the Antichrist and represents his control of the earth.

An Ancient Preoccupation

Throughout history, many have tried to figure out the identity of the Antichrist. This has been a preoccupation of believers through the ages, a sort of macabre game to guess who the Antichrist is. Way back in AD 37, some thought the Roman emperor Caligula was the Antichrist because he said he would put an image of himself in the Jerusalem temple. In AD 57, Christians thought Caesar Nero was the Antichrist because he violently persecuted Christians; they even called him "the beast." In the twelfth century, Joachim of Fiore predicted the arrival of the third age of the Holy Spirit and said that Frederick II, the emperor, was the Antichrist. Many others have offered their own guesses. Protestants have typically named past popes, such as Boniface VIII or John XXII. More modern guesses as to the identity of the Antichrist have ranged from Adolf Hitler to John F. Kennedy to Henry Kissinger to Mikhail Gorbachev. No doubt, unfortunately, such attempts at guessing will continue.

I believe the whole game to be futile, foolish, and a ferocious waste of time. I'm not looking for the Antichrist. I'm waiting for Jesus Christ to come back for His church! And I want to be ready to go when He arrives.

Don't you?

14

The Lamb Who Shepherds His People
Revelation 14

SUMMARY

God takes John to the very end of the Tribulation, right before the millennium, and gives him a vision of Jesus— the Lamb who is also the Great Shepherd—caring for a special Jewish remnant on Mount Zion. The ultimate winner, therefore, will not be the devil or the Antichrist, but the Lamb, God's beloved Son.

RELATED SCRIPTURES FOR STUDY

Isaiah 63; Jeremiah 51:33; Joel; Zechariah 14:2-3; Matthew 3:12; 9; 13:24-30,36-43

Revelation chapter 14 is like a breath of fresh air. After the horrors that are described in the preceding chapters and before the terrors that follow it, John sees a vision of the Lamb of God enjoying the company of His redeemed people. Here we learn that the Lord's grace and mercy do not in any way conflict with His holiness and judgment. And we remember that the time for getting right with God is *now*.

Sights Are Seen (14:1-5)

The first person who captures John's attention here is not a beast with seven heads and ten horns, not a lamblike beast who speaks like a dragon, and not a dragon, but rather the Lamb, Jesus Christ. And Jesus' portrayal as the Lamb contrasts vividly with the dictatorial, hateful, authoritative rule of the beast, as well as the false, lamblike demeanor of the second beast. *This* Lamb has true humility and embodies gentle, servant leadership.

But far more than that, Jesus as the Lamb symbolizes sacrifice. Jewish people, upon hearing this, would immediately think of the temple and the docile creatures killed there to cover sin. Every day in the temple, lambs were brought to the priest, hands were laid upon the animals, and their blood was shed in order to atone for the sins of Israel. All the way back in the book of Exodus, God told the Israelites to take a lamb at Passover, kill it, and place its blood around the front door of their homes (Exodus 12). In that way, those inside the house would find a reprieve from death when God sent the tenth and final plague upon the nation of Egypt.

The importance of the Lamb meeting with His people on Mount Zion (v. 1) cannot be underscored enough. The hearts of Messianic Jews would have leapt at this picture, for every Jew in history has looked forward to the time when the Messiah will return and rule from Mount Zion in Jerusalem. It's the capstone prediction of the Old Testament prophets, including Isaiah and Jeremiah. The Messiah will come—God's Lamb, Jesus Christ—and He will stand upon Mount Zion with those who belong to Him.

At the end of the Tribulation, Jesus and every one of the 144,000 Jews we first met in Revelation chapter 7 will stand on Mount Zion. The Lord miraculously gave a seal of protection to this group of 144,000 at the beginning of the Tribulation, and on the other end of this time period they will all come out unscathed and untouched. Of course, God has provided similar protection before. As we just saw a moment ago, He spared Israel's firstborn children during the final plague upon Egypt (Exodus 12). And later, He kept Daniel's three Hebrew friends safe in the midst of a fiery furnace (Daniel 3). Likewise, every one of the 144,000 whom God seals at the beginning of the Tribulation will still be alive at the end of it. Every one will be a conqueror, a victor with the Lamb. They will comprise an incredible force of loyal, godly, sacrificial, undefiled, truthful individuals who are eager to witness (vv. 4-5). God will preserve them all through the worst period in human history.

Sounds Are Heard (14:2-3)

John then hears a loud voice from heaven, which could be the voice of Jesus; we saw a similar description appear in Revelation 1:10. John also hears harpists playing their harps (literally, "lyres"). A lyre was a square or trapezoidal stringed instrument made out of fine wood and metal. One plucked the strings or strummed them like a guitar. Every time the Old Testament mentions lyres, they are associated with joy in worship. John also hears singers performing "as it were a new song" (v. 3) before God's throne and before the four living creatures and the twenty-four elders mentioned in chapters 4 and 5.

Notice what is present in this scene: voices, harpists, and singing that lifts up worship and praise to God. Shouldn't that be the response of all of God's redeemed people throughout all ages? We are to worship God in response to who He is and what He has done. The sound of voices and instruments and singing has always been and always will be exactly the right response of God's people to their God.

The Standard Is Described (14:3-5)

Next John describes a standard of life for God's people. God not only miraculously keeps the 144,000 safe all through the horrors of the Tribulation, they also adhere to a standard of godliness, character, and purity.

First, these individuals are "redeemed" (v. 3). That is always the basis for a godly, holy, and pure lifestyle. The real winner is the person who belongs to God, who's been redeemed from this age.

Second, John calls them virgins "not defiled with women" (v. 4). Some commentators suggest that the worship of the Antichrist will follow the pattern of many ancient cults, which were full of sensuality, sexuality, and prostitutes. These 144,000 will stay away from the depraved worship system of the beast and therefore won't get involved in the sexual promiscuity that characterizes his cult.

Another way to understand verse 4 is it's possible that John is referring to spiritual virginity or purity. The Old Testament called Israel "the virgin, the daughter of Zion" (2 Kings 19:21) and "daughter of Jerusalem" (Lamentations 2:13,15), and Paul picked up this imagery when he wrote to the Corinthians, "I promised you to one husband, to Christ, so that I might present you as a pure virgin to him" (2 Corinthians 11:2 NIV). James had a similar idea in mind when he wrote of "adulterers and adulteresses" in the church who lusted after material things (James 4:4).

Whatever the exact nature of the statement that the 144,000 are virgins, we can know with certainty they will not be involved in any way with the satanically energized worship system of the beast. They will remain undefiled and pure in their relationship to Jesus Christ.

Third, John calls the 144,000 "firstfruits to God and to the Lamb" (v. 4). Every year at harvesttime, the ancient Israelites offered the first and best of their fruits, grains, and vegetables to God. In doing so they were saying, "God has blessed us abundantly, and we want to give the first and the best to Him." The 144,000 are the very first persons saved in the Tribulation. They're saved, they're sealed, and they will lead others to Jesus Christ.

Fourth, they are faultless (v. 5). They do not lie or deceive, but testify fully to the truth. They are not ashamed of their faith or of their Savior, but are proud of their relationship to Jesus, the Lamb of God.

This is truly amazing: Even during the Tribulation, God will take a world in which sin and evil have run rampant and He will extract gold out of it. He will redeem 144,000 men, remake their lives, and change them so completely that they become the "firstfruits" to Him.

Angels Set the Record Straight (14:6-13)

During the Tribulation, God will send three angels who have special messages to deliver to the world. They will speak the words of heaven to every earth dweller. Almost everything the angels say will directly oppose the philosophies and assumptions of humankind and contradict what many people believe even today about the gospel, man's origin, Satan, death, and eternity.

In verses 6 through 11 these angels deliver announcements of tribulation, and in verses 12 and 13 they proclaim an announcement of triumph. In the first announcement, an angel preaches salvation (v. 6). The pulpit of this angelic preacher is the firmament of heaven, which is out of the reach of man. This angel flies in mid-heaven, which refers to the apex of the sun at noon, at its meridian, the time when the sun has its greatest visibility. The angel flies constantly, almost as if he hovers over the earth so everyone can see and hear him. He preaches the everlasting gospel, the greatest of all messages—the good news of Jesus Christ, which provides the means of everlasting life and free entrance into God's eternal kingdom.

This may be what Jesus had in mind in Matthew 24 when He said, "This gospel of the kingdom will be preached in all of the world as a witness to all the nations, and then the end will come" (v. 14). The Greek word translated "nations" is *ethnos*, from which we get the term "ethnic group." During this time, every tribe and tongue, dialect, and language in every corner of the earth will be able to hear the gospel. It's as if God will make one final, all-out attempt to reach the world for Christ. This is the heart of God. Before He buries the world in judgment, He will send out a message of the gospel with an invitation and an opportunity for people to turn to Him.

Remember that this angelic message goes out after the world's people have rejected the 144,000 Jewish witnesses. They will also have rejected the two miracle-working witnesses. They will have rejected the believers who end up as martyrs. And yet even after all that God will send a gospel-preaching angel who flies through mid-heaven, giving him the pulpit of greatest visibility for the benefit of every tribe, tongue, and nation on earth. That God will do this makes it clear, once and for all, that the gospel is not an exclusively Western religion. The gospel is for *every* ethnic group, *every* language, *every* tribe, *every* nation.

This angel will loudly urge people to "fear God and give glory to Him, for the hour of His judgment has come; and worship Him who made heaven and earth, the sea and springs of water" (v. 7). He will exhort people to worship God as the Creator—not mother earth, not Mother Nature, not father spirit, but Creator God. In effect, the angel will say, "As the Creator, God is the Judge. The One who started it all is the One who will end it all. The Maker is the Executioner."

The second angel will preach not the gospel, but doom (v. 8). He will pronounce judgment on "Babylon" and its evil system.

The third angel will preach neither the gospel nor doom, but damnation (vv. 9-11). He will proclaim that all who worship the Antichrist will be eternally condemned. He will say, in effect, "If you persist in drinking the cup of the wine of the evil city's fornication, then God will give you another cup—the cup of His wrath, the cup of His judgment." The destiny for people who reject Jesus Christ during the Tribulation will be exactly the same as for those who reject Jesus Christ at any other time in history: hell.

This angel thus clears up some additional false assumptions— namely, that hell is not real, that hell is not forever, and that hell is merely a metaphor for the unpleasant things that happen to us on earth. Jesus said that at the end of time, He would say to the unredeemed, "Depart from Me, you cursed, into the everlasting fire prepared for the devil and his angels" (Matthew 25:41). Jesus described hell as a place of unquenchable, unending fire where the worm never dies—a horrible, dark pit full of wretched people wailing and gnashing their teeth.

These proclamations of judgment, doom, and damnation will be followed by an announcement of triumph (vv. 12-13). Notice the enormous contrast that is made between the destinies of the followers of the beast and those who die in the Lord. The followers of the beast will be tormented forever and ever, never able to enjoy rest. Those who die in the Lord, by contrast, will rest from their labors. Better to follow the Lamb for a thousand years than the Antichrist for three-and-a-half years! During the Tribulation, believers may have to pay the ultimate price for their faith in Jesus Christ, but ultimately, they are the blessed ones. How opposite this is from the world's perspective that believes only the living are blessed, while the dead are cursed!

It sounds kind of odd, doesn't it? "Blessed are the dead" (v. 13). In fact, the word "blessed" means "very happy"—the kind of happiness that is to be envied. Such blessedness brings a potent feeling of inner satisfaction and bliss. These saints will know blessing both because of how they lived and how they died. Because they will live and persevere in the Lord, they will die with promise. That won't be the case for those who die outside of the Lord. Paul said that for a Christian, to be absent from the body is to be present with the Lord (2 Corinthians 5:8).

The unredeemed see nothing in a cemetery but hopelessness, tears, and loss. God, who lives on the other side of the time-space continuum, promises rest for the righteous, rewards, and the resurrection of the body—that is, the glories and the bliss of His heavenly kingdom (v. 13). If you're an unbeliever, death really is a curse. But if you're a believer, death is a blessing because one day you'll instantly be ushered into the presence of God.

It's Harvesttime! (14:14-20)

The Great Tribulation, which the Bible often calls "the Day of the Lord," is the dark time in earth's history when God will, to a large extent, put down His implements of grace and instead will deal with the planet in wrath and judgment. Think of it as heaven's harvesttime.

Three aspects of this harvesttime are revealed to us in this passage: the description (v. 14), the distinction (vv. 15-16), and the destruction (vv. 17-20). First, John describes the Son of Man, whom he sees sitting on a cloud with a sickle in hand, ready to reap a harvest. Second, he sees an angel appear, who also has a sickle and is ready to reap a harvest. The two figures harvest two distinct crops; the first, a grain crop, and the second, a grape crop. In the Bible, the idea of harvest is almost invariably a picture of judgment. Whatever you have sown, you will reap in divine judgment—which introduces the third and final aspect, the utter destruction.

Some people say that Jesus would never judge anyone, but Jesus Himself said, "The Father judges no one, but has committed all judgment to the Son" (John 5:22). One day Christ will judge the earth. Note that in this passage, He does not carry an olive branch or gesture toward a cross. Instead, He comes with a sickle. He intends to reap the harvest of the earth.

When Jesus came to earth the first time, He came as a servant; when next He comes, He will arrive as a sovereign King. The first time, He came in obedience; the second time, He will come as the Commander. The first time, Jesus came alone to live with a poor Jewish couple in an obscure Palestinian town. The second time, He will come with all the angels of heaven and will rule over the entire earth. The first time He came in humility; the second time He will come in glorious majesty, on a cloud and wearing a crown. The first time He came to seek and to save the lost; the second time He will come to judge and sentence the lost. The first time He came as the sower; the second time He will come as the reaper.

The word translated "ripe" in verse 15 means "dry, withered, overripe"—"rotten" might be a better term. The earth will have grown rotten, dry, and withered, more than ready for God's sickle. It will be ready for divine harvest. The world will have become useless, and God will hack it down in judgment.

In Matthew 13, Jesus makes it clear that today is not the age of the sickle of judgment, but rather the age of the net of evangelism. We are to preach the gospel of grace, for we live in a time of sowing, not reaping. In the age to come, however, angels will bring forth their sickles and reap a harvest of judgment. The good news is that in this present age, before the harvest, any tare can become wheat. That is, any unbeliever or false believer or hypocrite can become God's "wheat" by believing in the gospel and receiving Christ as Savior. At the time of harvest, however, the wheat will be separated from the tares, with the former kept as the Lord's prize and the latter burned in the fire.

The second harvest, a harvest of destruction rather than distinction, involves grapes rather than wheat. Historically, in Bible lands, grapes were harvested during the summer from July to September. People would pick the ripe grapes, put them in buckets, and take them to the winepress, where they would dump all their grapes without separating them. Then a number of workers would climb into this winepress—often a rock cistern with a channel cut into it through which juice could drain out and collect in vats—and jump, dance, and stomp all over the grapes. The resulting juice would spatter up several feet, all over the workers' clothes and surrounding rocks. That's the idea behind this harvest of judgment; it's not merely a separation, but a total wipeout. The wicked will be completely consumed.

Notice that the instruction to reap will come from an angel who emerges from the altar, an angel who has power over fire (v. 18). This may be the same angel as the one mentioned in Revelation 8:3. He says to the sickle-wielding angel, "It's time to reap!" No doubt we are to understand this angel as saying, in effect, "This time of judgment is the answer to the prayers of God's people. They've prayed for it, they've longed for it, they've said 'Thy kingdom come' for a long time, and they have suffered at the hands of the wicked. And now, in response to their prayers, the time has come for God to judge the earth."

The expression "fully ripe" (v. 18) differs from the previously used term that's translated "ripe" (v. 15). "Fully ripe" is a term used of grapes. There's so much juice spattering everywhere that it looks like a blood-bath is taking place.

Verse 20 tells us "the winepress was trampled outside the city," or outside of Jerusalem. In Revelation chapters 16 and 19 we read about the battle of Armageddon, in which the nations of the world will come against the city in a futile effort to destroy her and kill her inhabitants. The measurement noted, "one thousand six hundred furlongs," amounts to about 200 miles—roughly the length of Israel from north to south, from the Jordan Valley near Ezralon down to Edom. At the very end of time, the world's nations will gather outside of Jerusalem for battle. But their battle will end up becoming God's winepress, or a total wipeout. This scene pictures God's judgment at Armageddon, where the blood will flow up to the height of a horse's bridle (v. 20)—a staggering image of judgment.

They Need to Know

The world is in for a frightening future, but most people don't know it. They *need* to know that there's a God who loves them, who sent His Son to prevent them from falling into a destiny of destruction. We now live in the age of grace, but a time is coming when that age will come to an end. An angel will look at the earth and declare, "It's ripe. It's rotten. Hack it down! Trample it under in the winepress of God!"

One day, everyone will stand before God the Judge. The world will not be able to face the music. How much better to take part in the wonderful harvest of salvation now, rather than that great and horrible harvest then!

15

Getting Ready for the Grand Finale

Revelation 15

SUMMARY

This shortest chapter in the book of Revelation serves as an introduction to the grand finale. Just before the final and worst judgments of the Great Tribulation strike the earth, John witnesses a scene of worship and singing that takes place in heaven.

RELATED SCRIPTURES FOR STUDY

Zechariah 12:7-10; Romans 1; Philippians 2:9-12

An old joke tells of an airplane with severe engine trouble that was falling toward the earth below. The pilot contacted the nearest control tower and said, "Pilot to tower, pilot to tower—we're 400 miles from land, 800 feet above water, and losing fuel quickly. Please advise. Please advise."

The next transmission came through loud and clear: "Tower to pilot, tower to pilot—repeat after me: 'Our Father, who art in heaven, hallowed be Thy name.'"

Sometimes, there's just not much more left but the end. That's how it is with Revelation 15. We have arrived at the grand finale, with the final blow about to strike planet Earth. This chapter sets up the final seven plagues of judgment, which are described in chapter 16. In a very real sense, it serves as the introduction to the bitter end. It is time to say, "Our Father…"

Here we see two principal groups: some sentencing angels with a proclamation of wrath from God, and a singing multitude with a proclamation of worship to God. Judgment and worship go on simultaneously. It's an ominous chapter, but one filled with hope, prayer, worship, and singing.

A Group of Angels Proclaiming Wrath (15:1,6-8)

The series of judgments that occur during the Tribulation will grow in intensity as they take place; each series will be progressively worse than the last. First are the seven seals judgments, and when the seventh seal is broken, the intensity of God's divine judgment will rise to the next level. The breaking of the seventh seal will usher in the seven trumpet judgments, each one initiated when an angel blows a trumpet. Then the last trumpet judgment will be followed by yet more judgments of even greater intensity. These are the bowl judgments, which are also delivered by angels. When all of these judgments are finally exhausted, the Tribulation will come to an end, Satan will have been bound, and God will usher in Christ's 1000-year kingdom.

The period of the seven bowl judgments will be the most dreadful stretch of history the world has ever known. Jeremiah said, "That day is great, so that none is like it" (Jeremiah 30:7). Daniel called this period "a time of trouble, such as never was since there was a nation, even to that time" (Daniel 12:1). And Jesus declared, "There will be great tribulation, such as has not been since the beginning of the world until this time, no, nor ever shall be" (Matthew 24:21).

Why will the Great Tribulation be so devastating?

First, it will be a final period of judgment upon all the nations, who up to now have presumed upon the grace of God. For millennia on end, God has been gracious and merciful and patient. He has issued warnings to various generations in a variety of ways, leaving opportunity for people to repent and turn to Him. But the time is coming when He will say, "It's over. The day of grace and mercy has ended. The world has presumed upon My goodness for long enough. Now I will judge." Now, the judgments are progressive so that at least *some* residents of the earth may wake up and repent while there is still time. God wants godless men and women to tremble as they look into the teeth of His judgment and see the devastation to come. That's one of the primary reasons for the Great Tribulation—God will use it to shake the world and get its attention.

Second, the Bible calls this period "the time of Jacob's trouble" (Jeremiah 30:7). In Daniel's words, it functions in the national life of Israel "to finish the transgression, to make an end of sins, to make reconciliation for iniquity, to bring in everlasting righteousness, to seal up vision and prophecy, and to anoint the Most Holy" (Daniel 9:24). During this dark period of world history, Israel will be troubled as never before, but God will miraculously intervene to bring about the fulfillment of all His promises to His chosen people. The suffering of the nation will prepare the people to receive Jesus Christ as the Messiah, whom they rejected the first time He came.

God says, "I will pour on the house of David and on the inhabitants of Jerusalem the Spirit of grace and supplication; then they will look on Me whom they pierced. Yes, they will mourn for Him as one mourns for his only son, and grieve for Him as one grieves for a firstborn" (Zechariah 12:10). Paul says simply, "And so all Israel will be saved, as it is written: 'The Deliverer will come out of Zion, and He will turn away ungodliness from Jacob; for this is My covenant with them, when I take away their sins'" (Romans 11:26-27).

Third, God will use the Great Tribulation to pour out His wrath upon the Antichrist. After the beast exalts himself above God and forces the world to worship him, he will come to an abrupt end. The world will ask, "Who is able to make war against the beast?" and Jesus will respond, "I can." The Antichrist will amass the armies of the world against God and against His Christ, but he and his forces will go up in acrid smoke when God pours out His plagues upon them. Jesus Christ alone will be exalted in that day.

But here we bump up against a key question. If the Great Tribulation is the time of Jacob's trouble; and if it is the worst, most terrifying period in human history; and if Revelation 16 depicts the core of that most troublesome time—then why, just before all of this ferocious devastation breaks loose, does John call the sign that announces it "great and marvelous" (Revelation 15:1)?

Here's the reason: It's both great and marvelous because it's the *last*. It signals the end. God's wrath has been poured out upon the earth for some time now. But after this final sign, there's no more left. And *that* news is both great and marvelous.

God knows both when to begin judgment and when to end it. He's in no hurry to start judging people. He's patient. Peter tells us that He "is longsuffering toward us, not willing that any should perish but that all should come to repentance" (2 Peter 3:9). But when the time for judgment comes, it will come. And when it is time for judgment to end, it will end. God is in control of it all, from start to finish. And the angels who do His bidding during this time of judgment will do exactly what they're told, when they're told.

John says that the seven angels with the final seven judgments of God will come out of the "temple of the tabernacle of the testimony in heaven" (v. 5). All of the paraphernalia he mentions echoes in some way the ancient temple in Jerusalem. The term "tabernacle of the testimony" is a reference to the Holy of Holies, where the Ark of the Covenant was placed. After the Hebrews had fled from slavery in Egypt, and while they were camping in the wilderness, God commanded them to build a portable tabernacle. In the middle was the tabernacle itself, and it was surrounded by a courtyard. A fence enclosed the courtyard, and it had only one gate, or entrance. This taught God's people that there were not many ways to approach God, but only one—the one He had provided.

Suppose you were a priest who had been charged to represent your people before God. As soon as you walked through the gate, you would come upon an altar. At that altar, you were called to sacrifice certain animals and shed their blood, which would then be used to temporarily "cover" the sins of the people. Again, the point was clear: God supplied only one way to approach Him, and that was through sacrifice.

From there you would make your way into the tabernacle, a tent structure. In the first room, the Holy Place, to your left would be a seven-branched candlestick, and to your right would be a table with showbread on it, representing the twelve tribes of Israel. And then you would see a little golden altar right in front of a veil that separated the Holy Place from the Holy of Holies. On the other side of that veil stood a single piece of furniture, the Ark of the Covenant. This was a wooden box overlaid with gold, with a golden lid called the mercy seat. On top of this lid sat two golden angels whose wings hovered over the lid. This room, the Holy of Holies, was sometimes called the temple of the tabernacle of the testimony because the Ark was also called the Ark of the Testimony.

And why was it called the Ark of the Testimony? It carried that name because of the three things that lay inside of it: the Ten Commandments, chiseled in stone; a pot of manna, that odd "bread" that fell for forty years in the desert and so preserved the children of Israel during their wilderness wanderings; and a little rod, a piece of Aaron's staff, the symbol of his leadership. These three things testified to God's special relationship with the nation of Israel and reminded the people of the covenant God had made with them. The contents of the Ark testified to Israel's unique connection to God in both positive and negative senses.

Once a year, the high priest would walk into the Holy of Holies and sprinkle the blood of sacrificed animals on top of the Ark's lid. At that moment the box became known as the seat of mercy. It changed from an ark of testifying against them—people who had broken the commandments, grumbled against God's provision, and rebelled against the leaders God had given them—to a place of mercy extended to a guilty but repentant people.

In the New Testament, the writer to the Hebrews said the tabernacle of old was a shadow of what exists in heaven (Hebrews 9:23-24). God gave a blueprint of the tabernacle to Moses, and the Israelites built it as instructed. It was a model of what is in heaven itself. In his vision, John sees this "temple of the tabernacle of the testimony," and he sees that the place of mercy and salvation has been turned into a throne of judgment. *All* of God's judgments issue from this Ark of the Testimony. The time for mercy has come to a close.

The implements of judgment that the angels carry from the temple are golden bowls, or shallow saucers used for libations (v. 7). They are shallow so that the contents can be poured out quickly and completely.

In verse 8, we read that "the temple was filled with smoke from the glory of God and from His power." No one will be able to enter the temple until the seven plagues carried by the seven angels have ended. Not even the redeemed will be allowed to enter. This is very reminiscent of what happened to Moses, who could not enter the tabernacle when the smoke of God's glory (the *Shekinah*) filled it. This image declares that God's judgment is irreversible. God is saying, in effect, "I have nothing more to say about this. This is final."

No one will be able to enter the temple until chapter 16 unfolds, which reveals God's response to man's unwillingness to repent and turn to the Lord. To this point in Revelation, humankind has spurned God at every opportunity. People have not repented despite the judgments. They have rejected the testimony of the two witnesses in Jerusalem and the preaching of the 144,000. They have ignored the angel flying through the heavens and preaching the everlasting gospel. The hearts of these people have grown harder and harder. They refuse to repent. Mercy doesn't turn them. Grace doesn't turn them. Judgment doesn't turn them. So this is God's final response; He orders His angels to get ready to pour out their bowls.

With regard to the unrepentant the apostle Paul wrote, "The wrath of God is revealed from heaven against all ungodliness and unrighteousness of men," because "although they knew God, they did not glorify Him as God, nor were thankful, but became futile in their thoughts, and their foolish hearts were darkened" (Romans 1:18,21). That ugly process will intensify during the Tribulation. The rebellious response of man toward God—the clenched fist, the bitter and angry words, the self-sufficient attitude, the arrogant attitude that says, "We don't need God; we'll do it ourselves"—will be enshrined in the state religion of the time. And so the final and most severe judgment will fall without further delay.

A Singing Multitude Proclaiming Worship (15:2-5)

In stark contrast to the seven angels bearing the final seven plagues of God, John calls our attention to a multitude standing before the throne of God. He sees them singing or praying—or perhaps they're just bracing themselves for this final, devastating period of judgment.

What group is this? We were introduced to them in chapter 7 and recognized them as the Tribulation saints. They were martyred because of their allegiance to Christ and their refusal to participate in the corrupt worship and financial system of the beast.

And where are they standing? By a "sea of glass mingled with fire" (v. 2). They've gone through the fire of persecution. They've suffered all the atrocities and the persecutions of the beast. Yet they overcame the beast by the blood of the Lamb, by the word of their testimony, and they did not love their lives "to the death" (Revelation 12:11).

So here we see a group of believers who have been persecuted, tortured, and beaten. Because they refused to take the mark of the beast, they could not buy or sell, which means, no doubt, that many of them starved. They had marched through the fires of persecution, and yet they hadn't lost their song. Strongly and exuberantly they sing a song filled with worship to God. How different is their response to that of many people today, who become bitter when they face times of suffering!

Lord Byron and Sir Walter Scott were writers in the eighteenth and nineteenth centuries. Both fell victim to the same kind of disease. Though both became lame, only one became crippled. Lord Byron grew very angry and bitter. Sir Walter Scott, much to the contrary, never seemed to complain. One day Lord Byron wrote a letter to Sir Walter Scott. "I would give all of my fame to have your happiness," he said. What made the difference? Sir Walter Scott, of course, was a committed Christian who trusted God regardless of his circumstances. It's easy to see his commitment to Christ in many of his writings. That's what made the difference.

These two men teach us that while bitterness can strangle you and prompt you to lose your song, contentment in the will of God will train your voice to sing ever more sweetly.

Others respond to significant pain with resignation. The ancient Stoics thought that the pinnacle of maturity for a person was to shed all emotion. They congratulated themselves if a beloved child died and they showed no emotion despite the loss. But there's a better response to pain; it's called worship. After one major episode of tribulation, pain, and suffering, David wrote this paean of worship to God: "I will lift up my eyes to the hills—from whence comes my help? My help comes from the LORD, who made heaven and earth" (Psalm 121:1). No doubt David would have resonated with Paul's response to suffering: "I consider that the sufferings of this present time are not worthy to be compared with the glory which shall be revealed in us," he wrote; and even more famously, "We know that all things work together for good to those who love God, to those who are the called according to His purpose" (Romans 8:18,28).

The Tribulation saints in Revelation 15 loudly sing "the song of Moses, the servant of God" (v. 3), a reference that looks back to the events of the exodus, when God delivered Israel from Egyptian slavery and drowned Pharaoh's army. At the time of their deliverance, Moses and his countrymen sang, "I will sing to the LORD, for He has triumphed gloriously! The horse and the rider He has thrown into the sea!" (Exodus 15:1). In a similar way, God will deliver this group of Tribulation saints from the bondage of the Antichrist, and at this point in time, He is about to bring them into a new and glorious kingdom.

These saints also sing "the song of the Lamb" (v. 3). The words of this song all center on Christ—it's the revelation, or the unveiling, of Jesus Christ. So they sing, "Great and marvelous are Your works, Lord God Almighty!" They've seen God's judgments all through the Tribulation period. They've observed the miraculous works of God's two witnesses. They've noted God's protection of the 144,000. They've watched God's absolute control over the planet's environment. They've seen *all* of His works, and they say in response, "Great! Marvelous!"

They also sing to God, "Just and true are Your ways" (v. 3). Despite what happened to them during the Tribulation, they will refuse to accuse God of being unfair. They will have seen God's justice meted out, and they will have observed it's not arbitrary or unjust. God will judge the world based upon an accurate and honest evaluation of everyone's deplorable condition. His ways are both just and true.

Then this singing multitude asks a remarkable question: "Who shall not fear You, O Lord, and glorify Your name? For You alone are holy" (v. 4). They are saying, in essence, "Lord, after all that the earth has gone through, we just don't understand why the people upon it don't fear You!" One of the marks of a world that has pushed God aside is the total absence of any fear of God. When Paul lists the many sins that plague human beings—evildoing, unholy speech, deceit, cursing, bitterness, murder, destruction, misery, enmity—he sums up the whole sorry list by saying, "There is no fear of God before their eyes" (Romans 3:18). No fear of God: That's the principal mark of a world that wants nothing to do with the Lord.

And why is there no fear of God before their eyes? Probably because they live in a "me generation"—a time when people are utterly self-focused, self-indulgent, and self-promoting. The egocentric slogans abound: Serve yourself, be your own best friend, do it for you. These people believe that all of life revolves around them. So instead of holding to the principle in Revelation 4 that says God created us for His pleasure, this group figures that God is there (if He exists at all) for their pleasure.

And that's pretty much how it is with people today, isn't it? They gauge everything in life in terms of whatever personal pleasure it will bring their way: "I'll serve God if He gives me what I want. I'll go to church if the programs they offer are right for me." To them, the bottom line is, "What's in it for me?" Such a continual self-focus does not allow a person to focus on God, except perhaps as a personal gift machine.

A genuine fear of God, on the other hand, produces humble submission. It produces a willingness to submit to God because we revere Him so much. This fear recognizes that it is a dreadful thing to fall into the hands of the living God, even as we remember that at His right hand are pleasures forevermore. And so we fear Him. While it's true that God is love, He is also light, and therefore He is holy. These Tribulation saints know this, and so they declare, "We can't believe the world has yet to figure this out."

And these saints know what is about to happen! So they sing, "All nations shall come and worship before You, for Your judgments have been manifested" (v. 4). They eagerly anticipate the day when the whole world will be gathered together, either by choice or by force, and declare that Jesus is King. They look forward to the time when every knee will bow and every tongue will confess that Jesus Christ is Lord, to the glory of God the Father (Philippians 2:10-11).

So John shows us two very different groups that speak of two very different destinies. On the one hand are those who revere God and who are therefore on the worshiping end of God's activity. And on the other hand are those whom the sentencing angels will warn because they refuse to revere God and are therefore on the wrath end of God's activity. In this way, Revelation 15 declares we all have a choice to make. We can either lift up worship to God, or we can receive His wrath.

Be Where the Fire Can't Hurt You

One evening a dad went on a walk on the Canadian prairie with his little daughter. They had gone a long way when they saw in the distance a roaring prairie fire rushing their direction. The father knew they had one but one chance to escape the onrushing inferno, and that was to burn the ground around them. He quickly took out some matches, burned an area of ground, and then stood in the middle of that area, tightly holding his frightened daughter. As the flames of the prairie fire got closer and closer, his little girl's screams became louder and louder. Soon the flames surrounded them, but he comforted her with these words: "Don't worry, honey; the flames can't get to us because we're standing where the fire has already been."

Two thousand years ago, God's Son died on the cross, and God poured out upon Him all of His judgment against sin. Whoever would believe in Christ, God says, will not perish but have everlasting life (John 3:16). When you're in Christ, you're standing where the fire has already been. You have nothing to fear—at all. You have no wrath to fear. No pain can separate you from His love. You stand where the fire already has burned. Jesus took the flames upon Himself so that you will never have to face God's wrath.

But if you're not in Christ...well, watch out. The fire is fast approaching.

What's in the Bowl?

Revelation 16

SUMMARY

John describes the seven final plagues of divine wrath that lay waste to planet Earth. God uses this difficult chapter to warn people about what will happen in the future so that they might turn to Christ. During the Tribulation, men and women will have a number of opportunities to turn to God— but sadly, the vast majority of them will not receive Him.

RELATED SCRIPTURES FOR STUDY

Exodus 7–11; 20:2-7; Joshua 10; Ezekiel 38–39; Daniel 11; Malachi 4:1

Although I love preaching through the Bible, I can't say that I've ever looked forward to teaching Revelation 16. This is perhaps the darkest chapter in Scripture; it's filled with death, destruction, terrifying plagues, and unimaginable suffering. It's hard to get psyched up about teaching through all that!

But like all of the Word of God, this chapter has a divine purpose. We must remember that *all* Scripture is given by inspiration of God and is profitable (2 Timothy 3:16). Although Revelation 16 really stretches the imagination, especially with regard to human suffering, there is great profit in reading through it. I can understand why some people would want to skip Scripture passages like this and instead read a nice, comforting psalm or a Gospel parable. Yet this chapter exists so that people would realize that God knows the end from the beginning and is warning people everywhere to repent of their sin and to turn to Him. The plagues described in this chapter do not have to strike you; there is still time to receive Christ as Savior.

The Releasing of God's Wrath (16:1-11)

The plagues in this last series of divine judgments are meant to punish sin and remake the world. The plagues are poured out of seven bowls, shallow saucers that can be emptied quickly. This tells us that these final judgments will come very, very quickly and in rapid succession.

Contrast these judgments with the seven trumpet judgments, which were all "partial" in nature—that is, a third of the green grass was burned up, a third of the water was turned poisonous, a third of the seas turned foul, and a third of humankind died. These bowl judgments will make the partial judgments total. They represent an assembling of all of the horrors we have seen up to now, and this time they will inundate the whole earth.

The first bowl will strike human physiology. Men and women will get loathsome, painful sores upon their bodies (v. 2). Notice that God aims this judgment at only one group of people, the worshipers of the beast. God knows how to target His judgments and make them specific, in both kind and extent! Recall from the book of Joshua that when the nation of Israel fought the Amorites, God sent hailstones from heaven that killed the Amorites but never touched the children of Israel. The Bible says that more Amorites died from the hailstones than fell by the hands of Israel's army (Joshua 10:11). A similar judgment occurred at Mount Sinai when the people worshiped a golden calf during Moses' absence on the mountain. Scripture says the Lord plagued the people who worshiped the calf, but not those who refrained.

Why will God judge the worshipers of the beast? Remember the second commandment: "You shall not make for yourself a carved image— any likeness of anything that is in heaven above, or that is in the earth beneath, or that is in the water under the earth; you shall not bow down to them nor serve them. For I, the LORD your God, am a jealous God" (Exodus 20:4-5). During the Tribulation, those who worship the image of the beast will break the second commandment (and they will have broken the first as well). And God will judge them for it.

It may be that this first bowl judgment fulfills an as-yet-unfulfilled prophecy given in Deuteronomy 28:27, which predicts of unrepentant Israel, "The LORD will strike you with the boils of Egypt, with tumors, with the scab, and with the itch, from which you cannot be healed." The word translated "boil" means "an oozing sore." A boil is an outward display of an inward problem. Something bad is going on inside the body that causes the boils to erupt. And the cause of the problem in Revelation 16 is the world's worship of the beast.

Could it be that the mark of the beast is itself the source of the sore? That would certainly be biblically appropriate (see Psalm 35:8). Some people think the mark will actually be a little microchip embedded under the skin; similar devices already exist to help track down or identify missing pets or cattle. These chips are powered by tiny lithium batteries with built-in recharging circuits and are regulated by changes in body temperature. It turns out there are two optimal places on the human body where such a chip could be placed—locations where a person's skin temperature changes most rapidly. One is the forehead, just below the hairline; and the other is the back of the hand. According to Revelation 13:16, those are the same locations where the mark of the beast will be placed. And what would happen if the unit should fail? A doctor at Boston Medical Center said that the user would get "a grievous sore."[1] Could it be that the angel who goes forth from God in judgment will cause all of these units to fail at one time?

The second bowl judgment will turn the world's oceans to "blood," killing everything in them (v. 3). This reminds us of the second trumpet judgment, which caused a third of the sea to become blood and kill a third of all sea creatures (Revelation 8:8-9). It also reminds us of God's first plague upon Egypt, when He turned the waters of the Nile into blood, killing its fish (Exodus 7:15-21).

What is this plague in Revelation 16? While no one can say for sure, it has certain similarities to what's called a "red tide." Tiny microorganisms in the sea multiply, turning the ocean red and depleting the water's oxygen content, thus killing off vast swaths of sea creatures. When red tide hits, you don't want to go in the water; it stinks terribly. Back in 1949, Florida had a red tide that encompassed a huge area. By mid-summer, the sea had become red, like blood, and very viscous because of the presence of billions of these one-celled creatures, called dinoflagellates. They killed fish over many square miles, and anyone who ate the fish in that area got poisoned. When this plague strikes, something like the red tide will affect *every square inch* of the world's oceans, killing everything in them. What an unimaginable disaster!

The third bowl judgment will turn the world's sources of fresh water into blood (v. 4). Experts are already telling us that a worldwide crisis looms due to a shortage of fresh water. Right now, large bodies of fresh water are contaminated in certain parts of the world, especially in underdeveloped countries. People die because of the diseases carried in this dirty water. Add to that the pollutants in the atmosphere which come down via rainwater, as well as the toxic wastes and oil spills poured into rivers, and you end up with major problems with fresh water supplies. Then this supernatural plague will hit—and people will experience a major catastrophe that affects the entire globe.

The fourth bowl judgment will follow quickly on the heels of the third (v. 8). This angel will pour out his bowl on the sun, which will then scorch people all over the planet with "great heat" (v. 9). This scorching sounds a lot like a radiation burn. Wavelengths along the electromagnetic spectrum range from very long, like that of radio waves, to very short, like that of gamma rays. The shorter the wavelength, the more harm that is inflicted upon the human body. This judgment might bring about some alteration in the earth's atmosphere such that shorter wavelengths emitted by the sun pass through the air and hit the surface of the earth; or it could involve some kind of change to the sun itself, perhaps greatly increased solar flares, which even today cause havoc on earth. Malachi might have had this plague in mind when he wrote, "Behold, the day is coming, burning like an oven, and all the proud, yes, all who do wickedly will be stubble. And the day which is coming shall burn them up" (Malachi 4:1). Though this heat that scorches people will be unbearable, it will be only a foretaste of what awaits the unrepentant in hell.

The fifth bowl judgment will target the kingdom of the beast, cloaking it in darkness (v. 10). This plague will bring complete darkness, whereas the fourth trumpet darkened only a third of the sun (Revelation 8:12). The Bible says God is light, which means that the absence of light, or darkness, is a powerful metaphor for evil and for Satan. Even the world calls Satan "the prince of darkness." In the New Testament, God calls us to walk in the light as He is in the light; so to sin means to walk in darkness (1 John 1:7). Scripture also instructs us to "cast off the works of darkness, and let us put on the armor of light" (Romans 13:12). So it seems only right that the kingdom of the beast, which follows Satan, would be shrouded by thick and painful darkness.

The Babylonian Talmud claims that God will use darkness to judge the world for some unusually wicked sin. What is the greatest sin the world has ever committed? Without question, it was the crucifixion of our Savior, Jesus Christ. And remember that for three hours, when Jesus hung on the cross, darkness covered the land (Matthew 27:45). So it is perfectly consistent that darkness should envelop the domain of the Antichrist.

Both the prophets and Jesus predicted this fifth bowl judgment (Isaiah 60:2; Joel 2:2; Mark 13:24). In his Gospel, John wrote of Jesus, "In Him was life, and the life was the light of men. And the light shines in the darkness, and the darkness did not comprehend it" (John 1:4-5). Jesus Himself said, "This is the condemnation, that the light has come into the world, and men loved darkness rather than light, because their deeds were evil" (John 3:19). So with this fifth bowl judgment, it is as though God is saying, "You love darkness? Okay, then, you can have it. I'll give literal darkness to all those who follow the beast."

The Refusal of Man's Will (16:9,11)

Despite the severity and intensity and rapidity of the bowl judgments, the men and women of earth will refuse to repent. In fact, after the fourth bowl judgment, which scorches men "with fire," John says, "They blasphemed the name of God who has power over these plagues; and they did not repent and give Him glory" (v. 9). Amazing, isn't it?

Even more amazing is that these people will *know* who is causing these plagues. And yet they will refuse to repent. Isn't that the height of pride and arrogance and stubbornness? It's as if they say, "We know what's going on. We know that God is behind all of this. But we're not going to change. We will not repent!" Neither grace nor wrath can move these people. Bible commentator William Newell wrote, "Men who will not be won by grace will never be won at all."[2] By the end of the Tribulation, the world will have become so accustomed to spiritual darkness and the Antichrist's deception that evil is all they'll know. In response to these divine judgments, they will do nothing except curse the Light.

Even today people can reject Jesus Christ for so long that their hearts become too hardened to change. There eventually comes a point when it's too late, and they *can't* repent. That is what happened to the Pharaoh of Egypt. After each of the first five plagues that devastated Egypt, the Bible tells us that Pharaoh hardened his heart and refused to let the Israelites go. But after the sixth plague, the story changes. Then Scripture says, "The Lord hardened the heart of Pharaoh" (Exodus 9:12). Pharaoh had gone too far; he no longer had the ability to repent.

That's what will happen after the fifth bowl judgment, which will plunge the Antichrist's kingdom into painful darkness. Note how the people will respond: "They blasphemed the God of heaven because of their pains and their sores, and did not repent of their deeds" (v. 11). This is the last reference in Revelation to the world's unwillingness to change. We will read about repentance no more.

God sent the first five bowl judgments upon the world to move its wicked people to repent, but instead they blasphemed God. They simply refused to wake up and turn to God. The Lord had given them preachers, martyrs, and miracles. They would not change. Their hearts had become so hardened from rejecting God over and over again that they could see and hear the truth, yet not even respond to it.

Because it's too late.

The War of Armageddon (16:12-16)

Now we come to the very end. We've seen the seven seal judgments, the seven trumpet judgments, and now we have reached the final two of seven bowl judgments. The second half of the Tribulation, the Great Tribulation, has arrived. And as this final three-and-a-half years of the Day of the Lord winds to a close, two key things approach: a global war, and a cataclysmic shaking of the earth. Both will take place before Jesus Christ comes back in power and glory.

This final war will play out in several stages. The sixth bowl judgment will pave the way for the war of Armageddon, in which millions will die. When the sixth angel pours out his bowl on the great river Euphrates, its waters will dry up, making it easy for "the kings from the east" to march toward the Holy Land (v. 12).

Who are these kings? They are rulers from the Orient who intend to invade Israel and marshal their forces in the great valley of Megiddo. When the Euphrates River dries up, no doubt the soldiers in these armies will think, *Hey, this is great—this is miraculous!* It will be as if God is doing them a favor. In fact, it will be a trap. God will lead them as sheep to the slaughter. Just as Pharaoh's army thought it could follow the nation of Israel through the Red Sea but was drowned, so will these armies meet their doom in Israel when the Lord's trap snaps shut.

The kings of the earth and their armies will all be deceived by the satanic trinity, whose members will use both rhetoric and ruses to "gather them to the battle of that great day of God Almighty" (v. 14). John sees this take place in an interesting vision; frogs will jump out of the mouths of the devil, the Antichrist, and the false prophet, and will travel around the world to deceive the nations. John calls these frogs "spirits of demons, performing signs" (v. 14).

Most ancient peoples considered frogs disgusting; the Jews (and even the Persians) considered them unclean. So the image of slimy frogs hurling themselves out of the mouths of Satan, the beast, and the false prophet is especially noteworthy. Satan's henchmen will influence the world through their persuasive speech, which will be accompanied by lying signs and wonders.

But why will the nations gather? Remember what will have transpired over the course of the first five bowl judgments. The world will be shrouded in thick darkness, and everyone will have boils on their sun-scorched bodies—and yet these armies will march toward battle.

Why? Apparently they will have been deceived into believing that they have enough firepower to eliminate God. What utter deception! Psalm 2 anticipates this idiocy: "The kings of the earth set themselves, and the rulers take counsel together, against the Lord and against His Anointed, saying, 'Let us break Their bonds in pieces and cast away Their cords from us'" (vv. 2-3). And do you know how God responds to such arrogance? "He who sits in the heavens shall laugh; the Lord shall hold them in derision. Then He shall speak to them in His wrath, and distress them in His deep displeasure" (vv. 4-5).

Satan knows that Jesus' second coming is close at hand, and he will use the Antichrist and the false prophet to bring the military might of the world together in Israel. He will get the combatants to believe they can overcome God. But in reality, God will be in full control of all that takes place. He says through Zechariah, "I will gather all the nations to battle against Jerusalem…Then [I] will go forth and fight against those nations, as…in the day of battle" (Zechariah 14:2-3). Really, there won't be much "battle" in the Battle of Armageddon. God will simply put an end to it all. He will come and take over. The end.

Both Daniel and Ezekiel give important details about what will happen in this war. The initial attack will come from the kings of the north, Gog and Magog (Ezekiel 38–39). They will band together to invade Israel, but God will supernaturally wipe them out. This will leave the Antichrist in clear control of the world system, probably headquartered at Jerusalem. The remnant of the armies of the kings of the north will join the kings of the east and the north African alliance, and flood into Israel to do battle with the Antichrist and his troops. They'll all converge at Megiddo and surround Jerusalem; and then Jesus Christ will return (Revelation 19) to put an end to all this nonsense. At that point He will take the title deed to the earth, which is rightfully His.

And in a nutshell, that is the Battle of Armageddon.

The Wasting of the Earth (16:17-21)

One final plague remains—it will occur at the very end of the Tribulation, right before Jesus returns to set up His kingdom. The seventh bowl judgment will bring a series of cataclysms in the atmosphere above and upon the earth itself. They will be devastating, and evidently they will serve to restructure and renovate the wasted earth. And once the seventh bowl is poured out, God will announce, "It is done!"

Note that the angel will pour out his bowl "into the air" (v. 17). Recall that the Bible calls Satan "the prince of the power of the air" (Ephesians 2:2). So this bowl will pour out God's judgment upon Satan's demonic kingdom.

First, a super-massive earthquake will rock the entire planet. John calls it "such a mighty and great earthquake as had not occurred since men were on the earth" (v. 18). All of the prophets predicted this quake, and the writer of Hebrews quotes one of those prophets when he reports God as saying, "Yet once more I shake not only the earth, but also heaven." The writer then explains that this divine declaration "indicates the removal of those things that are being shaken, as of things that are made, that the things which cannot be shaken may remain" (Hebrews 12:26-27).

In fact, this final shaking of the earth may well put the planet back into the state it enjoyed before the Fall, the curse, and the Flood. In Genesis 6 and 7 we read not only about torrents of rain, but also the breaking up of "the fountains of the great deep" (7:11). I believe that's when continents and islands and oceans were formed and when the tectonic plates began moving across the earth. Since that time, the earth has continued to suffer earthquake activity that has reshaped the land masses.

We live on an unstable planet. The earth, as affected by the curse, is not destined to last. As hard as people work at trying to perpetuate this planet, they will fail. It's designed to break up once again. God will renovate it after the Tribulation. And then after Jesus' 1000-year kingdom on earth, God will start all over again with a new heaven and a new earth.

John says this massive earthquake will split the great city, Jerusalem, into three parts (v. 19). This may relate to the prophecy in Zechariah 14:8: "In that day it shall be that living waters shall flow from Jerusalem, half of them toward the eastern sea [the Dead Sea] and half of them toward the western sea [the Mediterranean]; in both summer and winter it shall occur." If there's one thing Israel needs, it's water.

And this great cataclysm that takes place in Jerusalem may well help to solve the problem.

John also says that every island "fled away, and the mountains were not found" (v. 20). Islands, of course, are nothing but mountains that rise out of the sea. This renovation appears to restore the earth to a more gentle terrain, like that which existed in the Garden of Eden before the Flood. So it seems that God is winding the tape backward, so to speak. Some commentators even believe that God will put a thick vapor canopy over the earth, as might have existed before the Flood. Ultraviolet radiation—which shortens lifespans—could not penetrate such a watery barrier, which might help to explain why people lived such long lives before the Flood. And it would also help to explain why people will live long lives once again during the millennium (see Isaiah 65:20).

The seventh bowl judgment will come to an end when God hurls huge hailstones at the earth, each one weighing a "talent," or about a hundred pounds (v. 21). That's the final act of judgment God pours out, it's the last element of His wrath.

Why hailstones? Well, what was the Old Testament penalty for blasphemy? Being stoned to death. And so God will carry out this punishment at the end of the Tribulation. Unregenerate men and women will once more blaspheme God "because of the plague of the hail, since that plague was exceedingly great" (v. 21). If you think signs and wonders convert people to Christ, think again. These men and women will know who is responsible for the hail, but they'll attempt to dodge these enormous chunks of ice and curse God to their last breath. Apart from Christ, man in his fallen state is bound toward blasphemy.

And finally, after all of this is over, Jesus Christ will come to reign on the earth.

A Final Assurance (v. 15)

Near the middle of this dark, dark chapter, Jesus breaks the gloom to give us a wonderful word of assurance: "Behold, I am coming as a thief. Blessed is he who watches, and keeps his garments, lest he walk naked and they see his shame."

· The Bible often compares Christ's coming to that of a thief's unexpected presence. Paul wrote, "You yourselves know perfectly that the day of the Lord so comes as a thief in the night" (1 Thessalonians 5:2). To come like a thief speaks of suddenness, of being unprepared, and of danger.

Now here's a key point to keep in mind: In the Bible, Jesus is never said to come as a thief for *believers*. After Paul spoke of Jesus coming on the Day of the Lord as a thief in the night—resulting in the sudden destruction of the ungodly—he wrote to the church, "But you, brethren, are not in darkness, so that this Day should overtake you as a thief" (v. 4). Jesus comes to us, His church, as a Bridegroom, not a thief. We're waiting and watching for Him, but the world isn't. His arrival will catch unbelievers completely off guard.

Trust His Promise

For generations, the book of Revelation has pointed readers to the warnings of God. It has also pointed to the cross, where God placed His judgment against sin upon His innocent Son, Jesus Christ. When our Lord accomplished our redemption by His work on the cross, He cried out, "It is finished!" (John 19:30).

And Revelation also points to the final judgment to come. It tells us that when God exhausts His wrath during the time of Jacob's trouble, He too will say, "It is done."

You can believe the warnings of Scripture! The smartest response you can have, of course, is to trust Jesus when He said, "It is finished!" When you believe Him and accept His final words from Calvary, you will never have to worry about God's final words at Armageddon.

17

The Coming World Religion

Revelation 17

Summary

World revival is coming—but not a Christian revival. The future will see a world religion that exalts man and minimizes God. Chapter 17 describes the development and destruction of what John calls "Babylon the great," a blasphemous world religious system.

Related Scriptures for Study

Jeremiah 3; Daniel 4

Karl Marx was right when he called religion the opiate of the masses. He discovered the truth that man is incurably driven to worship something, somewhere. If humans do not bow before the holy and true God, then they will devise their own method, their own system, their own god, and they will worship their own creation.

While the coming world religious system in some ways resembles Christianity, John calls it "Babylon the great"—a monstrous, ecumenical combination of everything that people consider "spiritual." And the world will buy into it—hook, line, and sinker.

Mostly sinker.

Its Representation as a Prostitute (17:1-2)

John sees a woman whom the angel calls "the great harlot" (v. 1).

In fact, John calls her a harlot four times, even "the mother of harlots" (v. 5). Her sin is fornication. In the Bible, harlotry consistently stands for one thing: idolatry. Whenever God's people turned from the true and living God, or when any group of people worshiped anything other than God, the Bible consistently labeled it harlotry.

For example, at one point in Israel's history God asked Jeremiah, "Have you seen what backsliding Israel has done? She has gone up on every high mountain and under every green tree, and there played the harlot" (Jeremiah 3:6). The wayward people of Israel made it a habit to visit groves of false worship, where out of tree trunks they would carve statues to worship. And so God said, just a few verses later, "So it came to pass, through her casual harlotry, that she defiled the land and committed adultery with stones and trees" (v. 9).

The entire book of Hosea is built upon this metaphor of an unfaithful wife who plays the harlot. Just as Hosea repeatedly tried to reach his wayward wife, so God tried again and again to draw His people back to Himself; and yet Israel was consistently unfaithful to Him. She played the harlot by following after other gods.

This is not the first time in Revelation that John has used the figure of a woman to symbolize a religious system. In chapter 2, Jezebel represents the false religious system at Thyatira (v. 2). In Revelation 12 we see a woman clothed with the sun, representing Israel, both nationally and spiritually. Then in Revelation 19, we will see the church represented as the virgin bride of Christ, a faithful woman.

I find it interesting that Jesus would choose to use the metaphor of a woman for His church. As the British novelist Mary Elizabeth Braddon asked in the late 1800s, "How are our churches beautified, our sick tended, our poor fed, our children taught and cared for and civilized? Women are the church's strong rock. As they were the last at the foot of the cross, so they have become first at the altar."[1]

So here in Revelation 17 we have a deeply unfaithful woman whom an angel calls "the great harlot." She represents a religious system that claims to be joined to God but, like a prostitute, is unfaithful to God. Her sin is spiritual fornication, the sin of turning from God and refusing to remain spiritually faithful to Him. James had the same imagery in mind when he wrote to some church people, "Adulterers and adulteresses! Do you not know that friendship with the world is enmity with God?" (James 4:4). James rebuked them because they lusted after and coveted illicit pleasures, which sparked a series of church fights. They had allowed worldly things to replace God in their hearts. So James admonishes them, saying, "Listen, you simply can't have an affair with the world. That's adultery, and God won't stand for it."

God will always judge adultery and fornication, whether literal or spiritual. And He has a special judgment in store for the great harlot of Revelation 17.

The Roots of the System (17:5)

The roots of this false religious system go far back in time, long before John wrote his book. John tells us the harlot had a name written on her forehead: "MYSTERY, BABYLON THE GREAT, THE MOTHER OF HARLOTS AND OF THE ABOMINATIONS OF THE EARTH" (v. 5).

Clear back in Genesis 10, a man by the name of Nimrod is mentioned (vv. 8-9). He is four generations removed from Noah; his grandfather was Ham, the wicked son of Noah. After the Flood, God told Noah's family to multiply and cover the face of the earth. But some of Noah's descendants, including Nimrod, thought they had a better plan. When they came to a plain in the land of Shinar, they said to one another, "Come, let us build ourselves a city, and a tower whose top is in the heavens; let us make a name for ourselves, lest we be scattered abroad over the face of the whole earth" (Genesis 11:4). Notice their rebellion: Whereas God had told them to "fill the earth" (Genesis 9:1), they decided to stick together in their city, "lest we be scattered abroad over the face of the whole earth." They acted in direct disobedience to a clear, divine command.

These people, led by Nimrod, conceived their city in open rebellion against God. Their whole philosophy was built on the idea of exalting themselves and degrading God. We could say it was the first human city built on the philosophy of secular humanism. They called it Babel, which later became Babylon.

And they didn't stop with philosophy. They also decided to create a new religious system. They said, "Let us build…a tower whose top is in the heavens." They recognized their spiritual need, but they sought to fill it with do-it-yourself religion. The tower they decided to build probably took the form of a ziggurat, a stepped platform with a shrine at the very top. Normally a priest officiated at the shrine, using the signs of the zodiac to try to predict the future for his people.

History tells us that Nimrod had a wife named Semiramis. Before her marriage she had a son named Tammuz, whom she claimed was not fathered by a man, but rather was conceived when a sunbeam from heaven shone on her belly. And so, she said, she conceived Tammuz, whom she and others declared to be the savior of the world—a virgin-born savior who would overturn the curse of Genesis 3.

There's an ancient story that says one day Tammuz was gored by a wild boar while playing in a field. He died. For forty days, Semiramis wept over her son's death. Then he suddenly rose from the dead. So we see that, even way back in the early days of Genesis, Satan was busily creating a false religion. He cleverly concocted a counterfeit faith about a virgin-born savior of the world who died and rose again. As people scattered over the face of the earth (after God put to an end their experiment at Babel), Semiramis and Tammuz began to be worshiped as mother and child. In fact, she later came to be known as "the queen of heaven."

Many ancient cultures worshiped this mother-son pair. In Nineveh, she was called Ishtar. In Phoenicia, they called her Ashtoreth and her son, Baal. In Egypt, she carried the name Isis, while her son was known as Osiris. Later, in Greece, she was called Aphrodite, while he was called Eros. In Rome, her name became Venus, and her son, Cupid. The cult finally ended in Rome, according to Alexander Hislop in his classic work *The Two Babylons.* The cult died out with the empire; but remember, that empire will be revived during the Tribulation.

This ancient false religion has given birth to all sorts of spin-offs. When Daniel was taken as a prisoner to Babylon, for example, he became a court official in the government of Nebuchadnezzar. In Babylon he found a motley crew of astrologers, magicians, conjurers, and dream interpreters, all employed by the king to give him advice. We still have their spiritual descendants with us today; we call them channelers. A few years ago it was estimated that 95 percent of the readers of *New Age Journal* were college-educated, representing the most affluent and successful segment of the Baby Boom generation.[2] Corporations spent an estimated four billion dollars a year on New Age consultants. All of these channelers and New Age aficionados trace their religious heritage all the way back to Babel. And John calls this false religious system "MYSTERY, BABYLON THE GREAT, THE MOTHER OF HARLOTS."

The Reign of the System (17:2-13)

Why is Mystery, Babylon called the mother of harlots? John gives it this name because it has spawned a host of other false religious systems throughout history. That system will reach its peak during the Tribulation. No doubt the final version will incorporate some elements of the church—Christianity in a perverted and apostate form. Paul the apostle wrote, "The Spirit expressly says that in latter times some will depart from the faith, giving heed to deceiving spirits and doctrines of demons" (1 Timothy 4:1).

At the time of the end, this religious harlot will have established a worldwide reign. In Revelation 17:1, the phrase "who sits on many waters" refers to all the people of the earth. This meaning becomes especially clear in verse 15, when an angel tells John, "The waters which you saw, where the harlot sits, are peoples, multitudes, nations, and tongues."

This blasphemous religious system will forge an alliance with the beast. Verse 3 depicts her as sitting on a "scarlet beast," the same beast that appears in Revelation 13—the Antichrist. The beast will support the woman and her false religious system. Using his political and economic clout, he will help her to become a worldwide force. Of course, because she is shown riding the beast, it seems that, at first, anyway, she controls the beast's direction. The world will look to her for direction rather than to the Antichrist, especially when the heavens and the earth fall apart and people's hearts begin failing them out of fear. They'll see no hope in politics or economics, and so will turn to religion.

This false religious system will make alliances with the entire world. Verse 2 tells us that the kings of the earth will commit fornication with her, and she will make the inhabitants of the earth "drunk with the wine of her fornication." Through these alliances she will become very wealthy, clothing herself in the royal colors of purple and scarlet, flashing baubles of gold and precious stones and pearls, and drinking out of a golden cup.

It's important to remember at this point that one of the things that makes the Great Tribulation so terrible is that Satan will be allowed to have more control over earth than ever before. The restraining influence of the Holy Spirit will be gone, so demonic activity will explode—which is, no doubt, the primary force behind the great deception and delusion that will grip the world. The point to be made here is that the world is *not* becoming more secular; in fact, it's becoming more religious—but *not* more Christian! The trend toward an amorphous kind of spirituality and a growing interest in religion means that at the time of the end, the world will become increasingly religious. That is no doubt why the Antichrist must rely, for a time at least, on the support of the false religious system. He will use humankind's natural desire for a connection to God in order to gain worldwide power for his own ends.

Don Feder of the *Boston Herald* said that as a significant portion of the population drifts away from traditional religion, Americans look for comfort from beyond the stars.[3] When a people has that kind of pervasive mentality—that something wise and powerful and superior is "out there," whether in the form of demons or space aliens or avatars or what have you—then the earth becomes ripe for deception.

This woman will make alliances not only with beast and with the kings of the earth, but also against God's people. John tells us she will be "drunk with the blood of the saints and with the blood of the martyrs of Jesus" (v. 6). Throughout history, every false religious system has persecuted God's people. And so it will be in the last days.

In fact, we see a conditioning occurring right now throughout the world, and even in America, toward the elimination of people. Abortion is legal in every state, in many cases funded and sanctioned by the government. The key idea behind this is that a mother can choose to eliminate her unwanted fetus. The next logical step, euthanasia, has already started taking root. If it's legal to eliminate an unwanted fetus, then what about unwanted adults—those who are sick, or elderly, or terminally ill?

The state of Oregon already has a law on the books that permits assisted suicide for terminally ill patients. Society is methodically paving the way to remove *any* human life deemed unwanted, unviable, or unproductive. With that sort of mind-set in place, it will be no great step for the Antichrist to move toward eliminating believers in Christ. After all, they will refuse to cooperate with his state-sanctioned religious system and will insist instead on preaching about Jesus. The beast's answer? "Remove them! The world will be better off without them." We're seeing that mentality developing and growing even now.

When John sees the woman "drunk with the blood of the saints and with the blood of the martyrs of Jesus," he marvels "with great amazement" (v. 6). The angel who is talking with John at this time immediately challenges him on this and begins to explain the true meaning of the woman and the beast she rides (v. 7). Now, John isn't marveling because of what he sees here; he has already seen the whole world worshiping the beast. What causes him to marvel, rather, is the fact the woman is controlling the beast. How is this possible?

The angel goes on to identify the beast as one who "was, and is not, and will ascend out of the bottomless pit" (v. 8). That's probably a reference to the beast having a fatal head wound and yet continuing to live. This beast also has seven heads and ten horns (v. 3). Verse 9 tells us the seven heads stand for seven "mountains," and verse 18 speaks of "that great city which reigns over the kings of the earth." Historically, the city set on seven hills has always been identified as Rome. We know that in the last days the Roman Empire will be revived, as Daniel foresaw (Daniel 2:40-45). And the beast at the head of this revived Roman Empire will lead a ten-power confederacy, as depicted here by the ten horns (v. 7).

Verse 10 provides some additional details. The angel mentions seven kings, five of whom had "fallen," one who "is," and the last king, who "has not yet come." From John's perspective, there had been five major world powers that had exerted a major impact on Israel: Egypt, Assyria, Babylon, Medo-Persia, and Greece. At the time John wrote this, the sixth world empire was then in power: Rome. John had been exiled to Patmos by the Roman government. And John tells us that there is yet another empire to come, one that Daniel foresaw as well. Daniel saw it represented by the feet and toes of a grand statue, and the ten toes were made of an unstable mixture of iron and clay. John sees seven heads and ten horns, which we're told represent nations. So the visions of Daniel and John are essentially the same. The last worldwide kingdom to oppress Israel will be the kingdom of the Antichrist, the revived Roman Empire.

The angel tells John that the final king "must continue a short time" (v. 10). In fact, the Antichrist will rule for just forty-two months, or three-and-a-half years, the last half of the Tribulation period. That's not long!

But what can the angel mean when he says, "The beast that was, and is not, is himself also the eighth, and is of the seven, and is going to perdition"? (v. 11). Let's consider this verse in light of what we already know. What will happen to the Antichrist? He will receive what seems to be a fatal head wound, and he will supposedly die and then be resurrected. When he "dies," his kingdom will die with him. That's the seventh kingdom. And when he is "revived," his kingdom will undergo a resurgence, and so the seventh kingdom will become the eighth.

At no point does John identify the ten kings who will yield their sovereignty to the Antichrist (v. 13). But interestingly enough, certain groups and world leaders already have documented plans to divide the world into ten geographical zones for ease of rule. It may be that the Antichrist will take advantage of just such schemes.

Replacement of the System (17:16-17)

The beast will have no interest in allowing the great harlot to ride him forever. When she is no longer useful to him, he will devour her. And he will have the full support of the ten kings who give him their authority (v. 16). None of them want to be ruled by religion either.

The Antichrist will befriend this religious system, support it, and perhaps even allow himself to be directed by it until it has fulfilled his agenda. Once he jockeys himself into position and the kingdoms of the earth yield their sovereignty to him, however, all the restraints upon him will be thrown off. He will be free to make *himself* the object of worship. And obviously, to make that happen, the harlot who had proven so useful in the past will have to go.

For the first half of the Tribulation, this false religious system will remain in place. But at the midpoint of the seven years, the Antichrist will debunk the harlot he has used to gain power, and will present himself to the world as God in the flesh. He will do so in the rebuilt temple in Jerusalem, thus breaking a seven-year peace treaty with Israel. His blasphemous act, as we have seen, is called "the abomination of desolation" (Matthew 24:15; see also Daniel 9:27).

In many ways, this tactic is nothing new. Communist and other regimes have done this for years. They come into an area, make friends with the local religious leaders, and even put them in positions of authority—until they reach a critical mass of power and no longer need those religious leaders. Then they start executing the leaders and persecuting and restricting the freedoms of the religious groups. This happened with Hitler, it happened in the Soviet bloc, it happened in Nicaragua, and it continues to happen today. During the Tribulation, it will happen on a worldwide scale.

Ruin of the System (17:14)

The ten kings who throw their full support behind the beast will, with their evil leader, oppose the Lamb (v. 14). They will try to wage war against Christ, but of course they will fail spectacularly. More details on this ultimate confrontation are given to us in Revelation 19, but in the end, Jesus will win. And those who belong to Him will win with Him. Together they will rule over His everlasting kingdom.

The Antichrist's final destruction was portrayed in King Nebuchadnezzar's mysterious dream about the huge, magnificent statue with a head of gold, chest and arms of silver, belly and thighs of bronze, legs of iron, and feet partly of iron and clay (Daniel 2). Each segment of the statue represented a world empire. At the end of the dream,

Nebuchadnezzar saw a stone cut without human hands strike the statue at its feet and pulverize the whole thing into fine dust. After the wind carried away the dust, leaving no trace of what stood there before, this stone grew into a gargantuan mountain that filled the whole earth. Daniel explained to the puzzled king that the stone represented a kingdom that God Himself would set up. It will wipe away all human kingdoms, and it will last forever.

Paul also had a take on the demise of the Antichrist. He succinctly compressed the end of history into one verse: "And then the lawless one will be revealed, whom the Lord will consume with the breath of His mouth and destroy with the brightness of His coming" (2 Thessalonians 2:8).

Returning to Revelation 17, we see that John makes a point to mention those who will come with Jesus when He makes His triumphant return to earth. As King of kings and Lord of lords, Jesus will obliterate the Antichrist and his forces; and John adds, "Those who are with Him are called, chosen, and faithful" (v. 14). John wants to show that the Champ will not be the beast, but the Lamb. He makes that clear in verse 8 as well when he contrasts the winners with the losers: "The beast that you saw was, and is not, and will ascend out of the bottomless pit and go to perdition. And those who dwell on the earth will marvel, whose names are not written in the Book of Life from the foundation of the world."

Which side would *you* rather be on? The side of the beast, and have your name not written in the Book of Life? Or on the side of the Lamb, who will ultimately overcome and reign over all?

Blurred Lines

We live in an age when the lines of truth are becoming increasingly blurred. It's become fashionable to refuse to take a dogmatic stand about anything, especially Jesus Christ. And so people everywhere are drifting from the truth.

I want to exhort you to cling to the truth at all costs. About a century ago, Charles Haddon Spurgeon wrote the following words:

> If the Lord does not speedily appear, there will come another generation, and another, and all these generations

will be tainted and injured if we are not faithful to God and to His truth today.

We have come to a turning point in the road. If we turn to the right, mayhap our children and children's children will go that way; but if we turn to the left, generations yet unborn will curse our names for having been unfaithful to God and to His Word. I charge you, not only by your ancestry, but by your posterity, that you seek to win the commendation of your Master, that though you dwell where Satan's seat is, you yet hold fast his name, and do not deny his faith.

God grant us faithfulness for the sake of the souls around us! How is the world to be saved if the church is false to her Lord?...Stand fast, my beloved, in the name of God![4]

That's the charge. The world is fast coming to a point of abandoning the truth. Don't go along with the crowd—stand up for the truth! It might cost you everything. But one day, if you stand fast, you're going to hear some beautiful words from Jesus' own lips: "Well done, good and faithful servant."

Get Out of Babylon!

Revelation 18

SUMMARY

Revelation 17 focuses on the coming world religious system, or spiritual Babylon. Chapter 18 turns our attention to yet another Babylon, a political and economic one. The chapter chronicles God's judgment on this corrupt system, describes its utter collapse, and records the Lord's admonition to His people to get out of Babylon before divine judgment falls.

RELATED SCRIPTURES FOR STUDY

Isaiah 13:17–14:23; Romans 12:1-2; 1 John 2:15-23

An old nursery rhyme does a good job of encapsulating what takes place in Revelation 18:

> Humpty Dumpty sat on a wall,
> Humpty Dumpty had a great fall.
> All the king's horses and all the king's men,
> Couldn't put Humpty together again.

The fallen world's final ruling emperor, the Antichrist, will be a lot like Humpty Dumpty. He will sit atop his political, economic, and religious wall, thinking he has the world at his command. Then suddenly he will have a great fall, from which he will not be able to recover.

And all of the king's horses, allies, and merchants will be powerless to do anything about it. They will stand at a distance and wail when they see his system crash into utter chaos.

But before it all happens, God tells His people, "Get out of Babylon!"

The Proclamation of Judgment (18:1-3)

The Great Tribulation will see the rise of a powerful and coercive global economic system. The Antichrist will come on the scene with some sort of economic plan, and through it he will orchestrate a peaceful takeover of the world (see chapter 6). His global economy will not be communistic; in fact, it will be capitalism gone berserk. A lust for luxury and materialism will reign as people feed on the compulsive desire to indulge themselves. But, like Humpty Dumpty, both this system and its creator will have a great fall.

God will herald the news of Babylon's fall by sending a glorious angel with great authority to make the announcement: "Babylon the great is fallen, is fallen" (v. 2). That is, it's done. It's over. The angel does not stutter; he repeats the announcement because he proclaims a double fall. Spiritual Babylon falls in chapter 17, and economic Babylon falls in chapter 18.

While both corrupt systems are called Babylon, there are reasons to view them separately. It is true that both are under the rule of the Antichrist, both are filled with blasphemy, and both hate the saints and shed their blood. But there are some significant differences that show us why God views them as two distinct entities deserving separate judgments.

Spiritual Babylon is given the titles "Mystery, Babylon" and "the mother of harlots," whereas the economic system is called "Babylon the great." Spiritual Babylon is depicted as a woman guilty of religious evil; economic Babylon is shown as a great city guilty of commercial greed. Spiritual Babylon is destroyed by the Antichrist himself so that the world might worship him. Economic Babylon is destroyed by God when Jesus Christ comes again to rule the earth.

This future Antichrist will be a remarkable person. He will be able, somehow, to build a powerhouse economic system in the midst of the worst time in human history. Think of the catastrophes that have already taken place so far: the earth has been burned, mountains have fallen from heaven, the sun has scorched men with fire, darkness has blanketed the earth, springs of water have become poisoned, the oceans have died, and so much more. And yet in the midst of all of that chaos, the Antichrist will build a world empire upon a materialistic foundation. John tells us that the world's merchants will become rich through this system (v. 3), that the system will produce luxury and enable opulent lifestyles (v. 7), that it will handsomely reward the rulers who cooperate with it (v. 9), and that it will produce mountains of expensive goods such as gold, silver, precious stones, pearls, fine linen, purple, silk and scarlet, every kind of precious wood and ivory, bronze, iron, and marble (v. 12) That's a lot of luxurious items being traded, bought, and sold! All of that indicates the world will become feverishly capitalistic.

There will be seemingly unlimited economic opportunities, which will fuel an insatiable lust for luxury and greed. Through his economic system, the Antichrist will lead the world into a materialistic stupor. Increasingly the nations of the world will chant, "Give me, give me, give me!" as they see opportunities to amass more and more. People will do almost anything for money. The world will get so caught up in the promise of riches that men and women will willingly take a permanent mark on their body and worship the beast so they can take part in this perverted economic system (Revelation 13:16-18). But in the end, all of it will go for naught. God will announce doom on Babylon, and everything will quite literally go up in smoke.

James wrote—in his book for Christians scattered across the Roman Empire—a passage that sounds prophetic for those living in the end times in Babylon. He wrote, "Come now, you rich, weep and howl for your miseries that are coming upon you! Your riches are corrupted, and your garments are moth-eaten. Your gold and silver are corroded, and their corrosion will be a witness against you and will eat your flesh like fire. You have heaped up treasures in the last days" (James 5:1-3).

Whenever people read Revelation 18, they inevitably find themselves asking this question: Is the Babylon spoken of here a literal city—whether a code name for a city like Rome, or a real name for a new city rebuilt on ancient ruins in Iraq? Or is the term "Babylon" being used as a potent metaphor for the Antichrist's godless system of commercialism?

There are some clues in the chapter that speak to that question. Three times Revelation 18 speaks of that "great city" and how various individuals mourn its utter destruction (vv. 10,16,18-19). It is also called "that mighty city" (v. 10). Because Scripture calls it a city, we have no warrant to go outside of Scripture and say it's not a city. Perhaps we're to understand the term Babylon both ways: Maybe it speaks of both the corrupt commercial system opposed to God as well as its headquarters, which is based in a literal city like Babylon.

Those who see the term as only figurative, not literal, often quote Isaiah 13:19-20, which says, "And Babylon, the glory of kingdoms, the beauty of the Chaldeans' pride, will be as when God overthrew Sodom and Gomorrah. It will never be inhabited, nor will it be settled from generation to generation." But these people are confusing the *overthrow* of Babylon, which happened in 539 BC, with the *destruction* of Babylon, which has not yet occurred. Isaiah 13:6 tells us the destruction of Babylon will happen on "the day of the Lord," which is another name for the Tribulation period. So it would seem that, according to the prophets, Babylon needs to rise again in order for it to be utterly destroyed. And because John calls it a city, we have some warrant to believe that this city may be a rebuilt Babylon in Iraq.

The late dictator of Iraq, Saddam Hussein, had a lifelong dream to rebuild Babylon and make himself the new Nebuchadnezzar, the ruler of the world, beginning with the Arab nations. A few years ago I stood in Babylon and saw the walls he had erected on the original site of that great, processional city. Charles Dyer saw those walls as well, and in his book *The Rise of Babylon*, he says this:

> It is a cloudless September summer night, and the moon casts its shining image on the banks of the gentle Euphrates River. Thousands of guests and dignitaries walk by torch-light to Babylon's Procession Street and enter the city from the north. Instructed to line the streets along the massive walls, the guests obediently follow orders. When the

audience is in place, the dark-eyed man in charge nods, and the procession begins.

Rows and rows of soldiers parade in, dressed in Babylonian tunics and carrying swords, spears, and shields. Interspersed among the ranks of soldiers are groups of musicians playing harps, horns, and drums. Clusters of children carry palm branches, and runners bear bowls of incense. Then come soldiers and still more soldiers in a seemingly endless line of men and weapons. After the procession, the guests attend a ceremony paying tribute to Ishtar, the mother goddess of Babylon.

Have I just described a scene of pagan worship from the time of Daniel? Perhaps, but it is also exactly what I witnessed when I returned to Babylon a second time to attend the International Babylon Festival held under the patronage of Saddam Hussein.[1]

John MacArthur noted that more than 60 million bricks, at the expense of hundreds of millions of dollars, have been laid to rebuild the city of Babylon. He went on to say, "*The Washington Post* reported, 'In the next few years, Director General of Antiquities, Dr. Mouhad Sayad, predicts the government will also redig and refill the city moat; close the city to all traffic but pedestrians and horse-drawn carriages, and maybe rebuild the Ziggurat.'"[2] The Ziggurat is the Tower of Babel. Right back where it all started, rebuilt again as the symbol of the great world empire.

Even though Hussein was put to death in 2006, the Iraqis have continued the reconstruction project, hoping to create a tourist attraction. What's more, the Obama administration, through the U.S. State Department, pledged to contribute $700,000 toward "The Future of Babylon" project. So it's very possible that the Babylon in Revelation 18 is the literal and rebuilt city of Babylon in Iraq.

Of course the name Babylon also has a worldwide umbrella, so perhaps it implies that the future commercial power center of the earth will be located in the Middle East. We have seen a shift in economic power over the last few decades as the nations of the Middle East have become increasingly rich through oil sales. It is not hard to imagine how Middle Eastern nations hostile to Israel could use their oil to turn the world against the Jewish state; and remember that the Bible does predict the nations will gather against Israel in the last days. The enemies of Israel could simply say, "Any friend of Israel is no friend of ours—you can't have any of our oil." So it's easy to see how the kings of the East could quickly turn and invade Israel due to a Middle East oil crisis.

Or could the name Babylon simply be a code word to refer to another city that is terribly evil in character? Earlier in Revelation, we saw John use the name Sodom to refer to Jerusalem (11:8), although there he also explicitly said he used the name symbolically, and then gave other clues that made his identification of Jerusalem clear.

The fact is, no one can say for sure whether the Babylon of Revelation 18 is the literal city by that name, a symbol for a power center in the Middle East, or a code name for another city elsewhere in the world. But whatever it is, it's in for a catastrophic fall.

To get a better idea of the nature of this Babylon, note that John calls it "a dwelling place of demons" and "a prison for every foul spirit" (v. 2). Wicked beings will feel right at home there, because whatever Babylon is, it epitomizes a value system totally opposed to God. And this, of course, accounts for its massive deception on a worldwide scale. This demonic deception will lure the world into a false sense of economic stability.

An Admonition to God's People (18:4-5)

In seven different places in the Bible, God calls upon His people to flee Babylon before He judges it. And always, in every age, God calls His people out of *any* godless system that opposes His plan, His love, and His plan of salvation.

Of course, conditions during the Tribulation will become so harsh and lethal that those who survive will no doubt feel sorely tempted to get involved in the Antichrist's system despite its godless, materialistic, hedonistic nature. After all, you need to live! And those who do not receive the mark of the beast will not be able to buy or sell. They will starve. Don't you therefore *have* to get involved in the system? And so through social pressures of many types—whether from family members, friends, or the authorities—the temptation to get hooked up with Babylon will grow very, very strong.

And yet God says, "Come out of her, My people" (v. 4). Why? Two reasons are given.

First, "lest you share in her sins" (v. 4). What sins does God specifically outline? In chapter 17, it's idolatry. In verse 7 of this chapter, it's pride and luxurious living. The people of that day will puff themselves up and live opulently without caring in the least for the disadvantaged. The evil political and economic system of the Antichrist will ignore need and indulge in greed. The sins of those who take part in this system will grow to such an extent that the angel says of Babylon, "Her sins have reached to heaven" (v. 5). That is an interesting description in light of the city's history! The founders of the original settlement, Babel, wanted to build a tower that reached heaven. They failed, but their spiritual descendants will succeed in reaching heaven with their sins. Their iniquity will grow to such monstrous proportions that their wickedness will reach to heaven.

And second, "lest you receive of her plagues" (v. 4). In other words, the Lord will say, "What Babylon is doing is rotten, and I'm about to destroy it—so get out!" This reminds me of the angels whom God dispatched to Sodom to instruct Lot to leave the wicked city. The angels asked Lot if he had any loved ones with him, and then said, "Whomever you have in the city—take them out of this place! For we will destroy this place, because the outcry against them has grown great before the face of the LORD, and the LORD has sent us to destroy it" (Genesis 19:12-13).

We Christians need to heed what John said in his first epistle:

> Do not love the world or the things in the world. If anyone loves the world, the love of the Father is not in him. For all that is in the world—the lust of the flesh, the lust of the eyes, and the pride of life—is not of the Father but is of the world. And the world is passing away, and the lust of it; but he who does the will of God abides forever (1 John 2:15-17).

Remember the beautiful story Jesus told about the sower? (Matthew 13:3-8,18-23). A farmer sowed seeds on four different kinds of soil. Some of the seeds fell upon ground infested with thorns, and although the seeds sprouted, the thorns choked them out and they remained unfruitful. Jesus then explained that the cares of this world can choke out the seed of the Word of God in a person's life, causing that individual's life to become unfruitful.

Beware! The world wants to replace your love for God with love of self. It will say, "You're the most important one of all—so do good things for yourself. Love yourself!" Paul recognized the constraining nature of the wicked culture around us, and so he wrote, "Do not be conformed to this world, but be transformed by the renewing of your mind" (Romans 12:2). Or as the Phillips translation has it, "Don't let the world around you squeeze you into its own mold."

Be a nonconformist, God says.

A tree is known by its fruit, Jesus says.

The Lord encourages us to be like Abraham, who left his own city in order to look for a city with *real* foundations, "whose builder and maker is God" (Hebrews 11:10). If you dedicate yourself to God and His kingdom, then you'll be involved in a system that has no end—and long after this world is destroyed, you'll still be with Him.

The Lamentation of Kings and Merchants (18:9-19)

When God judges Babylon with fire, utterly destroying her with "death and mourning and famine" (v. 8), her associates and allies will witness her destruction, and they will be impotent to help her or prevent her obliteration. And so they will give a long, emotional lament, grieving her loss.

Verses 12 and 13 give a partial inventory of the assets of this system, all of them lost in Babylon's destruction. John lists twenty-eight commodities, including several kinds of jewelry, four types of cloth, building materials of every sort, luxury items such as spices and perfumes, a variety of food groups, and finally labor and transportation. All of that will have "fallen." Everything that keeps the Antichrist's world going economically will disappear—forever.

Three groups of people will loudly lament the demise of Babylon: political leaders, merchants, and distributors (vv. 9,11,15-19). They will wail over the catastrophic hit to their pocketbooks. Business will be over. Their wealth and investments will be destroyed. We find especially foreboding and foretelling words in verse 14: "The fruit that your soul longed for has gone from you, and all the things which are rich and splendid have gone from you, and you shall find them no more at all." These captains of industry will desire and lust after their accustomed riches, but they will know they can never have them again. Shipmasters will stand at a distance from the smoking city and cry out, "Alas, alas, that great city, in which all who had ships on the sea became rich by her wealth! For in one hour she is made desolate" (v. 19).

Those who banked on the Antichrist's corrupt economic system and the pleasures of this life alone, apart from God, will forever weep and wail and mourn. That's what Jesus said: "So it will be at the end of the age. The angels will come forth, separate the wicked from among the just, and cast them into the furnace of fire. There will be wailing and gnashing of teeth" (Matthew 13:49-50). This is why the Master asked, "What will it profit a man if he gains the whole world, and loses his own soul?" (Mark 8:36).

Proverbs 11:4 reminds us, "Riches do not profit in the day of wrath." So what good will all the wealth of Babylon be to those who enriched themselves upon it? Only lunatics pursue luxury when divine judgment is coming.

A Celebration in Heaven (18:20-24)

While the people on the earth lament the loss of Babylon, heaven will rejoice. The four living creatures, the twenty-four elders, and the Tribulation saints who were martyred—an innumerable host—will react to Babylon's fall with great rejoicing. Not only will they throw a party, but their celebration will be commanded (v. 20).

Does that seem a little callous? It's really not. The gospel and Jesus Christ have been humiliated for so long, God's children have been persecuted all through the ages, and righteousness and purity and justice have been abused more than enough—and there is coming a time when it will all be over. Heaven will exult over the ruin of evil Babylon: No more wickedness! Jesus is about to descend.

One of God's mighty angels will provide a dramatic illustration of Babylon's fate. He will pick up "a stone like a great millstone" and throw it into the sea, declaring, "Thus with violence the great city Babylon shall be thrown down, and shall not be found anymore" (v. 21). His graphic object lesson reminds me of what Jesus said about those who might "offend" a young follower of His: "Whoever causes one of these little ones who believe in Me to sin, it would be better for him if a millstone were hung around his neck, and he were drowned in the depth of the sea" (Matthew 18:6). Babylon will have offended the whole world and taken captive the souls of men (v. 13)—and this will be God's righteous judgment against her.

Take Your Pick

You are either a citizen of Babylon or a citizen of heaven. Either you cooperate with the world system, or you belong to the kingdom of heaven. Either your name is written on the rolls of God's book, the Book of the Lamb, or it appears on the customer logs of Babylon. Take your pick.

I'm not saying that you can't be a Christian and be involved in commerce; that's nonsense. The question is, Do you love a system that would turn you away from God? By being involved in it, do you exalt yourself over the things of the Spirit of God?

There is a man who wrote an anonymous letter at the end of his life. He obviously had lived for this world, and as he saw the end coming, he expressed great remorse for his actions. Listen to his anguish:

> How foolishly I have employed myself. In what delirium my life has been passed. How I've wasted my life while the sun in its race and the stars in their courses have lent their beams, perhaps only to light me to perdition. I have pursued shadows and entertained myself with dreams. I have been treasuring up dust and sporting myself with the wind. I might have grazed with the beasts of the field or sung with the birds of the woods to much better purposes than any for which I have lived.[3]

What a sad way to end one's life! And so unnecessary. I have never met any person who, as the end approached, bemoaned that he was too spiritual. Not once have I heard someone say, "I feel so bad—I loved God too much! I was too devoted to the things of the Spirit and to world evangelism and to the church."

Recently I visited a dying man in a hospital bed. He looked at me and said, "I'm about to go to heaven. I'm about to go home. Would you pray for me?" And so I prayed that God would comfort him in the last days of his life. When I said, "Before he goes to heaven," he exclaimed, "Soon, Lord, soon!" He was ready. Babylon had no hold on him. His feet were already at the threshold of heaven.

People who live for God die wonderfully. People who live for themselves die miserably. It is, always has been, and always will be a fact of life.

19

A Marriage Made in Heaven

Revelation 19

SUMMARY

The first half of this chapter takes place in heaven and describes the marriage supper of the Lamb, when the church is united in glory to Jesus Christ. The second half gives a graphic portrayal of the second coming of Christ, when Jesus returns to earth to defeat the Antichrist, imprison Satan, and inaugurate His 1000-year rule.

RELATED SCRIPTURES FOR STUDY

Isaiah 11; 42; 63:1-6; 1 Thessalonians 1:7-10

On the day of my wedding, I felt both nervous and scared. People who saw me said I looked like I was in physical pain; and in fact, I was. Unfortunately, the tuxedo shop had given me shoes one-and-a-half sizes smaller than my feet. My toes were curled up like a monkey's.

After the wedding came our marriage feast—or really, our lunch. One of the great things about this lunch is that we had on hand not only the wedding cake—a triple-layer white number—but also a carrot cake, my favorite. It was a special gift to the groom.

After the ceremony, we briefly left the festivities to take pictures of the wedding party. I'll be honest; I couldn't wait to sit down and eat my carrot cake. The photographer couldn't snap those photos fast enough to suit me. When at last we returned to the feast, I made a beeline for the carrot cake...and it was *gone*. The guests had eaten my cake!

So I rebuked them all.

No, not really. (But it did cross my mind.)

Marriages and the feasting afterward are among the most joyful of human celebrations. And no doubt the happiest of all such parties will be the Marriage Supper of the Lamb, the great celebration that Christians of all ages have looked forward to since they said yes to Jesus Christ. The time is soon coming when we'll be gathered in heaven with our Lord and we'll feast with great joy in honor of our eternal union with Him.

In marked contrast to what we have studied so far in Revelation, we now come to a great celebration and a great victory—the alleluia chorus of heaven. You might call it a marriage made in heaven.

The Marriage Supper of the Lamb (19:1-9)

After all the loud wailing by earth's residents over the fall of Babylon, John hears an even louder "voice of a great multitude in heaven, saying, 'Alleluia!'" (v. 1). The Hebrew word translated "alleluia" simply means "Praise the Lord!" This is the first and only chapter in which the word is mentioned in the New Testament, and it's used four times. It's as if heaven has had to wait until now to use this word, and then its residents cannot help but use it over and over again.

Heaven will ring with unbridled joy, great enthusiasm, and unrestrained celebration. Different groups of celebrants will do different things. A "great multitude," presumably including angels, will raise their voices in joyful anthems of worship (v. 1). The twenty-four elders and four living creatures will respond by bowing and worshiping (v. 4). A booming voice from the throne of God will command all people and every creature to worship and praise God (v. 5). And then, once more, a great, heavenly multitude will sing aloud the resounding paeans of praise (v. 6).

They will celebrate for several reasons. First, they will rejoice in God's salvation (v. 1). They will honor God because of His authority, power, wisdom, and loving willingness to rescue them from destruction. The New Living Translation renders this verse, "Salvation is from our God. Glory and power belong to him alone." God is powerful enough to give us this kind of total salvation.

Usually we think of just one phase of salvation: "I'm saved from sin's penalty. I will never have to go to hell." But salvation is much more than just being saved from sin's penalty. We are also *being* saved, moment by moment, from the power of sin over our lives. And one day we'll be saved from the very presence of sin itself. That is the culminating effect of salvation.

Second, they will celebrate God's retribution (v. 2). For centuries, people have doubted God's fairness and have challenged God's choices. But someday, in heaven, people will say, "Amen" to God. They will not be saying, "Excuse me, God, that wasn't fair. I disagree with what You did!" No, after God pours out His judgments, all of heaven will shout, "Yes! That's right! That's righteous!" Oh, to have a leader who always does what is true and right! Well, one day we'll have one. It will be God Himself.

Third, they will celebrate God's dominion over the world (v. 6). Literally they will shout, "The Lord God All-Powerful reigns!" During the Tribulation, God will give evil men and wicked spirits a lot more freedom than they have even now; but by the end of the Day of the Lord, He will take complete charge of everything. He will have the ability to do so, for He possesses all power and unlimited might.

In verse 7 John begins to describe the marriage of the Lamb. The Lamb, Jesus Christ, is the Bridegroom, while the bride is the church, made up of Christians who came to faith anytime from Pentecost to the rapture. God chose the intimate picture of a wedding to describe the quality of relationship He wants to have with us.

Right now we are in phase one of this arrangement. We're engaged to Jesus Christ. We have no physical contact with Him and we don't see Him. But we love Him, we're courting Him, we're getting to know Him, and we live on the promise that one day He will come for us.

Soon—and I believe very soon—will come the second phase. We will meet the Lord in the air in what is called the rapture. He will take us to His home in heaven, and we will never be apart from Him again.

The third phase will be the marriage supper, in heaven, when the anthems of joy really break out. This will be the culmination of our salvation—when Jesus comes to the earth the second time and sets up

His kingdom. That will begin our 1000-year honeymoon with Jesus Christ upon the earth.

As John looks around at the festivities, he notices that Jesus' bride is "arrayed in fine linen, clean and bright" (v. 8). Every bride wears a gown, and John says this garment is the righteous acts of the saints. While it's true that we're saved by grace, through faith, it's also true that our faith is designed to be active, not passive. God means for us to put it to work. Some time ago a man told me, "I've been a dead weight for many years around the church's neck. I've let others carry me and always pay the check. I've had my name upon the rolls for years and years gone by. I've criticized and grumbled too; nothing could satisfy. I've been a dead weight long enough, and beginning *now* I'm going to take a wholly different tack. I'm going to pray and pay and work and carry loads instead. And not have others carry me like people do the dead." That man was putting on his marriage garments.

The Return of Jesus Christ (19:11-16)

The second coming of Jesus Christ is the capstone event that will inaugurate God's kingdom (v. 11). The first time Jesus came to earth, He did so to deal with the sin issue and offer salvation to the lost. Now He will deal with the sovereignty issue. He will be absolutely, totally in charge over His creation.

The second coming will be the climax of redemptive history. When Jesus rides out of heaven and returns to earth, He will stop the Battle of Armageddon and set up His kingdom. His kingdom *will* come, and His will *shall* be done.

For 3500 years the Jewish people have prayed that their Messiah would come. In fact, one Jewish prayer goes like this: "I believe with complete faith in the coming of the Messiah, and though He tarry, yet I will wait for Him every coming day."

The prophets anticipated this event. They all looked forward to the time when God's Messiah would set up His kingdom. Nathan told David that someone from David's own house would establish an everlasting kingdom (2 Samuel 7:8-16). Isaiah predicted that the government would rest upon the promised One's shoulders and that

His government, and the peace it would bring, would never end (Isaiah 9:7). Jesus affirmed to the Roman governor Pilate that yes, He was a king (Matthew 27:11). And He told His disciples that one day they would see the Son of Man coming on the clouds of heaven "with power and great glory" (Matthew 24:30).

All this, John sees. Heaven opens, Jesus appears on a white horse, and the armies of heaven follow Him to earth as He comes to reclaim His throne.

In this passage, John records four important titles given to Jesus Christ. First, He's called Faithful and True (v. 11), in stark contrast to the Antichrist, who is unfaithful and false. Jesus is faithful because He always keeps His promises. And He's true because He's absolutely genuine, the meaning of the term used here in the Greek text. He is the embodiment of truth—He doesn't merely tell the truth; He *is* the truth.

I can't reveal what His second title is, because John says, "He had a name written that no one knew except Himself" (v. 12). Part of the nature of Jesus Christ is unfathomable. Even in heaven, we'll be learning about Him. A part of His character is like the fathomless depths of an ocean; He cannot be contained. As God, He is infinite in His essence, and it will take all of the coming ages for us to grasp the incomparable riches of His grace (Ephesians 2:7).

He is also named "The Word of God" (v. 13). John called Jesus "the Word" in his Gospel (John 1:1). The Jewish people used the name *Memra* to refer to God, which means "the word." The Greeks used the term *logos* to mean "the word." So when John called Jesus "the Word," to the Jews it meant, "Here's the *Memra*, God's ultimate expression," while to the Greeks it meant, "Here's the divine reason that put the world in order."

And finally, Jesus is given the title of sovereignty: "KING OF KINGS AND LORD OF LORDS" (v. 15). That's His victorious name. That's why He wears many crowns (v. 12). And that's why everyone on earth, whether the Antichrist or kings of the earth or the false prophet, must submit to Him. He is about to usher in His everlasting kingdom, which He will rule "with a rod of iron" (v. 15).

As Jesus prepares to leave heaven and return to earth, He sits on a white horse (v. 11). The horse was the animal of ancient warfare, and kings sat on white ones. When Jesus rode into Jerusalem the first time, He came on a donkey, the animal of peace (Matthew 21:7). Kings rode donkeys in times of peace, but they rode white chargers in times of war—and especially after a victory. So John sees Jesus riding a white horse.

John also observed Christ's eyes, which "were like a flame of fire" (v. 12). That is, Jesus had a penetrating gaze; He will observe every action and every motivation. Fire also symbolizes judgment. This is a very different vision of Jesus than the one John had seen on earth. When the Lord walked on the earth the first time, He had eyes of compassion. But now He comes with eyes of fire, which are flashing in judgment.

On His head Jesus will wear the crowns, or diadems, of the kings of the earth (v. 12). That's very different from the crown of thorns He wore at His first coming, put there by wicked men. Now He alone rules, so He alone wears a crown—or more accurately, many crowns. How many crowns did Satan wear in Revelation 12? Seven. How many crowns did the Antichrist wear in Revelation 13? Ten. But at Jesus' second coming, only He will wear a crown—in fact, He will be wearing all of them.

In ancient times, when a military general conquered a nation, often he would symbolically wear the crown of the king he had just defeated. This action proclaimed that he was now in control of that kingdom. When Ptolemy conquered Antioch, for example, he wore two crowns: the crown of Egypt, and the crown of Asia. But when Jesus Christ returns, He will wear *all* the crowns of the earthly rulers.

When the Lord returns on His white horse, He will wear a robe dipped in blood (v. 13). Remember, He will descend during the great showdown on the earth, the climax of the Battle of Armageddon. Christ will come back to put a stop to this great battle that has been raging in the Middle East. He Himself predicted, "Unless those days were shortened, no flesh would be saved; but for the elect's sake those days will be shortened" (Matthew 24:22). His robe will be spattered red with the blood of His enemies.

The first time Jesus came to earth, wicked men judged Him. The second time He comes, however, He will judge wicked men. The first time He came, He stood before Pilate, Caiaphas, and Annas, and they all brought unrighteous verdicts against Him. The second time He comes, He will return as everyone's King, and He will render nothing but righteous verdicts.

At His first coming, Jesus healed the sick and ministered to the needy and cast out demons and brought peace to troubled hearts and released people of their burdens. At His second coming, He will descend not with eyes filled with tears, but with eyes flashing in judgment. He will not wear a crown of thorns forced upon Him in mockery, but will wear the diadems of all the rulers of earth. Instead of being bloodied by His enemies, He will wear a robe dipped in their blood. And instead of being abandoned by His followers, all the armies of heaven will accompany Him and return with Him in triumph.

And what can we know about the troops who comprise His armies? They will include the church, "clothed in fine linen, white and clean" (v. 14, cf. v. 8). His bride, His saints, will ride at His side to victory (Colossians 3:4). But I don't think the church will be alone. Notice that John says that "the armies" in heaven will follow Him (v. 14). So He will also be accompanied by the Tribulation saints who are martyred during the beast's reign. Jude 14 tells us that the Lord will come "with ten thousands of His saints, to execute judgment." No doubt he is referring to the prophecies of Daniel and Zechariah and many other Old Testament prophets, as well as to the word of Jesus Himself, who said He would return to earth "in His glory, and all the holy angels with Him" (Matthew 25:31).

With great power Jesus will destroy His enemies. He will cast the false prophet and the Antichrist, alive, into the lake of fire (v. 20). The hostile armies from around the world who have gathered in the plain of Megiddo to fight Him will be annihilated (v. 21). With one weapon, the sword of His mouth, Jesus Christ will wipe out all who oppose Him. Paul tells us that the Lord will consume these enemy forces "with the breath of His mouth and destroy [them] with the brightness of His coming" (2 Thessalonians 2:8).

There is much carnage in this portion of Revelation 19. The word "flesh" is used six times in just two verses (vv. 18,21). Through an angel, God will invite the birds of the air to gorge themselves on the dead bodies of the slain; this is called "the supper of the great God" (v. 17). Here is a world that has lived after its flesh, pampered its flesh, worshiped its flesh, and tried to lengthen the life of its flesh—and now, as Scripture says, "If you sow to the flesh, you will reap corruption" (see Galatians 6:8). All the people who will die at the time of Christ's return could have accepted His invitation to eat at the marriage supper of the Lamb. But they will refuse, and so they will become the main course for the supper of the great God.

Take your pick: Attend His supper…or be the supper.

The Sovereign's Invitation

Jesus Christ is coming back to this earth in power and great glory. He will return not as a meek Savior riding a donkey, but as the King of kings and Lord of lords riding a white charger. He will judge the wicked and destroy His enemies, and then He will sit on David's throne and rule His kingdom with a rod of iron.

The twenty-four elders in Revelation 4 demonstrated both their piety and their wisdom when they cast their crowns before the Lord and cried in unison, "You are worthy, O Lord, to receive glory and honor and power; for You created all things, and by Your will they exist and were created" (v. 11). But I wonder: Have you cast *your* crown, so to speak, before Him? Have you yielded the sovereignty of your life to Jesus Christ? Have you said, "Lord, I'm going to let You control my life and be the King over my affairs. I will make my decisions based upon Your will and not my own"? That's really what Jesus wants. He is the King!

Prior to her coronation in 1953, Queen Elizabeth II sent out "invitations." Why put the word "invitations" in quotation marks? Let me show you what it said, and you can see for yourself. This was sent to her relatives, friends, and chosen British citizens:

> We greet you well. Whereas we have appointed the 2nd day of June, 1953, for the solemnity of our coronation. These are therefore to will and to command all excuses set apart that you make your personal attendance upon us at the time above mentioned, there to do and to perform such services as will be required of you.

That's the "invitation." I trust you see the point. A queen doesn't *request* a subject's attendance; she *requires* that attendance.

How much more, then, the King of all of creation, Jesus Christ! He is coming back to rule and to reign, wearing the crowns of all the earth. What services does He require of *you*?

20

The Pax Messiah

Revelation 20

SUMMARY

Revelation 20 is one of the most important chapters in the Bible. Not only does it describe the kingdom age, which will last for 1000 years, but it also records the ultimate punishment of Satan, details the Great White Throne Judgment, and warns of the second death.

RELATED SCRIPTURES FOR STUDY

Isaiah 2; 11; 35; 65; Acts 5; 1 Corinthians 5; 7; 15; Ephesians 2; 1 Thessalonians; 2 Peter 3:7-13

A little more than two millennia ago, the Roman Empire brought its version of peace to the Western world—the Pax Romana. Men and women around the empire felt thrilled that finally a power had arisen that could eradicate thievery on the highways and piracy from the seas. Most people felt secure...for a period of time.

Centuries later, the Pax Britannica, the British peace, calmed the world for about a century. It, too, brought a level of economic prosperity to many nations.

What about today, though? Is it possible to have world peace? One former U.S. Secretary of State, John Foster Dulles, declared the world of today cannot be ruled.

He was wrong. It can be ruled, and it will be. It will be ruled in peace not by the United States, not by the United Nations, not by any earthly ruler, but by Jesus Christ. He will rule the world during the kingdom age, ushering in a thousand years of peace—let's call it the Pax Messiah. When Jesus returns to earth, He will bind Satan, invite the saints to reign with Him in the millennium, bring about a resurrection, execute final judgment on the unredeemed, and create a new heaven and a new earth.

The Destiny of Satan (20:1-10)

Some skeptics deny God's existence because they have a problem with the whole matter of evil. "If God exists," they ask, "why is there evil and suffering? Why doesn't He just bring a stop to all evil?" Then they reason, "If God really is all-powerful, then He could destroy evil. And if God really is all-good, then He would destroy evil. But evil is not destroyed; therefore, there is no God."

Revelation 20 answers their argument. There is coming a day when God will deal decisively with both evil and sin. At the beginning of the millennium, an angel will bind Satan for 1000 years (v. 2). The devil's power must be greatly diminished by this time if a solitary angel, a messenger of God, can perform this task all by himself. In fact, this is Satan's day of humbling. He will not be cast into hell, but rather will be incarcerated in the pit, the abyss, a place we've read about already (v. 3; cf. Luke 8:31; Revelation 9:1-2; 11:7; 17:8). For 1000 years he will be removed from the earth; his eternal torment in hell will come later.

Some wonder, *But why doesn't God just destroy Satan when Jesus comes back? Why incarcerate him, and then later release him for a short period?* The answer goes to the heart of what it means to be human.

God allowed a fallen Satan to enter the Garden of Eden at the very beginning of human history because He had given men and women free choice. Free choice implies the opportunity to choose from at least two options, even poles apart. How can you say you have free choice if you don't have more than one option? That would not be loving, equitable, or just. So the Lord allowed Satan to enter the garden and tempt Adam and Eve, to see if they would freely choose to obey God.

God will allow something similar to happen at the end of the millennium as well. God will release Satan for a short while in order to reveal what lies in the hearts of unredeemed human beings. And as we'll see in the next section, it isn't pretty.

Once Satan is released from the abyss, the first thing he will do is to organize a war against Christ. A thousand years of incarceration will not rehabilitate Satan; jail won't—and can't—change his evil nature. When Satan is let go, he will rush out to deceive the nations into believing they can throw off God's "yoke." As we'll see, he won't end up corrupting these people; he will merely reveal the darkness that is already in their hearts. Sin comes from the flesh, and Satan will simply create an environment that stimulates the flesh. So for one final time, Satan will create a massive deception that will appeal to fallen human nature. He will do then what he does today: spread lies, false religions, false cults, false ideologies, false philosophies, false doctrines, and false security.

John wrote, "We know that…the whole world lies under the sway of the wicked one" (1 John 5:19). The word traslanted "lie" means to lie like a stranded boat, stuck fast on a sandbar. The whole world will lie trapped, immovably wedged, and under the sway of the evil one.

In this final rebellion, Satan will succeed in gathering "Gog and Magog" for battle (v. 8, see Ezekiel 38–39). In the Bible, Gog is typically characterized as a ruler. Magog was the grandson of Noah, who settled in the regions north of the Black Sea—which is now part of modern-day Russia. But scholars don't all agree as to the exact meaning of this. Some feel the terms "Gog" and "Magog" are emblematic titles. Just as we might refer to any disastrous battle as a Waterloo, so too these terms may refer to a coming conflict that hearkens back to its historical forerunner.

The devil will assemble a huge force "whose number is as the sand of the sea" (v. 8). This massive army will surround "the camp of the saints and the beloved city" (v. 9), but that's as close as they'll get. John writes, matter-of-factly, that fire will come down "from God out of heaven" and devour them (v. 9).

So much for the final rebellion.

The devil will then be thrown into the lake of fire, joining the Antichrist and the false prophet, who arrived there 1000 years before. This wicked pair is still there, and still conscious, when Satan's turn comes ten centuries later. This should demonstrate clearly that hell is *not* a place of annihilation. John says, "They will be tormented day and night forever and ever" (v. 10).

While Satan's judgment was assured at the cross, it won't be fully carried out until the conclusion of the millennium. The prophecy of Genesis 3:15 that the Seed of the woman, Christ, would crush the head of the serpent, the devil, will happen when Satan is cast into the lake of fire. That will mark the end of Satan's career. The one who desired to usurp God's throne will instead spend eternity writhing in a lake of everlasting flame.

While we can rejoice that one day Satan will be chained and then judged, he's not yet bound, so be careful! Peter tells us he's like a roaring lion, seeking someone to devour (1 Peter 5:8). Paul said we do not have to fall into the devil's trap, however, "for we are not ignorant of his devices" (1 Corinthians 2:11). You and I do have a powerful spiritual enemy who seeks to kill and to destroy us (John 10:10); that is why we must remain vigilant. Don't underestimate him! He is a skillful enemy who has spent thousands of years studying human nature. He knows just how to attack.

At the same time, however, don't overestimate the devil's power, as so many Christians do. The Bible says, "He who is in you is greater than he who is in the world" (1 John 4:4). God is in charge! Everything is under the sovereign control of God. Satan has limited powers and operates only by permission of the Almighty. So be wary, be vigilant, but be confident in the Lord. Remember these assuring words from Paul: "The God of peace will crush Satan under your feet shortly" (Romans 16:20).

What's a Millennium? (20:2-7)

How one interprets this section of Revelation 20 provides the pivot point for interpreting the rest of biblical prophecy. Six times in six verses, John insists that the millennium will last for 1000 years. Despite this, not everybody agrees on what the millennium is, when it is, or who will be in the millennial kingdom. There are three major viewpoints.

I hold to the premillennial view, which the early church held as well.

I believe that Jesus will return to the earth at the end of the Tribulation (and thus before, *pre*, the millennium) in order to set up His literal 1000-year reign on the earth (vv. 4,6). This viewpoint says the world will get increasingly worse until Jesus finally intervenes and changes things.

The second is the postmillennial view. This perspective holds that Jesus won't come until after the millennial kingdom, which the church brings in. This viewpoint gained popularity toward the end of the nineteenth century and the beginning of the twentieth, but largely died out with the coming of the two world wars. It's hard to argue that the world is getting increasingly better while it's trying to kill itself.

The third is the amillennial view, which denies the existence of an earthly kingdom of 1000 years. It says the references to such a kingdom are figurative and that there will be no literal kingdom on a literal earth from a literal throne of David, or a literal revived Israel, a literal throne in Jerusalem, or a literal 1000 years. Rather, according to amillennialists, the church is the kingdom and the kingdom began at the cross and the resurrection. Satan was bound at the cross and we're now living in the millennium; we are the kingdom. The earth won't get either better or worse; it will stay essentially the same until God decides the time has come to end it all.

In my opinion, there are at least four critical reasons to believe that there *must* be a literal millennium. First, it is needed to redeem creation from the curse and from judgment. Second, it will answer the prayers of all the saints who prayed to God through all the centuries, "Your kingdom come. Your will be done on earth as it is in heaven." The millennium is the answer to those prayers. Third, the millennium is needed to fulfill all of God's promises to Israel (there are hundreds of them). And last, it will reveal the depths of man's rebellious nature and will highlight the absolute necessity of Christ's death. We'll get back to that final reason in a moment; for now, let's investigate the nature of the millennium.

Jesus will rule the earth in righteousness and peace for 1000 years, assisted by His saints. John sees "thrones," plural, which indicates a number of individuals ruling, reigning, and judging (v. 4). Who will sit on these thrones? John answers: "those who had been beheaded for their witness to Jesus and for the word of God, who had not worshiped the beast or his image, and had not received his mark on their foreheads or on their hands" (v. 4). These believers "shall be priests of God and of Christ, and shall reign with Him a thousand years" (v. 6).

Apparently they will have company. The Old Testament saints will join them; God had promised them this very same kingdom (Daniel 7:18,22,27). Those who comprise the church will also have a part in this kingdom (Matthew 19:28; 1 Corinthians 6:2-3; 2 Timothy 2:12; Revelation 3:21; 5:10). So the millennium will bring together Old Testament saints in their glorified bodies, the twelve apostles in their glorified bodies, the New Testament saints in their glorified bodies, and the Tribulation saints in their glorified bodies—all of them will rule and reign with Christ for 1000 years on earth. Think of it! The very place where Satan once ruled—the very place from which the devil will be expelled for 1000 years—is where the saints of God will rule and reign. John says that they all "lived and reigned with Christ for a thousand years" (v. 4).

"But who will they rule?" some people ask. "Who will be the subjects of their kingdom?" Remember that at the end of the Tribulation, those who have not died will go into the millennial kingdom in their earthly bodies. Although all the wicked will die in God's judgment, at least two groups of people will survive that terrible period. First will be the 144,000 Jews whom God sealed at the beginning of the Tribulation. They will enter the millennium in their physical, natural bodies. In addition, many righteous Gentiles will escape the tyranny of the Antichrist and will still be alive when Jesus returns in power and great glory. They, too, will enter the kingdom in their natural bodies. Some of these survivors will become kings, presidents, prime ministers, legislators, judges, media executives, teachers, engineers, office workers, farmers, scientists—the whole gamut of human vocations. All of them will be God's people. So there will be justice in the courts, peace and harmony in the educational system, honesty in the media. They and their descendants will have 1000 years to give birth to children and repopulate the earth.

Now, will these children be perfect? Are you *serious*? Are yours and mine? We are all born into this world as sinners, and that won't change during the millennium. Though righteousness will be enforced with a rod of iron, utopia will prevail, and all weapons will be forged into plowshares, nevertheless, sinful human nature will remain unchanged. Many who are born during this era will come to faith in Christ; many will not. The millennium will conclusively demonstrate that people reject Jesus Christ not so much because of their environment, but because of their depraved nature.

At the end of the millennium, when Satan is released to deceive the nations, humankind's fallen nature will reassert itself—with a vengeance. Not even 1000 years of peace will cleanse humankind of its inborn sin. This futile rebellion at the end of the millennium will demonstrate to the universe, in an unmistakable way, why Christ had to die. All of us have sinned and fallen short of the glory of God, and not even 1000 years of righteous rule can eradicate the sin in people's hearts. Only the crucified and risen Jesus Christ can perform that miracle, and it won't happen unless we choose to say yes to His call. Only then can we obtain eternal life.

The Last Judgment (20:11-15)

Once the point is made emphatically at the end of the millennium that Jesus had to die to cure people of their sin, God will immediately drop the curtain on the fallen days of our planet. All the unrighteous human beings who ever lived, from the beginning of time until the end of the millennium, will stand before God at the Great White Throne Judgment. It will be an awesome scene.

Before we continue, it's important to note that the Bible uses the word "life" in three entirely different ways. The first word is *bios*, from which we get the terms "biology" and "biosphere." It refers to the material world around us. The New Testament rarely uses this word, and almost always negatively whenever it does.

More often Scripture uses the term *psuche*. This refers to one's conscious life, one's inner person. Jesus said that whoever wants to save his life (*psuche*) must lose it (Matthew 16:25).

The third term is *zoe*, probably the most prominent of the three. It's essentially a theological term that shifts the focus from earth to heaven; it refers to life in the eternal sense, a divine quality of life that begins now and continues through all eternity (v. 12). Jesus said, "He who hears My word and believes in Him who sent Me *has* everlasting life" (John 5:24, emphasis added). This kind of life starts now and lasts forever.

All of us born into this world receive *bios* life, but no one gets into the millennium or into heaven without receiving *zoe* life. We must be born spiritually, just as we are born physically. That is why Jesus said, "Unless one is born again, he cannot see the kingdom of God" (John 3:3).

With that in mind, does it surprise you to learn that John uses the word *zoe* of unbelievers? He writes, "The rest of the dead did not live [*zoe*] again until the thousand years were finished" (v. 5). But really, that's not so surprising. John uses the term to let us know that these people do *not* have *zoe*, and so cannot enter heaven.

The unbelieving dead will be raised at the end of the millennium to be judged in their resurrected bodies. They will already have died physically; now they will die spiritually. They will not receive *zoe*, but rather will suffer "the second death" (vv. 6,14), something far worse than physical death. Physical death means separation; your soul or spirit is *temporarily* separated from your *body*. But the second death involves a far worse separation; you will be *eternally* separated from the *presence of God*. This is what Paul called "everlasting destruction from the presence of the Lord and from the glory of His power" (2 Thessalonians 1:9).

Those who have *zoe*, however, do not have to fear the second death. John declares the second death will have "no power" over them; that is, over those who take part in the first resurrection (vv. 5-6). Recall that the first resurrection occurs before the millennium and will include all the righteous, except for those Christians from the church age who have already received their glorified bodies. The second resurrection, by contrast, will occur immediately after the millennium and will include all the unrighteous throughout history.

Jesus spoke of both resurrections when He said, "The hour is coming in which all who are in the graves will hear [My] voice and come forth—those who have done good, to the resurrection of life, and those who have done evil, to the resurrection of condemnation" (John 5:28-29). And Daniel predicted, "Those who sleep in the dust of the earth shall awake, some to everlasting life, some to shame and everlasting contempt" (Daniel 12:2). Both spoke of two resurrections.

The Greek term translated "resurrection" is *anastasis,* and it invariably refers to a corpse rising from the grave. It is not a metaphor for spiritual renewal; it always refers to something literal and tangible. When a person dies—any person, whether saved or unsaved—the soul leaves the body. The dead body decays, but the soul, the "real you," continues in a conscious state. Believers go to be with Lord; unbelievers are separated from Him, causing immediate torment (Luke 16:23-24), although not nearly as severe as the horror they will suffer in their final state.

Revelation 20:11-15 pictures the most serious, sobering setting in the entire Bible—the final judgment of unbelievers. They will be judged "according to their works" (vv. 12-13). Picture the scene: a multitude of unredeemed people standing before God, apart from Jesus Christ. These are the people who said, "I don't need Jesus. I'm good enough. I'll stand in my own works, on my own record." At that time heaven's books will be opened, revealing everything these people have ever thought, said, or done. Because they refused the grace of God, they will be judged by the things written in the books. And all of these people will be found wanting.

You're judged either "in Christ," or you're judged on the basis of your own record, apart from Christ. It's one or the other.

Does that help you better understand why Scripture says it is a fearful thing to fall into the hands of the living God? (Hebrews 10:31). "For our God is a consuming fire" (Hebrews 12:29).

John sees the Book of Life opened, implying a diligent search to see whether an accused person's name appears in the book. In no case will that happen at the Great White Throne Judgement. And every person whose name is not found in the Book of Life will be cast into the lake of fire.

Remember, this is Jesus, the Savior, the loving One. He will say to the condemned, "Depart from Me, you cursed, into the everlasting fire prepared for the devil and his angels" (Matthew 25:41). How could anyone not tremble at hearing such horrifying words? Some may reply, "Now wait a minute, Lord. I prophesied in Your name. I did wonderful deeds in Your name. I went to church in Your name." They'll go through their entire litany. But Jesus will declare, "I never knew you. *Depart.*"

Oh, how those words will probably ring forever in the ears of the ungodly! "I never knew you…I never knew you…I never knew you." For all eternity!

How Is the Question

We all live, we all die, we'll all be resurrected—but *how* is the big question. We all have *bios* life, but not everyone has *zoe* life. We will all die, but you don't have to face the second death. We will all be resurrected, but Jesus said some will be raised to life and others to condemnation.

Remember that the lake of fire was not created for human beings. Jesus referred to hell as "everlasting fire prepared for the devil and his angels" (Matthew 25:41). Hell was designed for the devil after he fell; God never designed it for people.

Heaven, on the other hand, God *did* design for people. He meant heaven to be a glorious place where redeemed men and women created in His image could spend eternity with Him.

But God leaves the choice—heaven or hell—up to us. *We* choose our final destination. God, who gave free choice to men and women in the beginning, will honor our choices.

Choose well.

21

All Things New

Revelation 21

SUMMARY

Revelation 21 represents a shift in dimensions. It describes events after the second coming and after the millennial reign of Christ. With spectacular imagery it tells us about the eternal state and the New Jerusalem, where the saints of all ages will dwell together with their Savior in a city of perpetual light.

RELATED SCRIPTURES FOR STUDY

Ecclesiastes 3:11; Isaiah 65; 1 Corinthians 15:53-54; 1 John 5:4-5

Star Trek, the famous science fiction television series from the '60s, opened with the iconic words, "Space...the final frontier." Ah, but it's not. *Heaven* is the final frontier. It alone is the final culmination of everything.

No wonder, then, that God's people have pondered heaven since there have been God's people. Heaven is the anticipated end of all Christians. When we die, we expect to go to heaven because of what God has promised us in the Bible.

The book of Revelation mentions heaven 55 times, while the whole Bible refers to it some 532 times. It is a definite place, and our ultimate home. Paul wrote, "Our citizenship is in heaven" (Philippians 3:20).

Heaven is our home sweet home, and as Dorothy said in *The Wizard of Oz*, "There's no place like home." Our Father is there, our Savior is there, and our Comforter is there. Our reward is there. All departed believers are there. Because of all this, the apostle Paul could say, "For to me, to live is Christ, and to die is gain" (Philippians 1:21). Heaven is going to be *so* much better than anything we've ever had here on earth!

When we get to the eternal state, we will leave time itself. We often think of time as something linear, and so describe eternity as a line traveling infinitely in both directions. But Albert Einstein taught us rightly that time is relative; it varies with mass, acceleration, and gravity. God, however, is not constrained by time. He exists altogether outside of the time-space continuum. So rather than thinking of time as a line that goes on and on forever, we should forget about the line altogether. In heaven we will live with God, who dwells in a wholly different dimension—a state that we call eternity.

The New Heaven and Earth (21:1,3-8)

John pictures a future when the current heavens and the earth disappear and God re-creates everything. All that we have known—earth, atmosphere, stratosphere—will be removed. The old will be gone, the new will come. God sums it up when He says, "Behold, I make all things new" (v. 5).

The word translated "new" means "different, fresh, innovative in quality, novel in existence." God made the earth for us to live on, inhabit, dwell in, and enjoy. But from the time of Adam and Eve, the present earth has languished under a curse.

While the Bible gives us few details about the eternal state, in verse 1 we read that there will be no sea. That sentence alone tells us that the planet will differ markedly from today's version. We live in a watery world; two-thirds of the planet is covered with water. Our bodies are mostly water. Most of plant and animal life is comprised of water. Earth is the only planet in the solar system, so far as we know, with the water needed to sustain our biosphere. If you don't drink water, you'll die. But in the eternal state, there will be no sea, which tells us the new heaven and the new earth will not operate on the principle of water.

John brings this up because he wants to tell us that heaven will be profoundly different from what we know today. Seas separate people; but in heaven, there will be no such separation. All of God's people will live together in peace under the authority of Christ.

It has always been God's heart to enjoy intimate fellowship with His people. But something always has gotten in the way—sin. So in the Old Testament, God set up a tabernacle, where His presence dwelled in the Ark of the Covenant. In pillars of fire and smoke He guided the Israelites day and night through the wilderness. In the time of Solomon the people built the temple, and the Shekinah glory of God dwelled within that place. Still, no one but the high priest could enter the temple's Holy of Holies. The temple had various courts, separations, and ritual sacrifices, all of it placing some distance between a holy God and sinful man.

Ultimately, God sent His Son into the world—Immanuel, which means "God with us." The Word became flesh and "tabernacled" among us—and we saw His glory (John 1:14). No more veils, no more rituals, no more cloth tent in the wilderness. God dealt directly with His people, in intimate fellowship with His adopted sons and daughters.

In heaven, time will be no more and we will have reached the eternal state—immeasurable, perpetual, everlasting. Because God has set eternity in the hearts of every human being (Ecclesiastes 3:11), we all long to have eternal life. And all those who place their faith in Jesus Christ will experience that life in all its fullness.

Interestingly, instead of telling us what heaven is like, John spends most of his time telling us what it's *not* like (v. 4). He begins by saying there will be no sea; a bit later he tells us there will be no death or crying or sorrow. I find it interesting that of all the ways there are to describe heaven, John describes it in the negative. Why? I think it's because heaven will be unlike anything we know. We simply have no basis for comparison.

When Paul was caught up into the "third heaven," he saw and heard the glories of heaven; and when he returned to earth, he said that he heard inexpressible words, unlawful for a man to utter (2 Corinthians 12:4). He witnessed things so astounding they couldn't even be told! We lack the words to fully describe heaven and we have no frame of reference for fully understanding it. That's probably why John describes heaven in terms of what it isn't.

Life on earth often comes with tears and deep sorrow. We shed tears of loneliness, tears of misfortune, tears of poverty, tears of sympathy, tears of remorse. But in heaven all of that will be gone forever, for God will wipe away *every* tear. We'll have nothing to cry about. Tears will be part of the former things, and they'll be gone forever.

Death also will be missing. The greatest of all mortal curses—the "last enemy," as Paul called it in 1 Corinthians 15:26—will be abolished. Remember that Revelation 20:14 declares, "Then Death and Hades were cast into the lake of fire." Death will be no more!

Sorrow also will pass away. Sorrow is the common human experience throughout history. We all have our ups and downs, sometimes descending into depression. That's one reason we love the book of Psalms; we see the psalmists up and down and back up again, and we can relate to that: One moment we'll read, "I think I want to die!" And the next we'll read, "I praise God! I love Him!" All in the course of a couple verses!

And pain? Also a thing of the past. Many people today live with chronic pain; from the time they get up until the time they go to bed, they groan. But whatever your past with pain, good or bad, you've only just begun to live. So Paul could write, "I consider that the sufferings of this present time are not worthy to be compared with the glory which shall be revealed in us" (Romans 8:18). Think of it: no hospitals, no funerals, no broken homes, no broken hearts, no rehabilitation centers, no cancer treatments, no Alzheimer's disease, no wheelchairs—*ever again.*

By the time John finishes writing verse 5, it's almost as if he loses his concentration for a moment. Apparently he feels so overwhelmed by all he's seen—a new heaven, a new earth, a new presence of God, sorrow and pain and death and mourning all gone, forever—that the vision stuns him and prompts him to drop his quill. He can only think, *Wow!*

And so God, who is on the throne, says, "Pick up your pen, man! Write—you're not done yet. I have some more faithful and true words to tell you. You have a chapter and a half left to go, buddy. Hang in there; write it all down."

So John continues by describing two classes of people: the occupants of heaven and the nonoccupants. Who's going to heaven? What are the criteria for becoming a resident? John gives the first requirement in verse 6: "him who thirsts." To get into heaven, you must be thirsty. You must see your need to drink from God's well. This is what Jesus told the woman at the well of Samaria (John 4:13-14). And as the Lord said to some Jews in the temple, "If anyone thirsts, let him come to Me and drink" (John 7:37). Only those who feel dissatisfied with their present life apart from Jesus Christ—who are thirsty enough and have a soul parched enough to long for living water—will go to heaven. Heaven will be populated by those who thirsted after God.

The second requirement is found in verse 7: "he who overcomes." This same phraseology was used earlier in Revelation, in the letters sent to the seven churches. Jesus promised something good to each one who overcomes. Overcomes what? When you're born of God by faith—when you trust in Christ alone and in His provision alone—then God enables you to overcome sin and temptation through the power of the Son of God, our Savior.

And then in verse 8, John lists the outcasts. First he mentions the cowardly; this probably refers to those who refuse to take a stand for Jesus Christ. Such individuals don't endure; they never had saving faith to begin with. They may have raised a hand at a worship service, or shed a tear, or felt their heart beat faster at an altar call, but they never made a real commitment to Jesus Christ. This text ought to put to rest any notion that there's a second chance to become saved after death; there isn't. Our only chance is here and now.

John then lists the "unbelieving." These individuals lack saving faith, as demonstrated by their ungodly life. Next are the "abominable, murderers, sexually immoral." The underlying Greek word for "sexually immoral" is *pornos*, from which we get the term "pornography." It technically refers to fornication, or having sexual relations with somebody other than your spouse. By extension it covers the gamut of sexual immorality, from adultery to homosexuality or sodomy or incest or any other sexual sin. John then lists "sorcerors," using the Greek term *pharmakeus*. We get the word "pharmacy" from this term. This refers to the use of drugs often associated with worshiping pagan gods—in our age, spiritism. In a similar vein John mentions "idolaters," those who give supreme devotion to anyone or anything other than to God. Finally he lists "liars," which certainly would include those who say they're Christians but who fail to live in a way that honors God (see Titus 1:16). They may say to Jesus, "Lord, Lord," but at the Great White Throne Judgment Jesus will say to them, "I never knew you; depart from Me, you who practice lawlessness!" (Matthew 7:23).

The New Jerusalem (21:2, 9-27)

This future and very different world will play host to a very different city. The "New Jerusalem" will descend "from God, prepared as a bride adorned for her husband" (v. 2). This is the capital city of eternity, the headquarters of all that will be. And what a city it is! We're told it's 1500 miles cubed, just a little smaller than the moon. Some think it will orbit the new earth. But whatever the case, it's unlike anything we've ever known. Here it's called "the holy city" because all its occupants will be holy (v. 2).

Note that John describes the city as a bride prepared for her husband, another characteristic of its populace (vv. 2,9). The bride of Christ, the redeemed people of God, inhabit it. And it's beautifully adorned, just like a bride on her wedding day. Think of it as the bride city. Marriage is the closest possible relationship we can enjoy on earth, and God wants intimacy, not distance! The term "bride of Christ" closes any gap that may exist.

Did you know that the Bible sets Jerusalem apart from all other cities? It calls Jerusalem the City of God, the City of the Great King, and the City of Peace. Some have called it the City of the Soul or even the City of the Book. During His earthly ministry, Jesus often visited Jerusalem; the Bible records seven of His visits. And yet with all of its earthly beauty and charm, one day Jesus stood and wept over it because He saw its future destruction (Matthew 23:37-39).

In its long history, Jerusalem has been engulfed by war no fewer than thirty-six times. Seventeen times it has been reduced to ashes, and eighteen times it has risen from the ashes. Yet it always seems to be on the brink of some catastrophe.

In the Bible, Jerusalem is portrayed as the geographic center of the earth. When Scripture uses the terms north, south, east, and west, its reference point is always Jerusalem. Israel and Jerusalem lie on a land bridge that connects Africa, Europe, and Asia, and so in Ezekiel 5:5 God said of Jerusalem, "I have set her in the midst of the nations and the countries all around her."

Jerusalem also is the spiritual center of the earth. It's where Jesus was crucified; it's where the sins of the world were placed upon the Son of God.

It is also the prophetic storm center of the world. What happens in Africa or Asia or eastern Europe may have grave consequences, but they don't compare with Jerusalem in the quest for world peace. God has said, "I will make Jerusalem a very heavy stone for all peoples" (Zechariah 12:3)—and it's becoming that, isn't it? In the end times, Jerusalem will become the very vortex of geopolitical activity.

And ultimately Jerusalem will become the glory center of the world. Jesus will rule and reign from Mount Zion in the millennium and the nations will flow to Him. The law will go forth from Zion and the Word of the Lord from Jerusalem (Isaiah 2:3). And after the millennium, when God creates a new heaven and a new earth, the New Jerusalem will descend from heaven toward the new earth.

Right now in Jerusalem there is a kingless throne, the throne of David. No one has occupied it for 2500 years, even though God promised that a descendant of King David would sit forever upon it. At the same time, in heaven, there's a throneless King, Jesus Christ. And when this kingless throne and this throneless King come together—and one day they will—utopia will erupt. That's exactly what we will see happen in the New Jerusalem.

John calls the New Jerusalem "the great city" (Revelation 21:10), which implies you can look forward to a corporate and highly social eternity. God made us to be social creatures, to need one another, to live and work and play and interact with each other. Heaven is a real place of real activity with real people. You will stay busy there, you will probably travel, and you will serve the Lord (see 22:3).

John twice says that this great city will descend out of heaven (vv. 2,10). He sees it presented, not created, which means it already exists even now. God makes the new heaven and the new earth, and then, *voila*, out of God's heaven descends this astonishing city, the New Jerusalem, which reflects the glory of God. This is its overarching characteristic. John says its light—*phoster*, illuminator—seemed like it came from a precious stone (v. 11). The term *phoster* describes something in which light is concentrated and from which it radiates, like a lightbulb. It does not describe light reflecting off of or refracting from something else. John says the Lamb provides the light for the city (vv. 22-23). In eternity, Jesus Christ, the Lamb, will radiate the glory He had before He came to earth—a glory that He mostly hid during His years of earthly ministry. Remember that He prayed, "O Father, glorify Me together with Yourself, with the glory which I had with You before the world was" (John 17:5). Here that prayer is answered. The Lamb is the light of the city, radiating into all of eternity.

John says this brilliant light looked as though it burst from a precious stone he calls "a jasper." The modern-day jasper is an opaque, whitish-yellow stone, but in ancient times the term "jasper" referred to a stone that was crystal clear. The term may have been used for what we call a diamond. It dazzled John, like some immense, radiating, iridescent diamond complete with colossal walls and oversized gates.

The city has four sides and is set out something like the tabernacle in the Old Testament, which had three tribes on each of its four sides. The city has twelve gates, each corresponding to the names of the twelve tribes of Israel and each guarded by an angel. The twelve gates have the names of the tribes of Israel because that's our spiritual heritage. Through the prophets, God promised the messianic age to Israel. God established a unique covenant with the twelve tribes; and so to proclaim our spiritual heritage for all eternity, the names of the twelve tribes of Israel will be inscribed on the dozen gates of the New Jerusalem. All of this points toward God, who sits on His throne (vv. 12-13).

The city is set on twelve solid foundations, each made of beautiful stones and each bearing the name of one of the twelve apostles. This celebrates the covenant relationship God has established with the New Testament church (see Ephesians 2:19-20). Our faith is built upon the doctrines, the teachings, and the eyewitness accounts of the apostles, from the time of Jesus Christ. These men wrote the first documents of the church, and from a human standpoint, they form the very foundation of our faith.

The New Jerusalem is a gargantuan place, laid out foursquare; the Greek word is *tetragonos*, meaning "four-cornered." It appears to be a perfect cube, 12,000 furlongs in every direction. A furlong is 660 feet, which would make the city some 1500 miles wide, deep, and tall—roughly the distance from Florida to Maine. That's a volume of 2,250,000 cubic miles, or 150,000 times the size of London, the largest city by square mileage on today's earth. Henry Morris, a scientist from Southern California, said this city could house well over 20 *billion* people if only *25 percent of the city* was given over to residents. Each person would have a cube of seventy-five acres. And because the city is as tall as it is wide, you'll be able to move within it not only horizontally, but omnidirectionally.

The city's wall is 144 cubits wide; and since a cubit is about 18 inches long, it measures 216 feet across (v. 17), far thicker than any terrestrial wall. The wall is also made of jasper—a clear, hard, diamond-like divider, utterly unlike anything we have ever seen. Amazing! And the city gets even more astonishing than that.

Have you ever seen transparent gold (v. 18)? Terrestrial gold is opaque; but you can see right through this heavenly gold. And although you and I have never glimpsed it, we're going to live with it. Brilliant light will radiate outward from the Lamb and from God, bursting through the translucent gold of the city's streets and through its shimmering, diamond-like walls.

Each of the twelve gates of the city is fashioned out of a single pearl (v. 21). No doubt this is where the common idea of the pearly gates comes from. But notice it's not pear*ly* gates; they're *pearl* gates, each made of a single, solid pearl. If the walls are 1500 miles high, then those are some *huge* pearls!

When John looks for a place to worship in the city, he seeks a temple. Every ancient city had many temples; even Jerusalem had a temple. But this New Jerusalem has no temple. Why not? Because it doesn't need one. God will be ever-present eternally with His people (v. 22). So in essence, God will expand His temple so that the *entire universe* becomes His temple. You won't be able to get away from God's presence! Nor would you want to.

Everyone will have access to the New Jerusalem (v. 26). All the nations will walk in its light and bring their "glory" into it. The word translated "nations" comes from the Greek term *ethnos*, or ethnic groups. Gentiles, Jews, people from every tribe, every tongue, and every nation will gather in the city. In other words, heaven will not be limited to one group of people. Prejudice will not exist in heaven; class warfare will never occur. While its residents will have skin of various hues—black, white, yellow, red, and every hue in between—all of God's people will live together in perfect harmony without any hint of division.

Don't Miss It

What a city God showed to John! Really, it's hard to say much more about it. I could offer some conjecture, but already John has described the key elements of both the inside and the outside of the city. It's the Father's house, the place that even now Jesus is preparing for you and me, where we can walk forever with Him in holiness and light.

Have you chosen this city? Have you chosen Jesus, who wants to grant you your own place in this city? Whatever you do, don't miss it— for if you do, you miss *everything*.

22

He's Coming—Now What?

Revelation 22

SUMMARY

The final chapter of the Bible brings God's book full circle. Scripture begins in a garden and ends in a city with a garden-like environment. Genesis 1 describes the creation of the heavens and the earth, while Revelation 22 sees God creating a new heaven and a new earth. In the beginning, God distinguished the day from the night; at the end, there is no night, only light. In Genesis 3, the curse is pronounced; in Revelation 22, the curse is removed. In Genesis 3, man is driven from the tree of life and the paradise of God; in Revelation 22, the tree of life is restored in the paradise of the New Jerusalem. In other words, what Adam lost, Christ regained…and then some.

RELATED SCRIPTURES FOR STUDY
Ezekiel 37:1-14; Matthew 24; 1 Thessalonians 4:13-18; 2 Thessalonians 2:1-3; 1 Timothy 4:1-3

What makes a good novel so satisfying? As you open the book, the story is cast, the characters are introduced, and the hero takes center stage. Then as you progress, a plot twist changes things as some intrigue carries you along, never allowing you to feel quite sure how it's all going to turn out. You're a bit on edge until the last chapter, when somehow it all works out. When all is said and done, you leave the book feeling content and satisfied.

The Bible is very much like that. It opens with the stunning creation of earth and sun and Adam and Eve, and all the rest of God's beautiful handiwork. But then comes chapter 3 and the Fall. Satan is introduced, the plot thickens and darkens, and we see chapter after chapter of Israel's disobedience and longing for something better. We see the Messiah come and breathe a sigh of relief—but then He dies. Three days later, He rises from the dead, and shortly after that He says, "I'm leaving, but I'm coming back." As the rest of the Bible unfolds, you wonder, *When is He coming back? What's going to happen to the world?* Finally the last few chapters unfold and we breathe a sigh of relief as we realize, *Oh, this is where it's all going!* And when all is said and done, we know we've read a wonderful story. It ends something like it begins—only better. That which was lost is finally restored.

In chapter 22 we come to the end of the book of Revelation. Here we find John's concluding remarks. This is how it will all end for those who love Jesus Christ and are called according to His purpose. The Tribulation is over, the second coming is long gone, the millennium has ended, a new heaven and a new earth have been created, and the King of kings sits on the throne and reigns with His Father, and He will do so forever and ever.

Eternity has come.

The Main Street of the City (22:1-5)

Just before John gives us his concluding remarks and tells us how best to respond to the astonishing visions he has shared, he gives us one last glimpse of the glories of eternity. Every city has a main drag, and the New Jerusalem will have one as well. John mentioned it briefly in Revelation 21:21, where he told us it was made of pure gold, like transparent glass. Think of this main street as something like the most important red carpet ever laid out, only infinitely better. Eternity's Main Street leads to some remarkable city attractions.

First, John sees a "pure river of water of life, clear as crystal, proceeding from the throne of God and of the Lamb" (v. 1). Because of this river, you will always feel a sense of total satisfaction in this city. But John may not merely be talking about H_2O! This water flows from the very throne of God, graphically picturing the abundant, pure, joyful life that eternally flows from God alone. He is the source of all life, and He invites us to drink deeply from His endless supply. Jesus once said to those attending a feast in Jerusalem that if they believed in Him, out of their innermost beings would flow rivers of living water (John 7:38). In other words, through faith in Christ, the Spirit of God would supply them with a constant, never-ending supply of divine life.

When you put your faith in Jesus Christ, this spiritual refreshment is yours. No matter what you drink in this world, eventually you'll get thirsty again. True and lasting satisfaction comes only from joining your life to the life of God. A life of following Jesus will satisfy you *now* and fill you to overflowing *then*. This "river of water of life" speaks of the utterly satisfying nature of a vibrant, dynamic relationship with God.

And then John widens his lens even more. He sees the tree of life— once in the garden temporarily, now in the New Jerusalem forever— in the middle of Main Street and on either side of the river, bearing twelve fruits every month. Some readers have stumbled a bit over this description. They say, "Hey, wait a minute. I thought this was eternity. So how can John talk about months?" I think this proves that eternity is not some vast, never-ending track of featureless land that goes on and on without distinction and without variety. Apparently there will be cycles and seasons of a sort, even in eternity. There will be variety, difference, diversity, unique points of interest, even change. What else would we expect from a God who says, "Behold, I make all things new"? (Revelation 21:5). He doesn't make all things new just to let them all grow old again. The New Jerusalem will be a place of astonishing creativity and newness.

So the tree of life will constantly produce, in a regular cycle, fruit of various types. John describes all this in anthropomorphic terms so we can relate to it more easily. God will provide for the residents of His city through a regular cycle filled with variety.

Another question sometimes arises over what John says next. He writes, "The leaves of the tree were for the healing of the nations." Now, if sin and disease and pain and tears will no longer exist, then why will the nations need "healing"? In fact, the word translated "healing" might be more helpfully rendered "therapy." The leaves of this tree of life add vigor to life, something like taking supervitamins. Even now in our fallen world we don't take vitamins to cure a disease; we take them to supplement our intake of nutrients, to add vigor to our regimen and enhance our life experience. In a similar way, using these leaves will somehow enhance our experience of eternity, helping us to move from strength to strength.

John then adds, "There shall be no more curse" (v. 3). How could there be, since "the throne of God and of the Lamb shall be in it." A curse implies distance between God and man, and in the New Jerusalem that distance will shrink to nothing. The curse will be gone and the blessing will grow more and more with each new discovery of some aspect of God's boundless grace and love.

Very contrary to what some people think, eternity won't be boring. You'll be busy with all sorts of fascinating tasks. What will you be doing? Serving the Lord. How will you serve Him? I don't know, but you won't lack for interesting things to do. John says simply, "His servants shall serve Him" (v. 3). Certainly there'll be plenty of variety.

Do you remember Jesus' parable of the minas? He told a story about a nobleman who left his country to "receive for himself a kingdom and to return" (Luke 19:12). In his absence, the man gave each of his servants ten minas—a unit of measure that varied from one to two pounds of precious metal, or about three months' wages at the time—and told them to "do business till I come" (Luke 19:13). He expected them to increase the value of their portfolios by trading during his absence. Upon his return, his first servant reported that he had doubled his master's investment; the master replied, "Well done, good servant; because you were faithful in a very little, have authority over ten cities" (Luke 19:17). In other words, the reward for faithful service was not boredom, but extravagant blessing in a new and far richer environment. That's what we have to look forward to.

So again, what a city! Really, it's hard to say much more about it. We could conjecture about the rest, but what would be the point? This is the Father's house, the glorious place that Jesus is even now preparing for you and me to share with Him. What a city!

The Certainty of Jesus' Return

Once John finishes describing the New Jerusalem and the blessed future that awaits all faithful servants of Christ, he turns his attention to his readers. He wants them to get ready for the amazing future to come. And so three times he writes that Jesus is coming (vv. 7,12,20).

As we have seen, the key biblical text on the rapture of the church is found in 1 Thessalonians 4:13-18. Paul says that some Christians will still be alive on earth when Jesus comes back. And because He could return at any time, the apostle advises us to deny "ungodliness and worldly lusts" and to "live soberly, righteously, and godly in the present age, looking for the blessed hope and glorious appearing of our great God and Savior Jesus Christ" (Titus 2:12-13). Early Christians certainly believed that Jesus could return at any moment, and Paul encouraged them and us to live in that kind of expectancy.

While no one knows when Jesus will return for His church, the Bible does give us some indications of when that arrival is growing near. A number of key prophesied events have already taken place that should cause us to rouse ourselves. One of the biggest, perhaps, is the return of the dispersed Jews to Israel, and the establishment of the modern nation of Israel in 1948. Scripture also predicted the recapture of the old city of Jerusalem by the Jews, which occurred in 1967. The Bible also foresaw the rise of Russia as a powerful nation, along with the antagonism of the Arab states toward Israel. We are seeing, in the development of the European Union, the beginnings of a revived Roman Empire, unlike anything since the old Holy Roman Empire broke up—again, just as prophesied. Jesus' predictions regarding a worldwide increase in earthquakes, famines, wars and rumors of wars are coming to pass, as is the departure of many churches from orthodox, traditional, biblical beliefs, as Paul foresaw. Of course, we must be careful as we see and try to interpret current events. Although it's premature and irresponsible to precisely assign these newsworthy events as being the exact fulfillment of biblical prophecy, they nonetheless pique our interest and excitement. We are seeing the groundwork being laid for a one-world government and a one-world religion. All of these are important signs that indicate the Lord is coming soon.

The devil does not want us to see this truth, for nothing would wake up the church more than the conviction that the return of Jesus is near. Remember James's admonition: "Do not grumble against one another, brethren, lest you be condemned. Behold, the Judge is standing at the door!" (James 5:9). The moment a man or woman takes hold of the truth that Jesus is coming again soon to receive His followers to Himself, this world loses its hold on him or her.

It's great that Jesus is coming—but what should we do about it? John lays out five primary responses to the return of Christ.

Walk

Verse 7 tells us our walk with Christ should correspond with the truth of Jesus' return. Jesus says to us, "Behold, I am coming quickly! Blessed is he who keeps [or obeys or pays attention to and does] the words of the prophecy of this book." In verse 9 an angel commends "those who keep the words of this book." And in verse 14 Jesus proclaims, "Blessed [or 'oh how happy, to be envied'] are those who do His commandments." Our primary response to the soon coming of Christ ought to be obedience to His Word.

When we study and use biblical prophecy in the way God intends, it will help to purify us. That's what John meant in his epistle when he wrote that everyone who has the hope of Christ's return "purifies himself, just as He is pure" (1 John 3:3). And it's what Peter had in mind when he wrote, "Since all these things [the material universe] will be dissolved, what manner of persons ought you to be in holy conduct and godliness, looking for and hastening the coming of the day of God… Therefore, beloved, looking forward to these things, be diligent to be found by Him in peace, without spot and blameless" (2 Peter 3:11-12,14).

What we have read and studied in the book of Revelation should change the way we walk. As we see what is coming upon planet Earth and what God has in store for the future of the church and humankind, our choices and our perspective ought to become less temporal and more eternal. A Christian who understands the message of Revelation has no room to live duplicitously—no reason for choosing a double life or living a double standard. John says to us, "You've read these things. You've heard these things. You've seen these things. Now, blessed are those who do them, who keep them, who walk in them."

Worship

After John sees and hears the awesome things revealed to him, he confesses that he feels overwhelmed and falls down to worship at the feet of the angel who showed him all of these things. The angel immediately responds, "See that you do not do that. For I am your fellow servant, and of your brethren the prophets, and of those who keep the words of this book. Worship God" (v. 9).

Can any believer read this book without responding in worship? Can you hear of the coming kingdom of Jesus Christ, vanquishing all its enemies on earth and in the heavenly realms, setting up an eternal kingdom, and *not* walk away from that experience worshiping the Lord? When we read about what God has in store for us, how can we remain nonchalant and neglect to worship Him? That just doesn't make sense.

The Father seeks men and women to worship Him (John 4:23). God has prepared heaven for you and for me. How can our response fail to include worship?

Witness

Unlike what an angel told Daniel centuries before, an angelic messenger tells John, "Do not seal the words of the prophecy of this book, for the time is at hand" (v. 10). Daniel had been instructed, "Go your way, Daniel, for the words are closed up and sealed till the time of the end" (Daniel 12:9). But this angel declares, "John, the message that I have given to you is not to be hidden, as wild as it is. You are to herald it, not hide it. Get its message out to others. Don't seal it up and don't keep it to yourself."

Biblical prophecy can provide tremendous motivation for us to witness and share our faith with unbelievers. Prophecy can motivate us not only toward godly living, but also toward godly witnessing. How can we read about the Tribulation and hell and judgment, and not be moved by these awful things to warn people to avoid them?

It is in this vein that John writes, "And the Spirit and the bride say,

'Come!'" (v. 17). The Spirit is the Holy Spirit, while we, the church, are the bride. And what does the bride say? "Come!" Not only is the Spirit in the world, drawing people to Christ, but the bride who received and was changed by the gospel is also out in the world, preaching the gospel. We are to say to those currently outside the family of God, "Come! There is room. Jesus invites you to accept eternal life. So come!"

Work

One of the last things Jesus tells us, in the final book of the Bible, is this: "My reward is with Me, to give to every one according to his work" (v. 12). Heaven will be your reward, of course, but that's not all. You'll also receive rewards from Christ based upon your work for Him now. Good works don't save you, but once you are saved, Jesus expects you to serve Him and work for Him.

Paul wrote, "I also labor, striving according to His working which works in me mightily" (Colossians 1:29). To a church that had largely forgotten about the importance of serving Christ, he wrote, "Each one will receive his own reward according to his own labor" (1 Corinthians 3:8), and "I labored more abundantly than they all, yet not I, but the grace of God which was with me," and "Be steadfast, immovable, always abounding in the work of the Lord, knowing that your labor is not in vain in the Lord" (1 Corinthians 15:10,58).

One day you'll stand before Jesus Christ in heaven, and based on your service now, you'll be tested as to your work for Him. Based on that test, you'll either receive a reward or have a reward withdrawn. Paul said, "We must all appear before the judgment seat of Christ, that each one may receive the things done in the body, according to what he has done, whether good or bad" (2 Corinthians 5:10), and, "Each of us shall give account of himself to God" (Romans 14:12). Jesus is coming, and now is the time to work. Jesus Himself said, "I must work the works of Him who sent Me while it is day; the night is coming when no one can work" (John 9:9). There's not much time left!

Willingness

Jesus calls us to believe in Him and live for Him and work with Him.

But as always, He gives us a choice. He makes His generous offer and then says, "Who's willing?" Some aren't. In verse 11 John names a few in this category: "He who is unjust, let him be unjust still; he who is filthy, let him be filthy still." In other words, if you want to carry on in an unjust, filthy way, go ahead; that choice is open to you. Of course, it won't turn out well. But go ahead and choose it if that's your will.

On the other hand, John says, "He who is righteous, let him be righteous still; he who is holy, let him be holy still" (v. 11). Again, it's your choice. Jesus wants willing hearts, not reluctant ones. He's after wholehearted and eager servants, not halfhearted and disinterested ones. Every day you and I make choices about whether we will follow Jesus or go our own way, whether we will accept His will or reject it. These daily choices will mark our destiny. So if we're wrong in this life, we'll be more wrong after death. But if we're right in this life, we'll be more right in our new and glorious home than we can possibly imagine.

Dragonfly Theology

Below the surface of a quiet pond lived a little colony of water bugs. They were a happy bunch, and for many months they scurried over the soft mud on the bottom of their pond. Every once in a while they noticed that a member of their colony seemed to lose interest in bustling about with his friends. He took to clinging to the stem of a pond lily and gradually moved out of sight of the group.

"Look!" said one water bug to another. "One of us is climbing up the lily stalk. Where do you suppose he's going?"

Up, up, up slowly went the bug. Even as they watched him, the water bug disappeared from sight. His friends waited and waited, but he didn't return.

"That's funny," said one water bug to another. "Wasn't he happy here?"

"Where do you suppose he went?" wondered a second water bug. They were all greatly puzzled.

Finally, one of the water bugs, a colony leader, gathered his friends and said, "I have an idea. The next one of us who climbs up the lily stalk must promise to come back and tell the rest of us where he went and why."

"We promise," they all said solemnly.

One spring day not long afterward, the very water bug who suggested the plan found himself climbing up the lily stalk. Up, up, up he went. Before he knew what was happening, he had broken through the surface of the water and fallen onto the broad, green lily pad above. He promptly fell asleep. When he awoke, he looked about with surprise. He couldn't believe what he saw. A startling change had come over his old body. His movement revealed four silver wings and a long tail. Even as he struggled, he felt an impulse to move his wings. The warmth of the sun dried the moisture from his new body. He moved his wings again and suddenly found himself up above the water.

He had become a dragonfly.

Swooping and dipping in great curves, he flew through the air, exhilarated in his new atmosphere. By and by, he lighted happily on a lily pad to rest and chanced to look below to the bottom of the pond. Why, he was right above his old friends, the water bugs! There they were, scurrying about, just as he had been doing some time before. Then he remembered the promise: "The next one of us who climbs up the lily stalk must promise to come back and tell the rest of us where he went and why." Without thinking, he darted down, but the surface of the water stopped him.

"I can't return," he said in dismay. "At least I tried, but I can't keep my promise. Even if I could go back, not one of the water bugs would even know me in my new body. I guess I'll just have to wait till they become dragonflies too. Then they'll understand what happened to me and where I went."

And so the dragonfly winged off happily into his wonderful new world of sun and air.

A whole new world awaits us too—a world far more different from our present world than the dragonfly's new world was from his old one. Jesus said, "I am going to prepare a place for you," and for 2000 years He's been hard at work preparing it.

Are you ready?

A Final Word

After journeying through the book of Revelation you probably feel bittersweet. There is joy and pleasure mingled with pain and sadness. Even the apostle John himself found this to be so. When he was told to take the little book, the disclosure of how bad the future was still going to get, he wrote, "It was sweet in my mouth, but when I swallowed it, it turned sour in my stomach" (Revelation 10:10 NLT). That's how most folks feel after reading this book. I know I certainly do.

So what now? How can we use what we have read to better our lives and the lives of others? Living in the light of the future should have a way of transforming us—of making us better people. That's because the book of Revelation is a book that reveals Jesus Christ. Any study of Christ should be transforming by its very nature. The clearer Christ becomes to us, the clearer should be His calling and claim upon our lives and the more defined our role becomes in this world.

In this book we have seen Christ's majesty, His sacrifice, His rule over the church, His ownership of the universe, His coming judgment, and His future plans for both the earth and heaven. This book demonstrates these realities more clearly than any other book in Scripture.

So studying Bible prophecy helps us to understand what's coming down the road for planet earth. We realize that the events described in this final book of the Bible are real and will one day become history. But there's something more to studying Bible prophecy than just learning the schedule of future events so as to know what's next on the prophetic calendar. Studying prophecy should motivate us to live godly lives. To repeat what Peter said,

> The day of the Lord will come as unexpectedly as a thief. Then the heavens will pass away with a terrible noise, and the very elements themselves will disappear in fire, and the earth and everything on it will be found to deserve judgment. Since everything around us is going to be destroyed like this, what holy and godly lives you should live (2 Peter 3:10-11 NLT).

Prophecy can and should become a wake-up call. We should think of it this way: *If Jesus is coming back, and perhaps very soon, I can't just keep on living the same old way I always have!* Everything around is going to melt away, Peter says. That means cars, computers, houses, bank accounts, vacation spots, pets, people, and toys! We should take a realistic assessment of our lives and begin to live godly and holy lives.

As you read this, you are in one of two places: You either belong to Him as a child of God or not. That means your final destination will either be eternally pleasurable or eternally miserable. If you are not a follower of Christ, then of course you should be fearful of the future and make the appropriate changes. When the final curtain closes, you want to make sure you are on the right side of the Director and Producer of the universe. But more about that in a moment.

If you are a believer in Christ, then consider how this book has pointed out some key issues of life and ask yourself some questions:

- Has my understanding of God, His Son, and His plan deepened in the course of this study?

- How will I use this understanding in the future?

- Has my walk changed as a result?

- Am I willing to take more risks in sharing my faith with others?

- Has my worship of God been challenged by this book?

- Could that worship stand to become more sincere and fresh?

- Do I find myself anticipating Christ's return?

If you answer these in the affirmative, then you are wisely growing in God's Word and fulfilling the core goal of the book of Revelation (Revelation 1:3). Yes, future events will certainly cast their dark and ominous shadows, but until those future events are here, we can and should be about His business, living life to the brim by loving those around us and serving our great Christ.

But perhaps you're not yet a believer—that is, a real follower of Christ. If that's the case, now is the time to think clearly and soberly. If you are looking for the kind of hope you'll need for difficult days, the only place you'll find it is in God. Paul called God "the God of hope" (Romans 15:13), and he assured us that this is the kind of hope that "does not put us to shame" (Romans 5:5).

Are you still considering whether or not to take the step of surrender to Christ? Think of it—this could be the moment of your own personal revelation! Just as Jesus was revealed to John and his readers through this final book of the New Testament, He wants to reveal Himself to you personally. Why not let Him? Maybe throughout the course of reading this volume you've become convinced that Jesus alone holds the key to our eternal future. But you alone have the keys to your own heart. How about allowing Christ to come in? Toward the end of the book of Revelation Jesus reminds the readers, "I am making everything new!" (Revelation 21:5). If you want a new start, a new purpose, and you are willing to take these things to heart and for Jesus to change your life, then I invite you to pray this prayer:

> *Dear Lord,*
>
> *Thank You for revealing Yourself to me and for revealing to me Your plan for the world in this book. I know that I am a sinner, and I ask for Your forgiveness. I believe that Your Son Jesus died, that He shed His blood for my sins and rose again from the dead. I turn from those sins and leave my past behind me. I turn to You for a new and different future. Thank You for*

Your willingness to cleanse and accept me. Please come into my
heart and be the Master of my life. I want to trust You and fol-
low You now and into eternity.

In Jesus' name. Amen.

If you have sincerely prayed this and meant it, then welcome to a
brand new future! You are about to walk into an adventure with the
living God as your captain. As He superintends your life, you will discover more of His plan for you personally and you will come to know
Him more intimately. You will discover that He wants to reveal more
of Himself to you. Your journey will be one revelation after another!

Notes

Chapter 1—What Have We Got Here?

1. C.H. Spurgeon, *Morning by Morning; Or, Daily Readings for the Family or the Closet* (New York: Sheldon & Company, 1866), p. 286.

2. C.H. Spurgeon, "Love Abounding, Love Complaining, Love Abiding," a sermon preached at The Metropolitan Tabernacle on April 11, 1886, in *The Metropolitan Tabernacle Pulpit*, vol. 32 (London: Passmore & Alabaster, 1886), pp. 205ff.

Chapter 2—The Churches of Revelation, Part 1

1. John Stott, *What Christ Thinks of the Church* (Wheaton, IL: Harold Shaw, 1990), pp. 28-40.

Chapter 3—The Churches of Revelation, Part 2

1. Charles Finney, *Revivals of Religion* (Westwood, NJ: Fleming H. Revell, n.d.).

2. *Encyclopedia of 7700 Illustrations* (Rockville, MD: Assurance Publishers, 1979), p. 1152.

3. G. Campbell Morgan, *A First-Century Message to Twentieth-Century Christians: Addresses Based upon the Letters to the Seven Churches of Asia* (New York: Fleming H. Revell, 1902), p. 215.

Chapter 5—History's Greatest Real Estate

1. W.A. Criswell, *Expository Sermons on Revelation* (Grand Rapids: Zondervan, 1960), pp. 69-70.

2. William Temple, *Readings in St. John's Gospel (First and Second Series)* (London: Macmillan and Co., 1945).

3. A.W. Tozer, *Man—The Dwelling Place of God* (Camp Hill, PA: Christian Publications, 1966), pp.56-57.

Chapter 6—Four Riders with Bad News

1. Cited by Russell Chandler, *The Los Angeles Times* (September 20, 1990), at http://articles.la times.com/1990-09-20/news/mn-1057_1_persian-gulf/2.

2. John Stott, *The Cross of Christ* (Downers Grove, IL: InterVarsity Press, 2006) p. 327.

Chapter 9—When All Hell Breaks Loose

1. Henry Morris—this was mentioned in a sermon by John MacArthur at http://www.gty.org/ Resources/Sermons/66-33.

2. As cited at http://www.disastercenter.com/crime/uscrime.htm.

3. Henry Madison Morris, *The Revelation Record* (Wheaton, IL: Tyndale House, 1983), p. 174.

4. Malcolm Muggeridge, *The Very Best of Malcolm Muggeridge* (Vancouver, BC: Regent College, 2003), p. 74.

5. Quoted in David Jeremiah, *Escape the Coming Night* (Nashville: Thomas Nelson, 2001), p. 150.

Chapter 10—A Big Angel with a Little Book

1. Francois Mauriac, in the foreword of Elie Wiesel, *Night* (New York: Hill and Wang, 2006), p. 10.

2. J.I. Packer, *God's Plans for You* (Wheaton, IL: Good News, 2001), p. 39.

3. Walter Scott, *Exposition of the Revelation of Jesus Christ* (London: Pickering & Inglis, 1968), p. 223.

Chapter 11—Two Powerful Preachers

1. C.S. Lewis, *The Joyful Christian* (New York: Simon and Schuster, 1996), p. 138.

2. C.S. Lewis, *The Great Divorce* (New York: HarperCollins, 2001), p. viii.

Chapter 12—The Panorama of Spiritual Warfare

1. Charles Haddon Spurgeon, *Spurgeon's Sermons on Christmas and Easter* (Grand Rapids: Kregel Academic, 1995), p. 141.

2. C.S. Lewis, *The Screwtape Letters* (New York: HarperCollins, 2001), p. 171.

Chapter 13—The Coming World Leader

1. *Time*, Monday, January 15, 1979, at http://www.time.com/time/magazine/article/0,9171,9200 12-1,00.html.

2. Roger Kotila, "Constitution for the Federation of the Earth" (Democratic World Federalists), http://www.dwfed.org/pp_CFE.htm.

3. Quoted in Allan David Bloom, *The Closing of the American Mind* (New York: Simon and Schuster, 1988).

4. W.A. Criswell, *Expository Sermons on Revelation* (Grand Rapids: Zondervan, 1969), 4:120-121.

Chapter 16—What's in the Bowl?

1. In 1968, Dr. Carl Sanders, Ph.D. in engineering, headed a research group of more than 100 scientists, engineers, and medical doctors involving many institutions stretching from San Jose to Boston Medical Center. The group's project was to find a microchip that could be implanted beneath the skin, which would allow the government to quickly identify and locate the person who has the chip on the body. The project was funded partly by the U.S. Government and partly by private corporations among which were Motorola and General Electric—see at http://www.gjcn.org/2009/06/mark-of-the-beast/.

2. William R. Newell, *Revelation Chapter by Chapter: A Classic Devotional Commentary* (Grand Rapids: Kregel, 1994), p. 253.

Chapter 17—The Coming World Religion

1. Mary Elizabeth Braddon, *Hostages to Fortune* (London: John Maxwell and Co., 1875), p. 9.

2. Daniel P. Mears and Christopher G. Ellison, "Sociology of Religion," *New Age Journal* (2000), 61:289-313).

3. Don Feder, "Baptists Expose The Real Disney," *Boston Herald* (Wednesday, June 25, 1997), p. 27.

4. C.H. Spurgeon, "Holding Fast the Faith," a sermon preached at The Metropolitan Tabernacle on February 5, 1888, in *The Metropolitan Tabernacle Pulpit*, vol. 34 (London: Passmore & Alabaster, 1888), pp. 73ff.

Chapter 18—Get Out of Babylon!

1. Charles H. Dyer, *The Rise of Babylon* (Chicago: Moody, 2003), pp. 14-15.

2. John MacArthur, "War in the Gulf: A Biblical Perspective, Part 3," at http://www.biblebb.com/files/mac/90-50.htm.

3. The Telescope: Volume 1 (New York: William Burnett & Co., 1824), p. 159.

Other Good Harvest House Reading

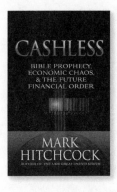

Cashless
Mark Hitchcock

Today's worldwide financial chaos, global interdependency, and modern technology are all converging in such a way that a cashless society and one-world economy are not only possible, but inevitable. Bestselling author Mark Hitchcock skillfully brings together current research and Bible prophecy as he addresses important questions such as...

- How is the stage being set for a cashless society?
- What is the mark of the beast?
- Are you prepared?

The Bare Bones Bible® Handbook
Jim George

The perfect resource for a fast and friendly overview of every book of the Bible! Here you will discover...

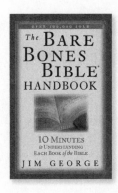

- The grand theme and main point of each book
- The key men and women of God and what you can learn from them
- The major events in Bible history and their significance
- Quick, simple, personal applications for spiritual growth
- Tips for Bible study and a one-year reading plan